THE GREAT ELECTOR'S TABLE

Studies in Early Modern German History

H. C. ERIK MIDELFORT, EDITOR

The GREAT ELECTOR'S TABLE

The Politics of Food in Seventeenth-Century
Brandenburg-Prussia

Molly Taylor-Poleskey

University of Virginia Press • *Charlottesville and London*

The University of Virginia Press is situated on the traditional lands of the Monacan Nation, and the Commonwealth of Virginia was and is home to many other Indigenous people. We pay our respect to all of them, past and present. We also honor the enslaved African and African American people who built the University of Virginia, and we recognize their descendants. We commit to fostering voices from these communities through our publications and to deepening our collective understanding of their histories and contributions.

University of Virginia Press
© 2024 by the Rector and Visitors of the University of Virginia
All rights reserved
Printed in the United States of America on acid-free paper

First published 2024

9 8 7 6 5 4 3 2 1

LIBRARY OF CONGRESS CATALOGING-IN-PUBLICATION DATA
Names: Taylor-Poleskey, Molly, author.
Title: The Great Elector's table : the politics of food in seventeenth-century Brandenburg-Prussia / Molly Taylor-Poleskey.
Description: Charlottesville : University of Virginia Press, 2024. | Series: Studies in early modern German history | Includes bibliographical references and index.
Identifiers: LCCN 2024020306 (print) | LCCN 2024020307 (ebook) | ISBN 9780813951614 (hardback) | ISBN 9780813951607 (paperback) | ISBN 9780813951874 (ebook)
Subjects: LCSH: Food habits—Prussia (Duchy)—History—17th century. | Food—Political aspects—Prussia (Duchy)—History—17th century. | Brandenburg (Electorate). Sovereign (1640–1688 : Friedrich Wilhelm) | Friedrich Wilhelm, Elector of Brandenburg, 1620–1688. | Prussia (Duchy)—Courts and courtiers—History—17th century. | Power (Social sciences)—Prussia (Duchy)—History—17th century. | BISAC: HISTORY / Europe / Germany
Classification: LCC GT2853.P78 T38 2024 (print) | LCC GT2853.P78 (ebook) | DDC 394.1/209431509032—dc23/eng/20240514
LC record available at https://lccn.loc.gov/2024020306
LC ebook record available at https://lccn.loc.gov/2024020307

Cover art: Still Life with Oysters, a Silver Tazza, and Glassware, Willem Claesz Heda, 1635. (Collection of Rita and Frits Markus, Bequest of Rita Markus, 2005, The Metropolitan Museum of Art)
Cover design: Cecilia Sorochin

CONTENTS

ACKNOWLEDGMENTS

Learning and writing about food never gets old, but nonetheless, I would have lost interest long ago, if it had not been such a social endeavor. It is a pleasure to reflect and acknowledge many of the debts I incurred along the way.

At Stanford, I had a strong academic triumvirate of advisors in Laura Stokes, Carolyn Lougee Chappell, and Paula Findlen and supportive classmates including Brad Bouley, Annelise Heinz, Gabriel Lee, Erin Lichtenstein, Josh Lobert, Julia Mansfield, Hannah Marcus, Lindsey Martin, Yair Mintzker, Sarah Murray, and Scott Spillman. At Middle Tennessee State University, I got to expand into the field of public history with the guidance of brilliant colleagues and students such as Emily Baran, Sean Foley, Victoria Hensley, Louis Kyriakoudas, Aliou Ly, Becky McIntyre, Susan Myers-Shirk, Lynn Nelson, Lisa Pruitt, Katie Rainge-Briggs, Victoria Richardson, Ashley Riley-Sousa, Carroll van West—really too many wonderful people to name!

The University of Virginia Press provided careful editing and I am grateful, in particular, to my editors Fernando Campos, Maura High, Wren Morgan Myers, and Nadine Zimmerli and the series editors Erik Midelfort (my *Doktorgrossvater*), Joel Herrington, and Tara Nummedal. Their reputations and specialist knowledge garnered two meticulous and insightful outside readers.

Karin Friedrichs, Sebastian Kühn, Mary Lindemann, Ben Marschke, Suzanne Sutherland, and Amir Teval were among the experts who generously read and commented on chapter drafts.

Jason Heppler was (and continues to be) a great inspiration in digital humanities and a terrific collaborator on the Königsberg Food Database during my year as a Design + Humanities Fellow at Stanford's Center for Spatial and Textual Analysis. Thanks also to Sage Schuster who helped me rebuild the database on my personal website.

Generous funding for the work was provided by the National Endowment for the Humanities, Middle Tennessee State University, the German Foreign Exchange Service (DAAD), the Central European History Society, the Stiftung Preußischer Kulturbesitz, and the Giles Whiting Foundation.

The librarians and archivists at Stanford University's library, the British Library, the Staatsbibliothek Berlin, the Herzog August Bibliothek, the Hessische Landesarchiv, the Landesarchiv Brandenburg, MTSU's Walker Library, Vanderbilt University's library, and the Bayerische Staatsbibliothek all greatly aided my research. The Prussian State Secret Archive in Dahlem was my research home, and many of my "discoveries" came from conversations with archivists and other researchers there, notably Thomas Fischbacher, Jürgen Kloosterhuis, Herr Tempel, and Wulf Wagner. My research in Berlin was supported emotionally by the *Geschichtswerkstatt* of Bonnie Begush, Alice Goff, Kate Horning, Sarah Goodrum, Gabriella Szalay, and Christoph Willmitzer.

I have benefited greatly from friendly and stimulating academic communities in Germany, and I am grateful to my hosts and friends, particularly Prof. Dr. Arndt Brendecke, Susanne Friedrichs, and students of the Frühe Neuzeit Oberseminar in Munich; to Claudia Ulbrich and Alexander Schunke for hosting me for two different stays at the Freie Universität Berlin; to Siegrid Westphal for welcoming me back to the Universität Osnabrück as a guest scholar of the Interdisziplinäre Institut für Kulturgeschichte der Frühen Neuzeit; and to Jill Bepler and Gerlinde Strauss for beautiful stays in Wolfenbüttel.

I was fortunate to have joined a diverse cohort of food scholars at the summer school of the Institut Européen d'Histoire et des Cultures de l'Alimentation at the Université François-Rabelais de Tours and particularly grateful to have found generous mentors there in Allen Grieco, Deborah Krohn, and Peter Scholliers. I developed German language and paleography skills thanks to Elisabeth Sobakken, the German Historical Institute, and the Franckesche Stiftungen Halle. The Congress-Bundestag Youth Exchange for Young Professionals funded the year in which I really learned German. This fellowship enabled me to study with and intern for Dr. Heike Düselder, who planted the seed of interest in the cultural history of the early modern German nobility. I am deeply indebted to my German host family, the Meyers. Anne Meyer, my daughter's namesake, was patient with my fumbling speech and introduced me to truly delicious German cuisine.

Many accomplished colleagues and generous institutions provided opportunities to share my works in progress and insightful feedback. Thanks to Helmut Walser Smith and Celia Applegate at Vanderbilt University's German History Seminar, David Goldstein and the "Food and the Book" conference from the Newberry and Folger Libraries, the Renaissance Society of America, seminars at German Studies of America conferences, the Research Center for the Theory and History of Science at the University of West Bohemia, Der Kreis workshop at UC Berkeley, Michael North at the Universität Greifswald, the Baroque Bodies Conference of the European Networks of Baroque Cultural Heritage, the Sixteenth Century Society Conference, the Institut für Geschichte der Medizin in Berlin, MTSU's Honors College, and Stanford's Center for Medieval and Early Modern Studies.

It was possible to enjoy both publishing and my children thanks to the loving, capable, and dependable care of Eliza Wofford and the teachers and staff at the Children's Center of the Stanford Community and the Anne Campbell Learning Center at MTSU.

Finally, I must acknowledge my family's unwavering support for this project. Bill and Carolyn Taylor sparked and sustained my interest in history and read multiple drafts. My children each got to come along for different parts of the process, whether they liked it or not. I think my husband has collected enough "weird factoids about early modern food" to last a lifetime. Hopefully that made all his sacrifices for this project worthwhile.

Family of Friedrich Wilhelm of Brandenburg-Prussia

Georg Wilhelm (1595–1640) *m.* Elisabeth Charlotte of the Palatinate (1597–1660)

       |

            Friedrich Wilhelm — *m.* Luise Henriette of Orange-Nassau
            (1620–1688)   (1627–1667)

                      |

                      Wilhelm Heinrich (1648–1649)
                      Karl Emil (1655–1674)
                      Friedrich III/I (1657–1713)
                      Amalia (1664–1665)
                      Heinrich (1664)
                      Ludwig (1666–1687)

                    — *m.* Dorothea Sophie von Schleswig-Holstein-
                        Sonderburg-Glücksburg (1636–1689)

                      |

                      Philipp Wilhelm (1669–1711)
                      Maria Amalia (1670–1739)
                      Albrecht Friedrich (1672–1731)
                      Karl Philipp (1673–1695)
                      Elisabeth Sophie (1674–1748)
                      Dorothea (1675–1676)
                      Christian Ludwig (1677–1734)

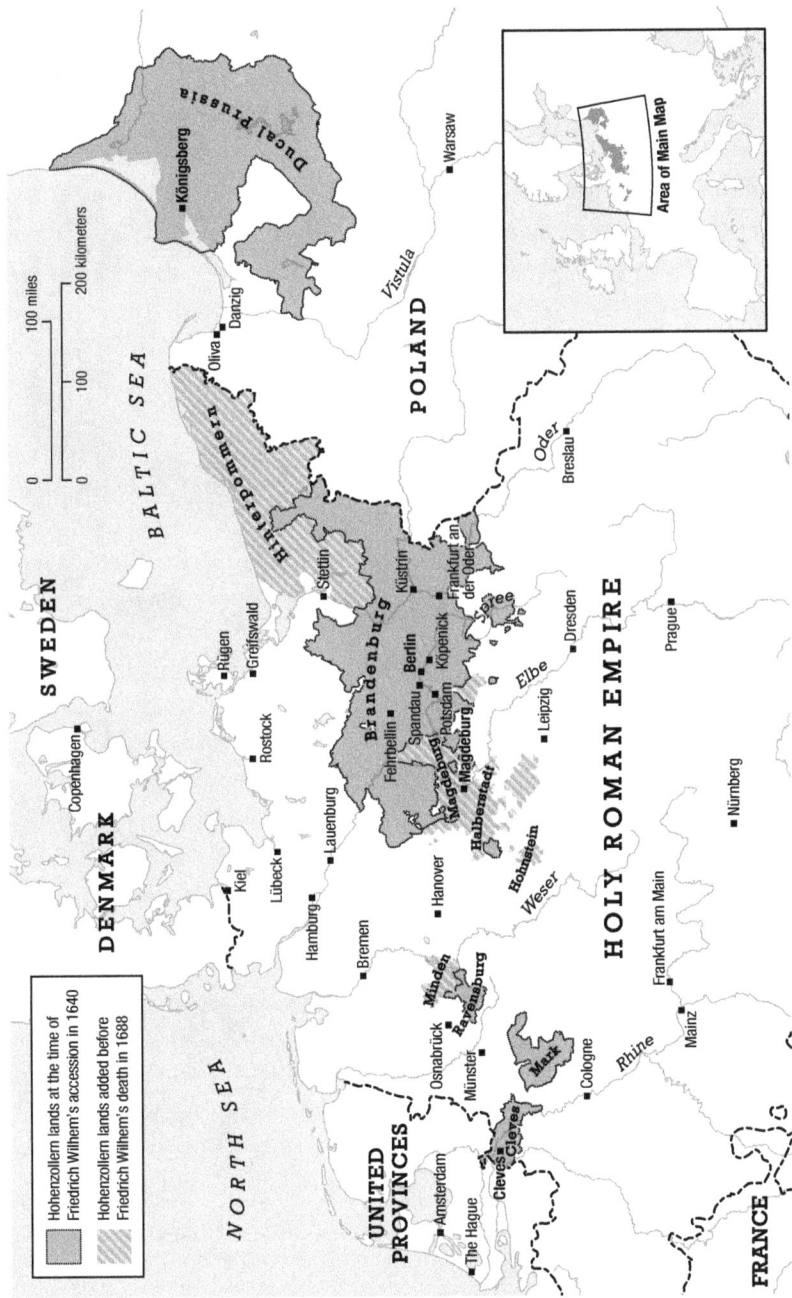

Brandenburg-Prussia in the 17th century. (Nat Case)

THE GREAT ELECTOR'S TABLE

INTRODUCTION

In 1640, Friedrich Wilhelm (1620–1688) became prince elector of Brandenburg-Prussia. With this, he inherited a set of diverse, nonadjacent territories in the northern reaches of the Holy Roman Empire that, over the course of generations, had come under one ruler variously through marriage, inheritance, armed conflict, and bargaining. The young elector found the heart of his holdings, the Mark Brandenburg, in shambles after decades of occupation by foreign armies during the Thirty Years War (1618–48). Its urban center, then known by the name of its combined cities, Berlin-Cölln, had dwindled to half its prewar population and even the elector's gardens had become a sandy wasteland. Indeed, the city palace on an island in the Spree River (Cölln an der Spree) was in such poor repair that Friedrich Wilhelm could not dine in the great hall when it rained because of the holes in the roof.[1]

By the end of his reign, however, instead of just one great hall (in the medieval palace tradition), the Berlin palace had a designated ceremonial hall at the fulcrum of the palace for receiving foreign visitors and for banqueting.[2] The 400-square-meter Alabaster Hall (Alabastersaal) contained statues of the previous electors of Friedrich Wilhelm's family, the Hohenzollern. Standing between exemplary historical leaders like Caesar, Alexander the Great, and Charlemagne, these twelve ancestor electors gained allegorical prestige by proximity. Moreover, the household budget for food skyrocketed, and the gardens outside the palace were burgeoning with native and exotic plants, supplying the kitchens with luxurious ingredients and projecting a message of a court in command of vast resources and refinement.

Beyond the island of Cölln, the streets were newly plastered and lit, and the city's population had grown from its postwar low of six thousand to nearly fifty-five thousand.[3] Brandenburg was again producing goods for export, and ships from Hamburg and beyond threaded throughout the region and onward to new markets via canals dredged under Friedrich Wilhelm. What is to account for this transformation?

The Alabaster Hall from Lorenz Beger's 1696 *Thesaurus Brandenburgicus*, p. 227. (Universitätsbibliothek Heidelberg)

The traditional response is that Friedrich Wilhelm (and his heirs) applied military acumen and bureaucratic exactitude to forge Prussia from the embarrassing ruins of the Thirty Years War.[4] This narrative provides a tidy origin story for later historians of the German Empire of the nineteenth century, but it obscures a fundamental truth about early modern European rule: power was communicated and reified by cultural gestures and ceremonial rituals.

This book offers a different view—a *cultural* approach to understanding this early modern court in a period of rapid change. "Culture" is an expansive and vague term. Furthermore, culture is constituted by often intangible elements that evade formal documentation. But one aspect of everyday culture was systematically tracked at court: food. Food is a material that is particularly salient for expressing cultural meaning because it is part of almost every aspect of the human experience. While food is a biological, individual need, its consumption is also a social practice in the sense that cuisine embodies shared values and expected behaviors in a given society. Food culture, then, encompasses the micro (for example, a single gardener's choice of which fruits to plant and how to nurture them) and the macro, as seen in large-scale provisioning of an army. Studying food culture means considering how humans associate with their food and with one another in order to obtain and share food.

The period under study saw centralizing governments throughout Europe settling into the forms they would maintain for the next century. As one classic interpretation puts it, seventeenth-century Europe was characterized by a "struggle for stability," as Europeans came to terms with upheavals in religious, scientific, medical, geographic, and environmental beliefs.[5] Changes in military technologies (referred to as the "military revolution") increased the cost of warfare. Only large, centralized governments could raise (or borrow) the funds needed to sustain the now standing armies. The large-state monopoly on violence required higher taxes, which in turn, required increased bureaucracy. All of this has been considered the origin story for later large modern European nation-states that came to dominate the Western political landscape.

The Hohenzollern were one of the ruling families in the Holy Roman Empire that were gradually able to consolidate territories and claim authority from local nobility and city leaders.[6] The rise of what would eventually become the Kingdom of Prussia and later the German Empire was not anticipated when the territories were ruled under the composite name Brandenburg-Prussia. Whereas France, Britain, and Spain had settled into their stable sizes and forms of rule by the end of the seventeenth century, Brandenburg-Prussia was still in flux. Although Friedrich Wilhelm has previously been called "the man who made Prussia," here he is "the prince elector of Brandenburg-Prussia." This book therefore examines his court culture not for traces of what Prussia would later become but for what we can learn about this early modern political culture. Principally, the takeaway is how interwoven were the concerns of knowledge, economy (in the expansive, older meaning of the word as the management of the whole household), and rule.[7]

The food culture of this court linked the representation of power to the practicalities of early modern rule. A banquet on an appropriate level of grandeur for a monarch, for example, had to be paid for and required bureaucratic innovations. When orchestrated correctly in accordance with mutually agreed-upon hierarchies and behaviors, a meal reified shifts in relationships as the Hohenzollern angled for status vis-à-vis the other seven electors of the Holy Roman Empire. Food fed the elector's "two bodies": his natural body and his body politic. On a domestic level, food was an integral part of the negotiations over central state power. While the ruler was dependent on subjects for most foods, it was also his prerogative to grant rights and privileges to certain citizens. This was a right that was used to take power from urban elites who had previously controlled local food trades.

Although the reign of Friedrich Wilhelm sets the parameters of this study, it is not a biography. Rather, it is a story about the whole court (mainly when it was in residence in Berlin, Königsberg, and Cleves) and how its different members negotiated their personal and shared interests to create a distinctive court culture. This speaks to the increasing bureaucratization of the state, but it also reveals hidden historical actors who had their role to play in the transformation of the state. The food culture required daily choices by many people: choices of procurement, economy, and manipulation of the environment, as well as choices of fashion, taste, religion, and tradition. These choices were shaped by the large and small mechanisms of early modern rule, and they, in turn, shaped those mechanisms.

The sources for this new assessment of the Brandenburg-Prussian court are the household records (including account books and merchant receipts) and descriptions of the food recorded in printed treatises, festival literature, and diplomatic reports. The household records are scarce and overlooked, mainly due to a nineteenth-century notion of separate private and public spheres, which resulted in an archivist's artificially dividing the archive into domestic and political papers. Then, in World War II, Friedrich Wilhelm's "political" papers were moved to a safe bunker, while his "domestic" papers were left in Berlin and largely destroyed in the bombing of Charlottenburg Palace.[8] The remaining annual accounts of kitchen expenses, letters, published treatises, and even a murder investigation have to be read against the grain to uncover the court's practices and beliefs about food.

As the largest expense of any premodern household and as a major cause of civil unrest historically, food was meticulously tracked and regulated at larger corporate institutions of early modern Europe including noble courts and religious communities.[9] Such corporations often left relatively systematic records about food supply, production, and shortage, and the present study uses computer visualization tools to look at change in consumption data over time. Although inspired by the Annalistes school of history in the mid-twentieth century, this dataset is comparatively small, and instead of making a *longue durée* argument, I use data wrangling and visualization as a means of deep reading to see shifts or absences. [10]

More recently, since the "cultural turn" in the 1980s, many historians have taken inspiration from sociologists and anthropologists to explore the cultural meaning of food, what Claude Lévi-Strauss called, "thinking with food."[11] As Georg Simmel wrote in a short article in 1910, eating is the most "egoistic" behavior (because we cannot share what we consume), yet it is also common to all people.[12] A meal is "natural" in that it fulfills a substantive physical need, but it is also "cultural" because in order to dine, we make plans (regulate time) and communicate in coded dining behaviors. Plates, for example, even uniform ones, communicate borders between those sharing a table and show the relationship of a group of equal individuals. Norbert Elias extended Simmel's argument about table manners to his study of Versailles under Louis XIV as an arena for monitoring minute distinctions of status, which set the Sun King apart from the rest of the nobility (a major shift in the "civilizing" of Europe).[13] In spite of Simmel's Eurocentrism and general snobbery, his ideas about socialization at the table are influential to the present study in seeing dining as an unifying *and* defining act.

Food studies blossomed for scholars of France in the 1980s, but was slower to catch on in other nations.[14] A sense of the superiority of French *haut cuisine* has led to a certain hierarchy of food culture, in which, among European food cultures, German food carries a reputation of poor refinement. Thankfully, Massimo Montanari has rebutted the idea that any cuisine is more civilized or cultured than another. All food is culture: the methods to harness and extract nutrients from the earth and transform them through cooking are known to us because of the human drive to control our environment, communicate know-how, and expand technologies. On the flip side, it is also a cultural myth that any food is more or less "natural" than another.

However, food history is not just about culture, it is also about politics. We have seen this in Steven Kaplan's exhaustive studies of bread in Enlightenment Paris, which document the monumental efforts the French government went to in order to satisfy the expectation of all French citizens for daily bread.[15] For Prussia, Lors Atorf has also made the classic argument that the state's ability to supply bread to soldiers differentiated the modern state army from a premodern, mercenary one.[16] A cultural reading from archival sources can take this line of questioning much further than the now outdated absolutism narrative.

One lasting influence from cultural historians of the past forty years is attention to how early modern life was documented and where we can implicitly hear the voices of marginalized actors who were silenced in those documents. Inquisition records, for example, document average citizens participating in larger political policies that consolidated the power of the Catholic Spanish monarchs when they testified about the food consumption habits of their neighbors.[17] Another tacit platform for political activity were the lavish banquets and festivals of premodern Europe, and historians do well to "read" the records of these events for political meaning.[18] Barbara Stollberg-Rilinger calls such festivals key political activities of prelegalistic European society at which whole populations played stipulated roles expressing their agreement to a particular social structure.[19] Power did not stem just from material resources and physical force (as has often been emphasized for Friedrich Wilhelm as the founder of Prussia's standing army), but from making power relations *visible*.[20] This is why the representation of a ruler was key to legitimizing the otherwise fictional social hierarchies that put them at the pinnacle.

Furthermore, political acts were not limited to those at the top of the social hierarchy—actors up and down the social scale participated in political negotiations.[21] These negotiations, Birgit Emich rightly points out, included not just the communication that happened at special ceremonial occasions, like diets and coronations, but also in everyday encounters.[22] As other historians have noted, this type of political revision is needed in Prussian history—particularly revisions that come from consulting archival manuscripts, not just the large source collections edited by Prussian archivists of the nineteenth and early twentieth centuries.[23] These collections were formed from a teleological idea about dominant modern nation-states. As Michael Rohrschneider recommends, a return to the full archival record is the way for scholars to determine *how* the early modern composite state of Brandenburg-Prussia worked.

Nonetheless, even with an anthropologically informed redefinition of early modern European political culture, the "Great Men" of history approach still dominates storytelling about Friedrich Wilhelm.[24] What his biographies from 1695 to 2020 have in common is a central concern with binary power.[25] Who dominated whom? Prussia or Austria, Friedrich Wilhelm or the estates, father or son (to name the most thoroughly discussed dichotomies)? Friedrich Wilhelm's negotiations were not so absolute, however: they were variously defensive, mutually beneficial, and improvised.[26] Food culture helps broaden the reductive tropes by expressing the shifting dynamics of human relationships and material resources. Examining the interactions of many actors involved in state formation with an *Alltagsgeschichte*, or history of everyday life, approach opens an understanding of early modern power as unstable and multidirectional.[27]

Food history challenges the conventional, top-down view of historical change by recognizing politics in the quotidian interactions between the elector and his subjects, servants, and suppliers. Sourcing food connected rulers with their subjects mainly as consumers, but also as producers. Building infrastructure to move foodstuffs over Brandenburg-Prussia both increased communication and collaboration between the different dominions of the Hohenzollern (a precursor to Prussian centralization) and integrated Brandenburg-Prussia more deeply into global trading networks. Of course, not all aspects of the food culture discussed here had a lasting impact on the subsequent Prussian kingdom and eventual Prussian empire, nor do they all have a traceable link to our own times. But, all of the food culture of Friedrich Wilhelm's reign exposes the particular values and ambitions of this court.

THE CHAPTERS OF THIS BOOK are thematic and progress in a loose chronology from the war-torn and recovery years of the elector's early reign to the power struggles both within Brandenburg-Prussia and with other European rulers to finally, his legacy building in the last decade his life. The first two chapters set the foundation for the subsequent chapters, which put the ingredients into context and ascribe meaning to them over the course of Friedrich Wilhelm's reign. While food consumption has been well studied in Italian and French archives, there have been few histories of food consumption in the German-speaking lands since the study by the agriculture historian Wilhelm Abel in 1935. Chapter 1, "To Dine with the Great Elector," addresses this by answering the foundational question "What did they eat?" Although some have argued that there was a unified elite culture across early modern Europe, even elite cuisine was not homogenous. While diners at the Brandenburg-Prussian court consumed imported ingredients (spices, dried fruits, and wines) that were common at tables of the wealthy throughout Europe in the late Renaissance, the majority of the foods reflect the local heritage and climate. Another finding from the records of food management is that each court office involved in food had their own food taxonomies. The vocabulary and categories each office used reflected their particular objectives and values. This specialization led to multiple meanings for the same foods.

Chapter 2, "Someone's in the Kitchen," introduces the Berlin palace servants who created the complicated dishes for banquets and labored daily to feed a court that numbered in the hundreds. These individuals blurred the line between the palace and the town as they were privileged with certain advantages to build and settle in the new neighborhoods of Berlin. The archival records suggest an increasing codification of the tasks of kitchen servants, yet creating those very records offered court clerks an outlet for complaining about the elector's focus centering on Brandenburg and away from his territories in East Prussia and Cleves.

Chapter 3, "The Field and Forest and River Richly Provide: The Regional Food System," deals with provisioning. In the reign of his father, war and weather could disrupt food deliveries between the dispersed territories of Brandenburg-Prussia. But the ability to source food from his different territories became a distinct advantage for Friedrich Wilhelm. No longer did he have to pay dearly, in cash, in a food shortage. Leveraging resources across the elector's dispersed territories required bureaucratic innovations and this was one way in which the heterogenous territories that Friedrich Wilhelm ruled in a personal union were haltingly drawn together. Coordinating food transfers from one region to another was a means of proto-centralization.

Food sourcing was not just a practical matter, but a symbolic one as well. As I show in chapter 4, "Prince of the Living World: The Berlin Pleasure Gardens," the palace gardens which supplied some foods to the kitchen were a representation of Friedrich Wilhelm's claims of refinement and dominion over all living things. The time and money he invested in the gardens signaled that the ruling family was laying down literal roots and would be a stable presence in Berlin after their extended absences during the Thirty Years War. Furthermore, cultivating exotic plants—including edible ones—on the prominent northern tip of the island of Cölln an der Spree signaled that Berlin was a center of learning about the natural world.

Chapter 5, "Feasts and Everyday Dining," considers the sociological and anthropological question of *how* people ate at court. Again, this question covers both representational power and practical concerns. Most scholarship treats ceremonial meals and everyday meals as distinct. However, court orders that dictated how everyday meals should proceed and festival literature that described meals for diplomatic purposes were both performances of hierarchy. Commensality was a means of defining and maintaining belonging within the court and among other European rulers. Members of the court and visiting dignitaries literally tasted their place within the social and political order.

Food was a means of imposing social control beyond the walls of the palace as well. Chapter 6, "The Northern War and the Prussian Bread War," tells the story of the cantankerous Königsberg court baker, Martin Hones, who was a local intermediary between Friedrich Wilhelm and city guild interests.[28] At a time when Friedrich Wilhelm was hotly debating the terms of his rule with the Prussian estates in parliament, Hones clashed with city bakers in the streets of Königsberg over local food production and sales. The elector's regular involvement in this street fight shows how well he understood that smaller conflicts impacted the consolidation of rule in Prussia.

Finally, for the elector who began his reign in a period of privation and uncertainty, increasing the cultural capital of the court was just as much a part of rule as military victories and gaining new territories. In line with other rulers of his age, Friedrich Wilhelm invested in scholarly projects and institutions while recruiting prominent scholars to Brandenburg and underwriting early scientific experiments. Chapter 7, "The Great Elector's Legacy," focuses on the work and life of one of the intellectuals drawn to Friedrich Wilhelm's court, Johann Sigismund Elsholtz (1623–1688), who wrote prolifically about botany and diet, among other interests. Dr. Elsholtz fit the mold of a seventeenth-century polymath: he had studied in the leading universities of Europe and he corresponded with a pan-European network of natural philosophers. He was initially hired to promote the Berlin palace garden. In cataloging and studying the plants there, he combined his interest in plants with his Renaissance humanist medical training to inform not just the court but a wider reading public. When compared with actual consumption, it is clear that Elsholtz's dietary theory influenced court consumption and was, in turn, influenced by existing court habits. This reciprocity confirms what historians of science have already argued: early modern medicine was frequently a product of networks of patronage.[29]

While all the chapters of the body of this book are about food and power, the conclusion instead explores food and vulnerability. In the last year of Friedrich Wilhelm's life, the court was shaken by a poison scare. Members of the electoral family turned against one another and suspicions reached a fever pitch until the Holy Roman emperor, Leopold I (1658–1705), intervened to reconcile the elector and his (then) oldest son and heir, Friedrich. Otherwise, the emperor feared the antagonism would destroy the only recently achieved peace in northern Europe. Friedrich Wilhelm's last will at this point would have broken up Brandenburg-Prussia among all of his sons (including those with his second wife) and Prussia might never have become a consolidated state. However, because the electoral prince Friedrich felt so threatened at his father's house, he negotiated with Emperor Leopold to ignore his father's will and recognize him as the sole ruler of all of the territories that Friedrich Wilhelm had ruled. This was an effect of the fear that came from the inability to guarantee the safety of food. The lack of an accurate test for poisoning (both during life and posthumously) left the ruler and therefore the state in danger. Because of the dual nature of the early modern ruler as a frail human and a divinely ordained leader of a state, a single bite of food could destabilize Europe.

Studying the food culture of the court of Brandenburg-Prussia not only transforms our understanding of that state, but also raises general methodological questions about the scholarship of early modern European courts. In this book, food draws the strands of early modern life together and offers a sense of how power worked at many levels of court society. Food cuts across almost every aspect of the human experience. As we are once again in a period of pessimism about future food security, the Prussian court diet offers fascinating lessons about food diversity and the construction of edibility. The history of food puts current food values into sharp relief and exposes the subjective natures of dietary theory, taboos, the construction of a meal, and taste. In doing so, it gives us a deeper appreciation for how the most basic necessities of life drive the rise and fall of states.

1

To Dine with the Great Elector

A MENU from the evening meal at the court of Friedrich Wilhelm in Cleves, January 3, 1652:

On the lord's table:

Pot barley
Mutton with white cabbage
White beef
Chopped roasted mutton with a vegetable mash
Prunes with wine and sugar
Boiled mutton tongues in egg porridge with lime
Chicken with wine and pomegranate
Chopped mutton roast with a vegetable mash
Plaice in butter
Plums
Boiled mutton marrow with deer ears
[illegible] with wine and mutton
Wild boar
Pickled salmon
Mutton with capers
Salad
Mashed carrots in butter
Pears with wine and sugar
Roasted mutton
Roasted stag
Roasted doe
Roasted partridge
Apple tart
Plum tart
Rice tart
Butter cookies

On the knights' side:

Beef
Mutton with white turnips
Sour mutton [illegible]
Prunes
Plaice in butter
Carrot mash
Salad

Imagine sitting down to the meal listed on this menu. Many questions arise when glancing over this list of dishes out of context. What were they? What did they taste like to the diners? How might they taste to a modern palate? Was this a "normal" meal? Where did the foods come from and why were they chosen? On its own, a list can only tell so much about the culture in which it was written. But the specific context of this winter dinner helps to answer some of these questions.

As the steward presented Elector Friedrich Wilhelm with this menu in Schwanenburg Castle in Cleves in the mid-seventeenth century, what was he thinking? Friedrich Wilhelm might have been relieved to focus on his physical appetite in the midst of many pressing political concerns. Not yet thirty years old, he had already made a name for himself as an ambitious ruler looking to increase his territorial holdings. His ambition, in fact, had earned him critics throughout northern and central Europe after his recent botched attempt to claim the United Duchies of Jülich-Berg in what was derisively called the "Düsseldorfer Cow War" (so named because Friedrich Wilhelm had seized a herd of cattle belonging to the wife of his adversary).[1]

Friedrich Wilhelm was also disappointed with the terms of the 1648 Peace of Westphalia, which, though mostly advantageous to his family, granted them only a small part of the territory of Pomerania. He desired the port of Pomerania to extend his commercial reach to the Baltic. Even in the face of these setbacks, though, a youthful optimism reigned at court. Cleves was at the center of important trade routes along the River Rhine and close to the hub of the riches of the Dutch golden age of the early seventeenth century that Friedrich Wilhelm had enjoyed growing up in the Netherlands. His new wife, Luise Henriette of Nassau-Orange (1627–1667), had not yet given birth to a living heir, but an earlier miscarriage proved she was fertile and the young couple's letters convey

Folio page, folded lengthwise listing how many dishes went to each table (left side) and what the dishes were (right side) for the evening meal in Cleves on January 8, 1652. (Hessische Staatsarchiv Marburg Best. 117 Nr. 2170) affection and trust. Taxes from the territories of Brandenburg, Cleves, Prussia, Pomerania, and Magdeburg were still slow to come in, but with the Thirty Years War over, rebuilding was happening not just at the electoral palaces but in their wider dominions.[2]

As the elector sat down for dinner on January 3, 1652, his ambitions were present even at the meal: his dinner table was yet another platform for the performance of rule. What does this meal mean? To begin: barley porridge seems a rather bland opening for a twenty-six-dish meal at the court of one of the seven prince electors of the Holy Roman Empire. But all walks of life consumed grain porridge during an average day in seventeenth-century Central Europe. The dishes that accompanied the pot barley, though, distinguished this meal from one at any other place and time.

The chicken with pomegranates and wine, the salad, and the rice pie contained expensive, imported foods and bestowed a cosmopolitan flair to the meal. Other dishes, though, were more traditional to the area. Cabbage, carrots, and turnips grew well in the colder northern European climate and were some of the few vegetables available in winter. Pickling fish was a common way to preserve fish in northern Europe, and the pickled salmon served here was considered the "noblest and tastiest [köstlichste] of all fish" by a physician at the electoral residence in Berlin, Johann Sigismund Elsholtz.[3] The preponderance of costly meat and particularly game on this menu confirms that this was a meal for the wealthy. Friedrich Wilhelm regularly enjoyed the exclusively noble pastime of the hunt and may have personally shot the roasted stag, doe, or partridge. Perhaps the boar was left over from the customary boar's head served at the previous week's Christmas feast.[4]

It is in the details—the precise ingredients and how and why they landed on the grand tables and modest boards of the court—that the contours of this culture emerge. The court was cosmopolitan and open to influences from other European courts and desired commodities from distant places. At the same time, though, the cuisine was rooted in the culinary heritage of northern Europe. As the main ingredient highlighted in the dishes of the above menu above, meat demonstrated the stature of the court. But not all of the ingredients were expensive: many locally grown, seasonal vegetables economically rounded out the meal. What Friedrich Wilhelm and the hundreds of other members of his court chose to consume reveals the characteristics of this court: where it stood in relation to other courts, what resources it could command, and what traditions or fashions it valued.

This chapter describes the Brandenburg court through its food. The archival evidence of consumption fills a gap in knowledge about elite cuisine in central Europe in the early modern period. Before delving into the less-tangible aspects of dining culture examined in the rest of this book, including labor negotiations, sociability, resource management, and beliefs about health and nutrition, this chapter sets the foundational knowledge of what was actually eaten and why. As a potent vector for meaning, food determines and expresses identity, and because it was so well documented, it is one of the most concrete ways to track the particular political-cultural history of the Brandenburg-Prussian court in the seventeenth century.

There is nothing to suggest that the meal on Wednesday, January 3, 1652, was out of the ordinary at the elector's table. What is extraordinary is that the menu survives. Only four such menus exist from the reign of Friedrich Wilhelm.[5] Other telling archival sources include the annual kitchen accounts from the Königsberg palace, of which thirty remain from Friedrich Wilhelm's forty-eight-year reign. This means these "East Prussian folios" are the most systematic of all the available food-related records. The regularity of these annual accounts enables a view of changes in taste over time.[6] The other evidence of food consumption at this court is more erratic and comes from the Hohenzollern residences of Berlin, Potsdam, Cleves, and Königsberg, among others, and include receipts, correspondences, and kitchen inventories.

In addition to the archival records of consumption, published sources from the period, such as cookbooks and dictionaries, indicate the social meaning of the foods mentioned in the court household records. The physician and botanist Dr. Elsholtz, published a vernacular dietary manual book, the *Diaeteticon* (1682), in which he presented the complex humoral beliefs about food for his readers and detailed the origins, contemporary views, and uses of different foods. The *Diaeteticon* also contains a French cookbook appendix. This and other contemporary cookbooks (both printed and manuscript) flesh out how raw ingredients, such as those inventoried in the Königsberg account books, were transformed into dishes.

In the Brandenburg-Prussian food records, servants employed their own food taxonomies depending on their purpose and interest with regard to food. Food categorization in both the manuscript and printed sources is significant in and of itself. Different actors communicated their particular *Weltanschauung* in the way they grouped foods. There is no natural order for food; even the designation of what is edible is culturally specific. The Königsberg kitchen clerks, Christoff Augustin, Gottfried (or Godfried) Augustin, and Caspar König, described foods according to their physical management. Foods that were handled in similar ways were grouped together, whether kept under the lock and key of the steward, broken down into parts, preserved, stored, or used fresh and immediately (so ephemeral that they might not even warrant recording in the accounts). The clerks' interests as they recorded food consumption lay in practical concerns of quantity and expense.

For the humanist Dr. Elsholtz, on the other hand, food categorization was part of the order of the natural world that medical practitioners and naturalists defined and redefined during the Renaissance and scientific revolution. In the 1652 menus, there is a third organizational model at work: courses. In this period in elite European cuisine, the fashion of progressing through separate courses in a meal was developing and we see this loosely underpinning the order of the menu here. Through cooking, ingredients were combined and chemically altered into new things that were organized along a different logic: that of soups, roasts, sides, and pies. Grouping food is an interpretive act that communicates underlying assumptions about how different actors thought about and interacted with food.

One example of these different classification schemes can be seen in the case of rice. The kitchen clerks treated rice as a spice because it was a luxury good imported from Hamburg or Amsterdam at great expense and the "spice chamber" (*Gewürtzkammer*) monitored its purchase.[7] Elsholtz, in his dietary treatise, described rice as a grain because "it was used in Asia to bake bread and all types of cakes, just as the Germans used their grains."[8] Both rice dishes from the 1652 menus were reserved for the high tables and not used in the lower knights' kitchen. Elsholtz, the worldly natural philosopher, took a universal perspective on rice, while the kitchen staff and clerks perceived rice according to how it was acquired.

The structure of this chapter follows actors' categories, from the most to the least valued foods—grains to spices—according to their value system. Although each individual had a particular way to categorize food, every member of the court, on some level, shared a collective food culture as they sat down together for a meal. The food consumed indicates a culture that accorded with European elite fashion but was also conscious of cost and imbedded in a regionally specific cuisine. In other words, food choice was informed by both the representation and the practicalities of rule. A "taste" for certain foods developed out of many overlapping values.

The Foods at Court

GRAINS

The most consumed food group was also the least expensive: grains. Grains were either combined with a liquid (and possibly other ingredients) to make a porridge or they were baked into bread, pies, and cakes. Whether as porridge or bread, grains had dominated the German diet since the thirteenth century, when grain consumption overtook meat consumption.[9] Grains fed even the nonhuman creatures at court: horses ate a combination of oats (40 percent), rye (30 percent), and barley (30 percent); pigs ate spent grain (*Malz*) through the winter; chickens were given barley; and geese and game received some oats.[10]

The historian Richard van Dülman claims that bread was not a regular part of the daily diet of ordinary people of the early modern period. This was not the case at the court of Friedrich Wilhelm, however, where even the most menial servants were doled out a portion of bread every day and Dr. Elsholtz designated grains in the "first order" of foods.[11] Bread consumption united all members of court—from the elector to the boy who drew the water. Even day laborers, who were not allowed to eat the food cooked in the kitchens still received beer and bread as part of their payment. Such daily bread and beer allotments were stipulated in long-term employment contracts as well, and the assurance of daily bread was likely a material incentive to court employment. Grains, as both beer and bread, contributed a large part of the caloric intake for members of court (particularly those lower in the court hierarchy, who had less access to meat).

Much of the grain used by the court came as taxes-in-kind from the local administrative districts and although bread was not particularly expensive, it was fundamental to the smooth running of the household and generally to the running of the state. Lack of bread was associated with the starvation so freshly imprinted in Brandenburgers' minds from the Thirty Years War.[12] Furthermore, as part of a Christian culture, members of court perceived their bread with implicit spiritual and local meaning.

As will be discussed in chapter 3, administrators in the elector's various dominions had to collaborate to ensure a steady grain supply and transported grains across great distances to whichever residence needed them. This need for grain, therefore, forced a connection between disparate holdings of Friedrich Wilhelm's personal union.

Millet, buckwheat, wheat, barley, oats, water manna grass, pearl barley, wheat flour, and peas are grouped by the clerks as the grains that were used by the cook in Königsberg. But it was rye that was the basis for most of the bread baked and consumed at court.[13] This was a particularity of northern Europe; German-speaking lands to the south, by contrast, such as areas of northern Italy, relied on wheat for their bread.[14] In fact, rye consumption was so great that it was managed by a different department: the cellar. Brewing and bread baking both required large quantities of raw grains. The bakery, too, was independent from the kitchen and required its own specific tools, spaces, and expertise. To give a sense of the importance in scale of each department: in 1672, the kitchen operated on 800 thalers per week and the cellars spent 700 thalers per week on wine, beer, and bread.[15]

This most common of all foods, though, was also a means of social distinction. Differences of grain type and fineness of flour translated to social distinctions. Fine white *Semmel* and *Herrnbrod* (the "lordly" bread) were for the highest members of court, and coarser rye *Gesindebrod* was given to all members.[16]

Bread did make its way into the kitchens, though, as stuffing and as a binding or thickening agent. It was likely a primary ingredient in the beer soup that Friedrich Wilhelm supposedly drank for breakfast every day. Beer soup carried a plebian, or *bürgerliche,* connotation according to humoral medical theory, which was specific to the needs of the individual patient. Physical constitution, age, gender, and caloric need (which was linked to class) affected what was considered healthy for each person.[17] The kitchen lexicographer Paul Jacob Marperger said that breakfast was the most useful to the young, the strong, and particularly for those doing heavy manual labor.[18] He added that the common man did well with a beer soup.[19]

The primary sources do not mention Friedrich Wilhelm's beer soup, but later Prussian historians frequently repeat this anecdote.[20] Whether or not Friedrich Wilhelm actually began each day with such a simple dish before attending to his work day at 6 o'clock is less important than the historiographical awareness that this quotidian detail helped nineteenth-century

Prussian historians to project an image of a Calvinist ruler with assiduous work habits and simple tastes, with cultural beliefs like those of Max von Weber.[21] Friedrich Wilhelm's European contemporaries also began the morning with a drink. Charles II, upon being restored to the throne of England, was reported to have brought the habit of drinking a *restaurant*, or beef broth, during his elaborate morning dressing ceremony, known as the *levée*. Other members of the Brandenburg-Prussian court (including the young prince and princesses) probably broke their fast with a similar *Früh-trank* of beer as everyone—high and low, young and old—received at least a quart of beer per day.[22]

Grains were such an assumed part of life in this culture that it was really only disturbances that generated mention in the historical record. For instance, when the citizens were struggling to pay for bread in Königsberg in the Thirty Years War, his chief officer there sent Friedrich Wilhelm an actual bread roll contaminated with inedible ingredients as self-explanatory evidence of the desperate situation.[23] The ability to procure needed grains was the sign of a healthy household and a healthy state (as well as a state that could maintain a standing army), especially in the wake of the financial crises (the so-called *Kipper und Wipperzeit*) of the Thirty Years War, when grain harvests were uncertain due to both climate and marauding armies, and debased currencies sent grain prices skyrocketing.

Meat and Fish

While every member of the court ate bread, it was meat that signaled this society was elite. And the accounts indeed reflect that this court consumed a tremendous quantity and variety of animal flesh. In the 1652 menus, meat was the primary component for most of the dishes. Bread, on the other hand, was such an assumed part of daily consumption that it was not listed on the menu (*Küchenzettel*) at all. Consuming meat was a metaphor for both man's dominion over all other beasts and the ruler's dominion over other members of society. For this reason, it was not just consumed at the court table, but paraded around: a courtier, trained in the noble art of carving, presented the roasts in their recognizable animal forms and gracefully sliced and served the individual portions before the eyes of the diners.[24]

Although this was certainly conspicuous consumption of meat, it was not wasteful consumption. This theme runs through all of the evidence of

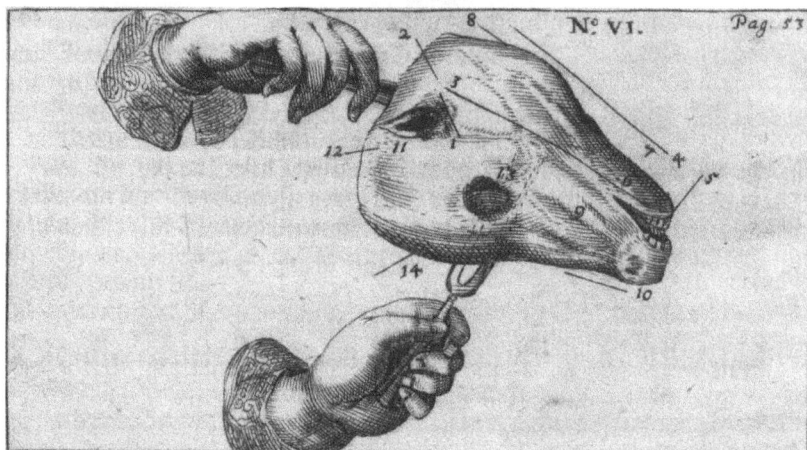

Image of pig's head being carved in midair, from Andreas Klett's 1677 carving manual, *Neues Trenchier- und Plicatur-Büchlein*, p. [80]. (Sächsische Landesbibliothek—Staats-und Universitätsbibliothek Dresden)

court dining: food was a representation of power and status, yet practical concerns weighed equally in food choices. Almost all parts of these expensive animals were put to use. Roasting was the most common preparation, but meat was also pickled, dried, processed into a terrine, cooked into soup, and baked into pies.[25] The Brandenburg-Prussian court consumed parts of animals that are not universally considered edible. The Königsberg clerk accounted for cow tongues and pig heads separately once the animals were slaughtered—a testament to their continued value. Cow's tongue might be smoked and filled with other meats and spices, making a type of sausage. It might add flavor to a roast, or be baked into a pie with raisins, butter, ginger, salted lemons, and a pastry cover.[26]

Cooks had many uses for the heads of livestock (usually either swine or cattle): the brains could be cooked into a dish served warm that was "good and tasty" (*gut und wolgeschmack*), according to the famous cookbook author and Mainz court chef Marx Rumpolt.[27] When cut into small pieces and cooked with the hooves, the boiled skull made a useful aspic. The leftover meat and broth from the cooking process, Rumpolt suggested, could be given to the poor. Only when foods were *too* ruined by rats, were they ever thrown away in Königsberg.[28]

Of all the meats, the wild boar and venison on the 1652 menu particularly conveyed noble status. The exclusive legal right to hunt gave young knights in the feudal period a chance to practice and demonstrate combat skills. While it provided an arena for primal displays of masculine power, it was also a form of elite sociability that became increasingly performative in the seventeenth century. Along with exercise, hunters had to know and perform proper behaviors and thus demonstrate their belonging in a certain caste.[29] Elector Friedrich Wilhelm was himself a keen hunter who spent many afternoons in the Tiergarten in Berlin or one of his other hunting parks.

While wild game was a fixture of noble banquets across early modern Europe, it carried particular significance in Prussia. For one thing, hunting was closely tied to ancient Germanic ideals of nobility. It was only when German tribes had conquered parts of the Italian peninsula after the fall of Rome and then became the ruling elite there that hunting took on a noble connotation in southern Europe.[30] Furthermore, as opposed to the rest of Europe, humans had only encroached on Prussia's great forests to a limited degree by the seventeenth century, leading to a particular hunting heritage. With low human density, its virgin, biodiverse forests sustained abundant wildlife.[31] The Königsberg records list foods such as rabbits, birds, wild boar, and the most highly prized meats from elk, roe deer, and stags that arrived at the palace kitchen from court hunters in Prussian forests.[32]

The Teutonic characteristics of Friedrich Wilhelm's cuisine are highlighted in the story of the mysterious *Auer* that appeared in the Königsberg palace. The common translation of *Auer* is aurochs (*Bos primigenius*), or wild cow, the first animal recorded extinct in history.[33] Deforestation and overhunting elsewhere had limited the species to areas of Poland, Lithuania, and Prussia until supposedly the last aurochs died in Poland in 1627.[34] However, in 1645, an *Auer* was recorded in Königsberg as coming in from the ducal hunting lodge, *Jagerhoff.* Perhaps von Berbisdorf presented it as a particularly rare and valuable gift to the elector.[35] Two quarters of that *Auer* were used fresh in the kitchens and the other two quarters were sent to the *Pökel* (the picklery?) to be processed into two and a half tons of pickled *Auer.*

It is impossible to say for sure whether von Berbisdorf's *Auer* really was the last living aurochs, as the term was also used to refer to bison at the time.[36] In any case, *Auer* (whether bison or aurochs) were extremely rare. Serving bison or aurochs meat would have brought honor to the court, highlighted a local delicacy, made reference to the noble hunting tradition, and presented a topic of conversation and delight for a limited number of diners and a larger number of voyeurs.[37] Indeed, *Auer* had been one of the local delicacies sent from the Prussian forests for the 1594 wedding that had given the Hohenzollern their initial claim to Ducal Prussia.[38] The presence of the *Auer* on the menu was underscored by *Auer* table sculptures that would have leveraged the symbolism of Prussian natural resources at the celebration of the union.[39] In this case, it was not the expense that made this food elite: it was a combination of placemaking and rarity.[40]

Like large game, many birds were served at the court table that contributed to the spectacle of dining. Along with the larger, fleshier wild birds, there were thousands of small birds, including thrushes, sandpipers, fieldfares, quails, curlews, snow buntings, yellow hammers, larks, waxwings, coots, starlings, finches, sparrows, skylarks, and generic "small birds."[41] While these provideded only a modicum of flesh, they also provided symbolic and entertainment value. Baking twenty-four blackbirds into a pie in order to have them fly out (as in the nursery rhyme) was actually something medieval and Renaissance chefs did to make a meal entertaining. The small birds in Königsberg may have been part of such an *entremet* intended to stimulate multiple senses with the local twist of birds particular to the Prussian forests.

There was likewise a tremendous variety of both fresh- and saltwater fish. Fifty-two types came into the Königsberg kitchens fresh, pickled, smoked, salted, and even jellied. Many of these fish—including vimba bream, Wels catfish, sturgeon, chameleon loach, tench, gudgeon, and burbot—are unlikely to be found on a German menu today. One historian attributes the comparatively limited selection of fish for culinary use today to humans' destruction of fish habitats.[42] While it is true that many waterways are polluted or have been diverted and many stocks of wild fish have been overfished, this is only part of the story. Many of the fish listed in Königsberg still exist—mainstream Western society has simply ceased to view them as food. Yes, industrialization has spurred ecological and even genetic changes for fish, but there has also been a cultural shift in what is considered food. Supply of certain fish could never be guaranteed, but in some ways, early modern (elite) diners had more choice and variety in their diet because they were not constrained by homogenized industrial production methods.

However, despite the wide number of fish species listed in Königsberg accounts, fish was not a large part of the court diet. In the four 1652 menus, only 6 of the 108 dishes included fish. In a purchasing record, expenses for fish constituted 8 percent of costs for half a year in 1652.[43] The physician Elsholtz did not have a high opinion of fish and, in accordance with Galen, thought they were less healthy than other animal flesh because they were "further from man's nature" and therefore harder to assimilate into the body.[44]

Furthermore, as devout Calvinists, Friedrich Wilhelm, his wife Luise Henriette, and their family were not compelled to abstain from meat and eat more fish on the Catholic fasting days. During the Reformation, in other European Calvinist enclaves, ignoring the prescribed Roman Catholic fast day was a form of protest.[45] Eventually the secular princes of the Holy Roman Empire determined their own replacements for Catholic fasts, which later also included corresponding feast days.[46] Elector Johann Georg I of Saxony, for one, proclaimed a penance and prayer day in 1633 due to the "general hardship" of the Thirty Years War.

Friedrich Wilhelm, motivated by war with the Turks, proclaimed a "general fast, penance, and prayer day" the first Wednesday of every month of 1664 and 1683 for Brandenburg.[47] His trusted counselor Otto von Schwerin described the first of these days: "The 4th of May [1664], arose at 6 o'clock, prayed and went to church. Because it was the first penance and fast day, [electoral prince Karl Emil] could not hold table; instead he only took a soup and an egg in his chamber. Afterward we read a penance sermon in Saxon and sang. At 2 o'clock, we went to the church again, at 5 o'clock, the table was laid, and [Karl Emil] ate with the elector."[48] As a result of this Calvinist fasting culture, fish mattered less in the Brandenburg court diet than it would have in the diet of contemporary Catholic courts. Food, therefore, was a way to assert religious identity. The minor importance of fish in the Brandenburg cuisine likely stemmed from intermingling values of nutrition, expense, and religious confession.[49]

Dairy and Fats

Animals provided not only their flesh but also their milk for the court table. Butter and cheeses were of medium monetary value in the Königsberg accounts, and were therefore listed between the meat (domesticated animals and birds) and fish. As with meat, the use and choice of butter and cheese reflected the particularities of this place. Once again, a mixture of both expensive, foreign cheese and inexpensive, local dairy were eaten. For example, of the three cooking fats used in the court kitchens—butter, lard, and olive oil—butter was overwhelmingly the most consumed.[50] At the meal on January 3, the court used an astonishing fifty-five pounds of butter.[51] Marperger's kitchen dictionary mentions that the biggest courts had a dairy close by that would supply the lordly table daily with fresh butter.[52] Butter took on the taste of the particular *terroir* as the local cattle ate local grass, which meant that a dish cooked in Berlin or Königsberg or Cleves would have tasted different anywhere else. Butter flavored the traditional baked goods of the Easter *Mundbrodt, Putterkuchen,* and *Streuzel,* and most recipes for that *bürgerliche* beer soup start with a pat of butter in the pan.[53]

The court's butter use had significance beyond the taste and saturated fat it imparted to diners. First, it reflected the traditions of the area: animals were easier to farm in this area than oil-producing plants. Second, preference for butter, as with fish, distinguished the Calvinist court of Friedrich Wilhelm from the courts of Catholic princes. Dairy was an indulgence prohibited during Catholic fast periods, when olive oil was typically substituted. This was an expensive form of abstinence for Catholics living in colder, northern areas. But, no longer beholden to fast prohibitions on dairy, the Hohenzollern were able to (cheaply) consume a fat more suited to their climate.

This particularity, in turn, affected the flavor of the food because olive oil was often rancid by the time it reached northern European consumers.[54] Olive oil, referred to as *Baum-oel,* or tree oil, in court accounts, carried a certain prestige as an expensive import from Mediterranean lands. But it was used in such small quantities compared to the other fats that it was considered a condiment, rather than a cooking fat.[55] Elsholtz listed it as a "liquid condiment" (between honey and vinegar) in his *Diaeteticon.*[56] He noted its use as a dressing on salad but added that "as the oil from Spain and Italy was usually old and yellow instead of fresh and green, Germans preferred to make their salads with fresh butter."[57] He would have noticed the difference from the fresh olive oil he would have enjoyed while a student in Padua. But, when it came to choosing a fat, taste, freshness, and local habit took precedence over cosmopolitanism and exclusivity.

The third reason butter was significant in Brandenburg-Prussia was its link to the commercial and agricultural initiatives of Friedrich Wilhelm's reign. The rebuilding efforts in the lands surrounding Berlin included enticing Dutch dairy farmers to transplant their methods and prolific

Holstein Friesian dairy cows to Brandenburg. Cow and sheep butter was available in Berlin either from the local estates or transported from Prussian farms to the elector's other residences.[58] Electress Luise Henriette's own estate in Oranienburg, for example, supplied butter to the Berlin residence.[59] Beyond its uses in the kitchen, butter made up part of the *Deputat* (food allowances) of the court staff and dependents, including the university supported by the elector in Frankfurt an der Oder.[60] It was a small source of income when the court sold excess butter.[61]

Just as meals in France still often conclude with a cheese course, butter and cheese were served to diners at the higher tables in Brandenburg-Prussia as a stand-alone dish. A carving manual printed in 1670 instructed the butler (*Mundschenk*) to serve cheese and butter after the third course and before the confections.[62] In one week in December 1655, the Berlin residence used 2¾ small vats (*Feßlein*) of cow butter. Of that, 1¼ vats went to the steward, ¾ vat went to the pastry baker (*Pastetenbecker*), and the final ¾ vat landed on the plates (*"uf die Teller"*).[63] Dr. Elsholtz acknowledged this practice as a habit specific to "our northern lands."[64]

The cheese that accompanied the butter course at the end of the meal was another material manifestation of Brandenburg's far-reach and cosmopolitan tastes. The court regularly bought *"hollandische Kees"* (Edamer cheese) from Hamburger merchants.[65] Since the collapse of the Roman Empire, cheese had been considered by some Europeans as barbaric.[66] The Dutch were finally able to rescue the reputation of cheese during their golden age thanks to the high-quality cheeses that came out of this period of Dutch agricultural development.[67] With Edamer cheese on their table and Friesian cows increasing Brandenburg dairy production, this shift in the perception of cheese benefited the court's reputation and its commercial enterprises.

Aside from expensive imported cheeses, however, cheese was quite common fare, given the traditional cheeses of the region.[68] In Königsberg, fresh quark (recorded by its Prussian name, *Glumse*) was a payment in kind from local domains.[69] The local Brandenburg hard cheese made from sour milk, known as *Knapkese,* was eaten and paid out as part of the *Deputat* for court day laborers.[70] The selection of cheeses found in Berlin, Cleves, and Königsberg reflect the influence of Dutch industry and tastes in particular. At the same time, more traditional cheeses still held an important place in the court diet, particularly to lower orders, who were not consuming the expensive, imported cheeses. Interlocking concerns of religion, tradition, climate, agriculture, and economy determined the choice of food, and in this case, the very particular types of cheese.

FLAVORINGS

In terms of quantity, flavorings made up the least volume of the foods at court, yet their cost and impact on the flavor of the food were substantial. Elsholtz used the expansive Latin term *condimenta* to connote anything needed to "complete a dish," and included spices under this heading.[71] Of a total expense of 482.5 thaler for the week of the menus in January 1652, only 15.75 went to spices, and only 69 thaler went to flavorings in general (including nuts, preserved fruits, and vinegar). The four 1652 menus hint at the flavorings in these dishes: acidic citrus cut the richness of beef tongue, sheep organs, or a tough leg of mutton; spices like caraway and ginger accompanied strong-tasting beef and mutton; and saffron colored a beef and bacon dish a brilliant yellow. The expense account for that first week in January 1652 lists other spices not found in the menus including cloves, cinnamon, mace, nutmeg, and, in great quantities, pepper and sugar.[72] Anise was also in the Cleves records of 1652 and was purchased occasionally by the court at other times, but was never listed among the other "spices."

Because condiments have an outsized impact on taste, food scholars have used changes in spice use to mark the different eras of European food history: heavy spice use characterized elite cuisine of the medieval and Renaissance period.[73] The market for spices was so strong in the late medieval period that it fueled the nautical discoveries and the invention of navigational tools of the fifteenth and sixteenth centuries.[74] As merchants began sailing faster routes to the East, however, prices fell and spices lost the prestige they had carried in France since the time of Catherine de Medici. French chefs developed a new style of cooking, *haute cuisine*, which promoted fewer exotic spices and more local herbs and complex sauces.[75] This new taste marked the Baroque food culture found at the court of King Louis XIV.

This periodization does not reflect the food history of all of Europe, however. Although often thought to have followed the French trends in cooking, German diet and cuisine only adopted significant spice use in the fifteenth century.[76] Spices impacted habit so much in the German-speaking lands that reformers, including Luther, railed against their use in food and medicine and against the merchants who traded them. Luther and like-minded reformers criticized the spice trade as detrimental to the community: as spices were an unnecessary luxury, their trade did not benefit the common good and its consumption made Germans dependent on foreign goods. Nonetheless, as evidenced in the records from Brandenburg-Prussia, spices were still used consistently through the reign of Friedrich Wilhelm.[77]

Whereas the division between using imported spices and local herbs may have been stark in France, herbs and spices were used concurrently in Brandenburg-Prussia. Elizabeth Schmidts worked as an "herb woman" (*Kräuter-frau*) at the Berlin residence in 1683 (although her work may have had more to do with medicinal herbs).[78] Elsholtz cataloged forty-eight varieties of herbs and leafy greens in his 1652 *Hortus Berolonenis*, and occasionally the clerks recorded additional purchasing of herbs. In one case, marjoram, parsley, dill, and rosemary were bought with cash for the homage feast at Königsberg in 1663.[79]

According to the kitchen account books, pepper and ginger were the most consumed spices, accounting for 65 percent to 75 percent of spices used (not including sugar, which was still recorded as a spice).[80] Ginger, for one, was adopted relatively late into German cuisine, and pepper continued to be popular in German areas long after its use had declined in neighboring countries.[81] Elsholtz recognized the prominence of pepper, but mistakenly wrote that it was the "most common condiment among us."[82] For one thing, he overlooked that ginger was used in similar proportions and, for another, he neglected to mention sugar.

This apparent oversight, however, indicates that, in Elsholtz's mind, sugar was in a different food group altogether (another epoch-marking shift). Even though the kitchen clerks were still accounting for sugar with the spices described above, sugar had otherwise evolved into something new in the minds and diets of members of the court.[83] The increase in sugar available on the market because of enslaved labor in the Americas and Europeans's growing addiction to and familiarity with sugar accounts for the jump in sugar consumption in the seventeenth century.[84] During Friedrich Wilhelm's reign, sugar consumption was so high that if it is included in graphs of spice consumption, it completely obscures the relatively small use of other "spices."[85]

Previously, sugar had been part of a medieval flavor profile that mixed sweet and savory. The concentration of the fruit pies and cookies at the end of the 1652 menus indicates that during Friedrich Wilhelm's reign, a distinct sweets course was developing.[86] Along with its use as a seasoning and in sweet baked goods, sugar was used as a preservative for fruits (by a special court confectioner). Wooden molds in the Königsberg kitchens of such delightful shapes as a springing deer and a swimming swan were probably used to make sugar or marzipan sculptures for the table—a forerunner of the ceramic table figures that would become popular in the eighteenth century.[87] Old labels and accounting practices sometimes endured after the use and understanding of an object shifted, but food categorization could also adapt with changing tastes and markets.[88]

In spite of Europe's increased consumption of sugar, the older, sweet and savory flavors profile were still present in the seventeenth century. Many of the savory dishes in Cleves, for example, were sweetened with sugar or fruit, as was the case with the *Sauerbraten* with large raisins from the Wednesday, January 3, midday menu. In the French cookbook appended to Elsholtz's *Diaeteticon,* sugar is repeatedly listed as a possible addition to meat roasts (sometimes along with cinnamon, cloves, or pepper).[89] Sugar was also sprinkled on dishes as a seasoning (sometimes interchangeably with salt, as in many of the *Diaeteticon* recipes). Culinary shifts, such as that seen with sugar, were gradual and new dishes shared space on the elector's table with more traditional ones.

Certain traditional foods, indeed, had remarkable staying power. Long after the spike in sugar consumption in Europe, the customary cakes for Christmas, New Year's, Easter, and Pentecost were still sweetened with honey, the preferred sweetener in the region prior to plantation production of sugarcane.[90] Otto von Schwerin, recorded in his diary that Friedrich Wilhelm's own sons baked these *Lebkuchen* at New Year's and were thus personally participating in and perpetuating Prussian traditions dating back at least to the fourteenth century.[91]

Foods from Plants

Whereas spice consumption was monitored very closely because of its expense, native plant foods, by contrast, were rarely recorded in the clerks' account books. Plant foods cost little or nothing for the court, and their handling indicates that different value systems were, in fact, connected. The monetary value of plant foods corresponded with poor nutritional assessments and loose handling and accounting practices. Vegetables were supplied to court fresh and locally and thus, like dairy, tasted of their particular terroir. However, following the transoceanic voyages of exploration by Europeans, many of the foreign foods that entered the court were plant foods. In other words, vegetables were emblematic of the local place, but, they too, presented an opportunity for novelty and for expressing cosmopolitanism.

Etymologically, vegetables have undergone a transformation in the German language since the seventeenth century. The story of the development of the German word *Gemüse* highlights the historical specificity of food categorization. In modern German, the word *Gemüse* covers all edible plants and is the direct translation of the English word "vegetable."[92] During the early modern period, however, *Gemüse* did not refer to lettuce, carrots, turnips, cabbage, or other items we know as "vegetables" today. *Gemüse* evolved from the Middle High German word *Mus* or *Muos*, which meant grain porridge.[93] *Zugemus*, or "that which went with the *Mus*," first referred just to turnips and various types of cabbage, and later included other produce now considered vegetables.[94] The eighteenth-century lexicographer Johann Heinrich Zedler defined *Zugemüse* as "everything green or baked and dried fruit, cereals, groats, porridge, general egg dishes, garden and cabbage herbs, and roots that were of use in the kitchen."[95] These, he said, were served after the meat, fish, or roast. The root of the German word *Gemüse* as an accompaniment to other foods indicates the lower status of vegetables in early modern cuisine.

Neither Elsholtz nor Marperger used the terms *Gemus* or *Zugemus* in their works on cuisine. Instead, they used *Küchen-Wurzeln* (root vegetables) or *Küchen-Kreuter* (mostly leafy vegetables grown above ground).[96] The court household records also do not refer to *Gemüse* as such. In account records, the rather broad language of *Gartengewächs* and *Grungewächs* (garden, or green, growths) describe any green vegetables. The roots of the English word, "vegetable," were similarly expansive coming from the Latin (via medieval French) for "living" or "capable of growth."[97] Indeed, the first recorded use of "vegetable" to describe plant foods was not until 1767. Before that, the term connoted any plant, edible or not.

The etymological evolution of vegetables suggests that they were freely available in one's garden or in the wild. In fact, it is impossible to quantify vegetable consumption at court because vegetables were not accounted for individually since they cost little to nothing. In instances when vegetables were purchased, only a total price, not a unit price, is recorded.[98] Since most vegetables came from the court's kitchen garden, no budgeting was needed; the accounts simply state, "for all types of plants, take them from the gardens, as needed."[99]

Plant foods were considered peasant food in the early modern period because they were so cheap (with some rare exceptions). This hierarchy of worth translated to their perceived health qualities. In his study of Renaissance ideas about food and the humors, Ken Albala found that root vegetables were largely considered poor foods, "except when they have an effect on the body, such as horseradish, which has an incisive quality."[100] Dr. Elsholtz divided plant foods into five groups, the first of which, grains, was the most consumed. He arranged the other four divisions in order of the height of growth, starting with roots and moving up to food from trees. This typical Renaissance hierarchy of plant foods was imbued with analogies to human society.[101] The closer to heaven something grew, the more highly it was esteemed. Fruits from the trees, for example, were reserved for nobility, while root vegetables were associated with the lower orders.

The nutritional and social assessment of plant foods aligns with the 1652 menus in which few plant foods are mentioned. Vegetables would not have been featured in table sculpture, as fruit confections were at prominent banquets. More exclusive ingredients overshadowed the presence of vegetables in court cuisine: on a menu for a meal at a royal court, only one out of ten dishes (in this case, kale with sausages and chestnuts) named a plant food.[102] Other plants were almost certainly used, but they added no prestige and are not named.

The only exception to this ambivalence about local vegetables was the Teltower turnip, a white root vegetable that was exported from Brandenburg to wealthy households as far away as France.[103] Elsholtz claimed Teltower turnips "were desired far and wide."[104] He recorded these *Rapa sativa oblonga* in his 1656 catalog of the Berlin palace garden and described them as, "small, but sweet."[105] The delicate and highly sought-after turnips were, in Elsholtz's assessment, beneficial to health, and he deemed them to have a "somewhat warm or moderate temperament."[106]

Given the climate of the region, it is not surprising that, in addition to the Teltower turnip, the records list many other hearty varieties of cabbage and root vegetables including carrots, parsnips, radishes, and beets.[107] But, while the stereotypical cabbage had been consumed in northern Europe since antiquity, there were also "new" vegetables entering the court diet. As will be discussed in chapter 4, growing nonnative plants in the palace gardens signaled that the elector could control resources from all over the world. It was also a representation of his knowledge of the natural world, which supported the argument for his divine right to rule. The scholars he brought to court enabled this image, and Dr. Elsholtz's writings, in particular, demonstrate how erudition was used to promote new foods.

It is hard for a new food to be adopted into a cuisine—instinctively, unfamiliar foods are unappetizing or even nauseating. For this reason, new foods in Brandenburg-Prussia were couched in familiar terms. This is the same slow, sociointellectual process that finally enabled tomatoes to become mainstream in European cuisine hundreds of years after their initial introduction in the fifteenth century.[108] In Berlin, the story of the sunchoke, or Jerusalem artichoke, exemplifies this back-and-forth process between naturalists, gardeners, and the kitchen. Artichokes (native to Italy) had been known in elite northern German cuisine for centuries by the time sunchokes (native to the Americas) came to Europe in the seventeenth century.[109] The term Elsholtz uses for sunchokes, *Erdartschocken*, literally meant "earth artichokes." The Königsberg kitchen accounts record that *Obererdtschocken* were purchased in 1630 while *Artschocken* were purchased 1663 and 1670.[110] Elsholtz put sunchokes and artichokes in different sections of his *Diaeteticon* (sunchokes were root vegetables, while artichokes were "herb fruits"), but otherwise, he claims that they had a similar taste. The *Diaeteticon* recipe for sunchokes says, "They acquire the taste of artichokes, only they are softer."[111]

Elsholtz could not refer to ancient dietary theory to determine their health properties because the ancients knew nothing of sunchokes. Instead, he quoted from a near contemporary horticulturalist who claimed sunchokes provided swift nourishment and were good for the body. "For this reason," Elsholtz writes, "we often eat sunchokes, in spite of their flatulent properties."[112] Thus, scholarship could be deployed in the service of diet. Their similarity to artichokes is likely not the only reason sunchokes were adopted more quickly into Brandenburg cuisine than other American foods such as tomatoes and green beans. Tubers grew well in the northern European climate and could be cooked similarly to native foods. The decision to eat sunchokes, as with everything else consumed by the court, was influenced by many factors.

FROM THE *AUER* (whether bison or indeed aurochs) to the earth artichoke, the food of the Brandenburg-Prussian court was particular to that culture. The cuisine projected power both representationally and through the control of financial, natural, and human resources. At the same time, elite foods were balanced with frugal, locally grown staples. Even though

Friedrich Wilhelm's reign started with drastic disruptions in court culture from the Thirty Years War, long-standing food traditions and administrative practices persisted and gradually blended with new foods and practices. Contemporary published descriptions of food provide clues of the values underpinning their choice while the archival records show that this food culture did not neatly fit the periodization of European food fashion. It is not that Brandenburg-Prussia was behind culinary developments in Italy or France, instead, heterogenous early modern European food histories emerge when we look beyond hierarchical comparisons of cultures.

The dishes presented on January 3, 1652, were served to a court in transition. After being disappointed in his bid to be regent for his nephew, the Dutch stadtholder, Friedrich Wilhelm turned his attention in the opposite direction: east to Brandenburg. This foundational moment in Friedrich Wilhelm's court set the tone for its culture for the next thirty-five years. The changes in this period following the Thirty Years War were evident in the administrative correspondences regarding budget that discussed the size and expense of the household as well as leases of sources of tax revenue. There is no indication that changing the types or quantities of food was part of any solvency debate—taste and plentitude were nonnegotiable. However, the food itself was not the only representation of the court's ambitions and values: the people who created and served it also played their role in creating the image of this court.

2

Someone's in the Kitchen

THE JANUARY 1652 meal described at the start of chapter 1 consisted of twenty-six dishes for the lord's table and a further six dishes for the knights. The meal would have been announced with trumpets calling to the hall all the members of court who received board (*freie Tisch*) as part of their salary. Once there, they would sort themselves into their departments at the prominent *Tafeln* or simpler *Tischen* (two German words for table that were distinguished according to status in the archival record). The room would be lit and heated in the winter months with a roaring fire. The high tables would be laid with cloths, candles, and dinnerware. When all were seated and prayers said, the hot dishes would be brought out from the kitchen—a mixture of boiled and roasted meats, mashed carrots and fruits cooked in wine and sugar. The cold dishes—salad and maybe the pickled salmon and fruit tarts—would be served from a tiered credenza off to the side. As dishware was removed from the table, it might be returned to the kitchens to be refreshed and reheated or washed and set back up on the credenza to add to the glitter and rich spectacle of the hall.

The experience was full of sensorial delights. Diners and spectators were transported from a mundane occasion for sustenance and camaraderie to a realm of fantasy. At a banquet, attention was directed toward the prince's table on a raised stage and canopied by a baldachin where a forest tablescape of springing deer, running horses, or the lord's coat of arms might be twinkling in sugar or marzipan. The tablescapes might have echoed pastoral or ancient noble hunting themes referenced in other parts of the room: in paintings, tapestries, and theatrical masks. The dining ware, too, contributed to the sense of wonder with miniature masterpieces of northern Renaissance sculpture on spoons or elaborate goblets with moving parts bringing an element of play to the table. The objects and images might even have been changed throughout the meal to provide new sources of stimulation.

IT IS AS IF THE MEAL appeared by magic. But it was not magic at all. It was work. If one includes all of the court offices involved in dining and the food allowances paid to servants, food accounted for up to three-quarters of annual court expenses.[1] It is the elaborate presentation of a meal that contemporaries were meant to remember, and that is why they are described in rich detail in the festival books that were published as a means to record and broadcast the occasion to other courts across Europe. In the same way that modern televised cooking shows feature an individual cooking in a clean, open space, most early modern depictions present a filtered story. The banquet was far removed from the toil of the fields, the stench of the chicken coops, and the heat and sweat of the kitchens. For the dozens of "officers of the mouth" at court, the early modern kitchen was not a place of miracles, but of expertise applied in daily labors. Yet, court studies have primarily focused on the representative power of early modern banquets rather than looking behind the curtain to see how the gastronomic feats of court dining were accomplished and *by whom*.[2]

There are a few celebrity chefs of early modern Europe who are remembered largely because they published popular works on their craft, notably Bartolomeo Scappi (1500–1577) and Cristoforo di Messisbugo (late 1400s–1548). Both Scappi and Messisbugo served at prominent Italian courts, were famous in their time, and published cookbooks that elevated the profession in the eyes of the literate population.[3] The personal chef to the archbishop of Mainz, Max Rumpolt, also published a cookbook in German that went through multiple editions, though little else is known about him.[4] Some court chefs became the stuff of legend, such as François Vatel, chef to Prince Louis II de Bourbon-Condé, who ran himself through with a sword when he thought he had botched a banquet for two thousand people (including King Louis XIV). However, in spite of the status afforded to these few notable stewards and cooks, they could not work alone and they were not the only servants at court who had political and cultural agency.

Some early modern images of large kitchens, however, do depict busy crews engaging in a variety of individual and collaborative tasks such as the unnamed men leveraging a cauldron in Scappi's *Opera*. More scholarship is needed to understand the corporate nature of these early modern professional kitchens and the ties of loyalty and influence between members of the court up and down the social ladder. As Sebastian Kühn writes, when we take the constant presence of servants in the houses of power seriously, we understand the relational nature of power in early modern

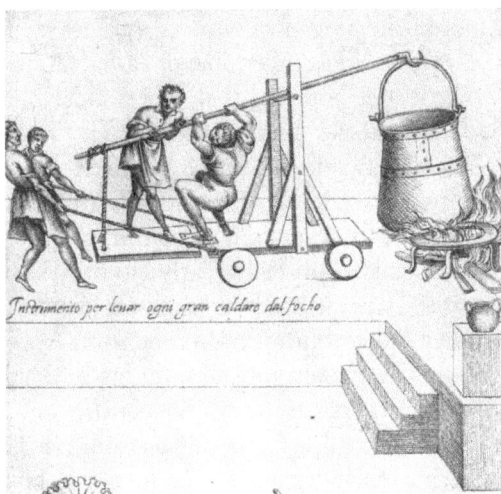

Unnamed cooks at work, from Franz Philipp Florin's 1702 *Oeconomvs Prudens et Legalis*, p. 136 [1477] (*top*) and Bartolomeo Scappi's 1570 *Opera*, p. [947] (*left*). (Bayerische Staatsbibliothek and Hathi Trust)

society more generally.[5] The records for the court of Brandenburg-Prussia convey reciprocal, though unequal, bonds of obligation between the elector and servants of the kitchen that impacted urban development in residence cities.

Without a doubt, recovering the history of these hidden actors is difficult: food is largely ephemeral and so many records pertaining to dining in the past are lost. Particularly for Friedrich Wilhelm's court, few traces remain from daily life: there is little furniture from his reign in the Brandenburg palaces, the great halls have been renovated, palaces and their records bombed. Only a handful of table objects remain.[6] Not only have the edible springing deer and running horse sculptures been lost, so too have the molds used to make them, leaving only descriptions in archived documents.

And yet those archival records contain a great deal of information, not just about the table ornaments themselves, but about the people who used them. From the lack of mentions of individual court servants in the countless books about Prussia, one might think that there is no historical trace of them. But the archives hold specific and contextual clues about their lives and their roles in larger shifts in seventeenth-century Brandenburg-Prussia.[7] Focusing on the servants counters the idea of a dichotomous system of rule, in which a single individual or ruling family imposes dominance on others. Without implying that others were not oppressed under Friedrich Wilhelm, stories about a broader set of actors in Brandenburg-Prussia show "network building by both parties," whether rulers or servants, behind the running of the state.[8] The term "empowering interactions" was coined to describe how communication between central agencies and local societies propelled early modern state formation, and it may also be a useful term to describe what was happening here on the local level.[9] Within a single court, servants had some measure of influence over their masters and could pursue interests of their own concomitantly with those of the corporate body of the court.

There are two purposes to following unknown individuals from Friedrich Wilhelm's court through their archival remains. The first is to humanize invisible laborers by naming them and acknowledging their role in early modern political culture. The second purpose is a meta-analysis of the documentation of food-related tasks and what these documentary processes reveal about proto-legalistic state formation. In recording the minutiae of hygiene, hierarchy, and the division of household labor, the work of the kitchen clerks reflects a codification impulse that marked many European polities in the seventeenth century.

Following the Thirty Years War, European rulers sought new ways to set themselves apart from their subjects to justify their elevated position, leading to a "new ceremonial grammar." In order to gain or solidify sovereign standing, a ruler had to be recognized as sovereign by a peer and documented as having all the fitting titles, crown, and ceremony. "Above all, however, [a ruler] could no longer get by without complete written records," writes Barabara Stollberg-Rilinger.[10] This encompassed documentation of the subtle gestures and language of a banquet. If status had to be *seen*, then the servants who documented that display were key to that status.[11]

This chapter begins with an overview of the offices in the court responsible for procuring, processing, and serving food. The beer and wine cellars, the bakeries, the silver chamber (*Silberkammer*), and the apothecary were adjacent offices to the kitchen that also performed essential work for the court meals. We then move to the stories of individuals who filled the three leadership roles in the kitchens: the steward (*Küchenmeister*), the clerks (*Küchenschreibern*), and the cooks themselves. Their duties to the court are described, as are their opportunities for social mobility, and their role as mediators between the town and crown.

The kitchens of Elector Friedrich Wilhelm's court were continually busy. Days in the kitchen began and ended with the fires. In Berlin, at least five kitchen fires kept dishes simmering, boiling, baking, roasting, and frying, depending on the implements, ingredients, and distance from the fire. One servant was responsible for bringing in the wood and another the coal (a *Holtzträger* and a *Kohlenschweler*) to keep those fires burning.[12] These positions would interact with the silver chamber, which along with maintaining linens for the meal, managed the lighting of the court.

The kitchen servants listed in the court rolls were of a mixture of ages—largely, but not exclusively, male.[13] Family names reappear in the records over many years, and some people move up and down the hierarchy and from one residence to another, showing job mobility was possible in every direction. The number of servants in the kitchens fluctuated. In 1655, there were ten menial kitchen servants listed for the electoral prince: two pot boys (*Topfjungen*), another young boy, a pastry chef's boy, the boy servant of the knights' cook, a female dishwasher, two boys employed to turn the spit, a room heater (probably responsible for keeping the fire going), someone to guard the pantry, and someone to draw water.[14]

A new order for the running of the court a few years later, in 1659, listed a similar group of thirteen kitchen laborers, who were to be served two dishes to share at their table at mealtimes. While most of the positions remained the same, there were a few changes to this list: the "pot boy" was replaced with a "roast boy" (*Bratjung*, responsible for turning the spit and basting the roast), the butcher had a boy servant, the guard was specifically associated with the "wild boar vault," and a woman was employed as a shopper. Instead of a "room heater," the position became a "wood and coal carrier," and lastly, there was a kitchen door guard.[15] By 1672, there were only eight menial kitchen staffers (listed without specific jobs), as well as six people who washed the silver- and tinware.[16] In 1683, thirty of the 424 "civil servants" at the court in Berlin were listed as working in the kitchens. Additionally, there was a confectioner, Abraham Chedomme, whose name suggests he was the only person in the kitchen of French origin and he earned an astonishing 600 thalers per year. Only one woman, Eva Grasnicks, was named in the kitchens. She was a dishwasher, earning 11 thalers annually, with no board or food allowance.[17] As the size of the court fluctuated, though, even at its smallest, it always included spit turners (usually two *Bratjungen*) and two children to mind the pots (*Topfjungen*).[18]

The kitchen of a peer court in the region, that of Duke Georg Wilhelm in Celle in 1682, by comparison, employed nine cooks, not including two roast masters (*Bratmeistern*), a fish cook, two kitchen boys (*Küchenjungen*), two kitchen women (*Küchenfrauen*), and three confectioners.[19] In total, there were thirty kitchen servants in Celle, led by the steward, whose name was given as "Barreau," who received a salary of almost 1,400 thalers. He was not the only kitchen servant with a French last name: two of the personal or privy chefs (*Mundköche*) did, as well as two of the three confectioners. This is to say that, although the Berlin court increased the resources in the kitchen as the court grew overall, Celle spent more proportionally on their kitchen staff and employed more French chefs and confectioners. This could indicate that Georg Wilhelm kept a more stylish table or that Friedrich Wilhelm resisted French cultural influence.[20]

Besides maintaining the heating sources for food, a primary task of the kitchen staff and of the steward, in particular, was to acquire and safely store food, which brought him into contact with suppliers from within the residences and beyond. Specific servants, such as the *Speise-meister* (the pantry manager), the kitchen clerk, and the *Kuchentürknecht* (kitchen guard) were charged with monitoring the goods coming in and out of the pantry. Furthermore, there was typically a butcher, a fishery steward, and someone (usually a woman) to tend the chickens.

In addition to the kitchen staff, a number of parallel departments collaborated with the kitchen to provision and prepare food and drinks at court. As was the case with the steward, these were directly under the senior butler (*Oberschenk*) in the official court hierarchy and the lord marshall (*Hofmarschall*) in practice. They included the silver chamber, the beer and wine cellars, the office of the *Mundschenk* (who managed the bakers and the confectioners), and more tangentially, the apothecary.[21] The relative importance and budgets of these offices is suggested in an ordinance of 1680 when the overall expense of running the court household (across all the elector's residences) was estimated at 172,000 thalers.[22] From this annual budget, 30 percent went to the kitchen (41.5 percent, if food allowances are included), 5.8 percent went to the cellar, 1.7 percent to the confectioner, and 2.9 percent to the silver chamber.[23]

Even though the supervisors of the cellar, kitchen, silver chamber, and stables all carried the title *Meister,* only the steward and stable master were afforded a higher degree of social prestige due to their position.[24] Members of this rank of court officer were expected to dine together. The 1656 ordinance of the electoral kitchens dictated that the steward, the kitchen clerk, the privy chef's servant, the pastry chef, the silver master, a servant of the kitchen chambers (*Küchstüben*), one court butcher, one house fisherman, the cellar master, the cellar clerk, and one pantry manager dine at a table together in the kitchen on eight prepared dishes.[25] The leftovers from their table would be eaten by the subordinates in their respective departments.

The officers of the silver chamber maintained and provided all the nonedible accouterments of dining, such as cutlery, dishes and other tableware, table linens, and lighting (candles, torches, and candelabras). The silver chamber had its own master, scribe, and servants. Two of these silver chamber servants were female: one was an unnamed "silver and tin washer" and the other a "table equipment washer" (*Taffelgeräth-swäscherin*) named Martha Rhader. The care of the dining equipment involved both ceremonial tasks (displaying the silver and tin equipment on a tiered buffet in the dining room during meals, bringing it down as needed, washing it and returning it to the buffet for later use during the meal) and practical chores (inventorying and guarding equipment). According to Rainer Müller, the dishes and table silver were the most valuable items at court after textiles.[26] The task that likely commanded most of the silver chamber scribe's time, however, was recording the daily distribution of lighting (either in the form of tallow and wax candles or torches) to the various offices of the court and to the servants who received lighting as part of their salary.

The baking master in Berlin worked in a detached building, most likely at the manorial estate in Mühlendorf, which handled much of the provisioning and was located very close to the city palace in what was to become the neighborhood of Friedrichswerder (in current-day Berlin Mitte).[27] He baked bread not only for the meals served at court but also for the servants who did not receive full board but were still allotted daily beer and bread.[28] The court bakers were likely subject to the regulations of the local bakers' guild: in 1696, when the court travel baker wanted to be elevated to the status of master, he had to bake the guild's definition of a masterpiece and pay them 10 thalers.[29]

There were specialist bakers, too, who baked mainly for the high tables. Each residence had a *Pasteten* baker who made a variety of meat and fish pies.[30] A Königsberg *Pasteten* baker, Nicolas Löckel, petitioned the court for better compensation and compared his living to that of his counterpart in Berlin. This petition resulted in his official appointment in Königsberg in 1647 with an annual salary of 30 thalers and the same livery as the privy chef. His contract stipulated that he never use old or foul smelling foods, whether meat, wild boar, or seafood. In 1680, he was (finally) promoted from travel *Pasteten* baker to *Pasteten* baker in Potsdam (with a salary of 40 thalers per year) once Matthias Burhardt retired from the role after fifty years of service. Even when the court was not present at a residence, the *Pasteten* baker made Easter, Christmas, and Pentecost cakes for the servants who remained behind.[31]

The apothecary and the kitchen may not, at first glance, seem to have much overlap, but as maladies in the early modern period were often treated with herbal medicine and diet was considered to be crucial to overall health, the apothecary's art was closely tied, in theory, to that of the cook.[32] The two were also associated with each other in practice, as they used some of the same ingredients, namely sugar and other spices.[33] The same spice merchant might supply both the apothecary and the kitchen.

Since the sixteenth century, the Berlin apothecary had been located in a corner of the palace along the River Spree. This was fortunate for the steward in the summer of 1674 when he unexpectedly ran out of spices in the kitchen and could buy them at a moment's notice from the apothecary. But he paid a premium for the convenience and was admonished when the elector later wrote to the councilors in Berlin instructing them to purchase the spices more economically elsewhere in the future.[34]

The kitchen office most closely tied to the apothecary was the confectioner (*Konditor*).[35] Early in the century, the finances of these two departments were even jointly managed, although later the confectioner fell under the authority of the privy chef along with the other bakers.[36] The confectioner was charged with the preservation of fruits and roots in sugar and with making the tabletop sculptures.[37] When Johann Tiegel was appointed to the position in Cleves in 1647, he received an annual budget of 700 thalers in cash, 960 fresh eggs from the court kitchen, flour, as much local wine and herbs as he needed, and a thousand each of fresh lemons and pomegranates to preserve or prepare fresh, as he chose. It was furthermore specified that he prepare confections for celebrations of life events (baptisms, funerals, and weddings) and whenever the elector was in residence.[38] In 1659, then working in Berlin, Tiegel was granted the right to set up a shop to sell his wares to city residents on the Stechbahn, an arcade next to the city palace with various shops.[39] Preserving fresh produce this way was one way for the court to economize, since purchasing preserved fruits in the off seasons was expensive.[40] At least in one instance, a woman, Regina Tiegel, was a court confectioner.[41]

The communications between these different departments were overseen by the steward. Unlike the office of the butler (*Oberschenk* or *Mundschenk*), which by the seventeenth century had become an honorary, ceremonial position for noblemen, the steward was a commoner and responsible for the very real labor of managing the kitchen staff and ensuring that the correct ingredients were available.[42] A court steward held morning meetings to discuss the plan for the day with his team of assistant cooks (the terms *Mundköchen* and *Kavaliersköchen* were used for the high table cooks, and *Beiköchen* and *Unterköchen* for the lower servants' cooks).[43] For exclusive dishes at special occasions, specialist pastry chefs with the various titles of *Hofzuckerbäcker, Konfektmeister, Konditoren* or *Pastetenköche* were at the disposal of the steward. Further special services might be handled by roasting masters (*Bratmeistern*), a baking master

(*Backmeister*), a court butcher (*Hofmetzger*), *Zehrgeber* (perhaps a pantry clerk), and keeper of the fowl (*Geflügelwart*).

The steward was the most immediate manager of the court meals and it was he who, in consultation with others, decided on and organized the dishes and the mode of their service. The steward was on what Peter Bahl calls the "third rung" of the overall court administrative hierarchy. He was directly subordinate to the head court marshal (*Oberhofmarschall*), who oversaw all court personnel.[44] Officers above him, most likely with the elector, determined his budget and the food allowances he divied up for the servants' salaries. In one instance, Friedrich Wilhelm stepped in to order the steward to buy his butter and cheese from his wife's own estate, Oranienburg, which gave her dairy enterprise there a decided advantage![45]

A 1628 appointment contract for a steward during the reign of Friedrich Wilhelm's grandfather lists many of the position's expected duties. In essence, the steward was a barrier between the electoral family and contaminated food as well as a manager of food resources. Specifically, the contract entrusts the Brandenburg-Prussian steward in typical Baroque run-on style to

> strictly maintain the kitchen order, ensure the spices and other foods be available in the kitchen and maintained in a responsible and frugal manner, uphold high standards of cleanliness in the slaughterhouses and control that the animal skins are not pilfered. Furthermore, the steward should ensure that meat is honestly weighed, accounted for, and delivered uncontaminated, and that only fully-cooked, clean food be served to the electress, the princes, and all the servants dining at court. Any leftovers should be accounted for and not removed. From time to time, if it does not detract from his duties at court, he should make sure that the fisheries are not overfished, that the lox season is observed so that our waters are not empty [*verwüstet*] and fish can be brought to the court when needed and that our kitchen clerk record the harvest accurately. He should also care for the wild boar so that the meat never spoils and is on hand when needed. So too, should he safeguard all the kitchen utensils and keep them clean and tidy. He is charged with going to our court warehouse in Hamburg and buying food there that is of high quality and will be useful to us.[46]

The wide-ranging duties stipulated in this excerpt encompass resources management, delivery and purchasing coordination, personnel management, theft prevention, and fiscal accountability, as well as monitoring sanitation. Some of these instructions were likely specified to guard against the eight possible ways that cooks could cheat, according to the "fraud lexicon" of Georg Paul Hönn, who claimed the only way to prevent kitchen theft was to hire trustworthy servants and carefully monitor the stores.[47] This complex job was crucial for the safety and sustenance of courtiers, high and low on the social ladder, and therefore, care would have been taken to hire a capable and loyal steward.

Indeed, during Friedrich Wilhelm's long reign, there were only two stewards in Berlin: Erdmann Schmoll (steward 1640–64) and Daniel Graupius (ca. 1623–1706).[48] Graupius's career can be traced from appointment records as he moved up the ranks over his nearly six decades of service, finally becoming *Oberküchenmeister* under the succeeding elector, Friedrich III. Graupius is first mentioned for his installation as "travel steward" in 1656 working in the kitchen of Erdmann Schmoll in Cleves. In 1657, he sent a request to the elector for a promotion and more money to cover his expenses. He claimed he had already served the elector for seventeen years, which meant from the beginning of Friedrich Wilhelm's reign in 1640. One of his justifications for the change was the hard journeys he had already made through Prussia and Cleves during which he had often "worked more nights than days" and had incurred large debts.[49] He asked for another position in the exchequer's office (*Rentkammer*) or the kitchen in Prussia. His services were apparently appreciated as Friedrich Wilhelm replied favorably in his own hand. In acknowledgment of his good service and in order to prevent his leaving, the court promised him a promotion to steward in Prussia, when the position became available and granted him a one-time payment of 200 thalers to cover his debts (in comparison with the 188 thaler salary he was to receive when he later was installed as steward in Berlin 1664).[50]

Graupius became the steward in Königsberg in 1659 and lived in a free apartment in the smokehouse until it burned down in 1660. He must have been doing well for himself, because he was in a position at that point to lend the exchequer 1,000 thalers to rebuild the smokehouse.[51] Next, Graupius lived in an apartment in the garden (the *Lusthaus*).[52] When Erdmann Schmoll died in 1664, Friedrich Wilhelm summoned him from Königsberg to fill the position of steward in Berlin.[53]

Although Graupius had earlier complained he was exhausted from traveling with the court, when he became steward in Berlin, his contract specified that he still travel with the elector.[54] Peter Bahl wrote that the two offices of steward in Prussia and steward in Brandenburg were only separate posts under Schmoll and Graupius (perhaps Schmoll was too old at the point of Graupius's installation as Prussian steward to travel back and forth).[55] As dictated by his new contract in 1664, the duties of the steward expanded to travel with the elector and management of his kitchen, whether in Königsberg or Berlin. For this, the salary was to increase from Schmoll's 150 to 188 thalers (not including the value of his free board and allowances in kind).

Along with his professional advancement, Graupius was integrating himself into the urban fabric of Berlin. He lived a few blocks from the palace on Gertraudenstraße. Although, this was not one of the prominent boulevards that drew the eye on a straight axis to the palace, where mostly high court officers lived, it was full of activity: home to the island's fish market and to many Berliners who did not work for the court. He lived behind St. Peter's Church (Lutheran), where he was eventually buried with his wife, Johanna Brandt (d. 1673), and their child (d. 1666). There were a number of Brandts variously employed at court: as court marshals (*Obermarschall*), foresters, and other advisors. One Heinrich Julius Brandes (1635–1691) succeeded Graupius as kitchen clerk and fish master and worked under him in that position. Graupius's own origins are unknown. It is possible his family was from Halberstadt where one contemporary, Nicodemus Graupius, was a dyer (*Schwartzfärber*).[56] The principality had been one of the territories ruled in the personal union under Friedrich Wilhelm since 1648.

This is to say that while Graupius may not have had a long family history of court kitchen service, he could, assuming those other Brandts at court were related, leverage his wife's kindship network to his professional and personal advantage. His house in Berlin was purchased from court servants, surrounded by them, and sold to them (after Graupius died without an heir).[57] Graupius was part of the influx of court servants in the new suburbs near the palace island. His overlapping personal and professional circles likely furnished trust that would be an advantage in carving out his place in the community. Furthermore, the influence of court servants outside of the palace gave the elector another point of access to monitor Berlin urban life just as a court servant offered their neighbors a point of access to palace life.

In his career, Graupius played an inadvertent part in the long process of the consolidation of Prussia. Like many other kitchen servants, he moved between the disconnected territories ruled in a personal union under Friedrich Wilhelm, from Cleves to Königsberg to Berlin. His job required him to travel further afield too: on campaign with the elector and up to Hamburg to manage the court's warehouses there and liaise with merchants in order to procure goods from the far reaches of the globe. In performing his duties in the elector's different residences, he bridged the cultures in the heterogenous territories.

In 1692, "in recognition of his fifty years of service," Graupius's title was elevated to *Oberküchmeister.*[58] With his advanced age, his more strenuous duties were passed to the travel steward (*Reisekuchmeister*). This promotion not only honored his long service but likely also served the ambitions of the next elector, Friedrich III. A larger court with grander titles for its highest officers, more closely approximated a *royal* court and therefore aided the new Elector Friedrich III's rise in stature, leading to his coronation as king *in* Prussia in 1701.[59]

There is no evidence of how Graupius first became connected with the new Elector Friedrich Wilhelm in Cleves. Furthermore, it is a mystery how he developed the skills needed to balance the desires of his superiors with the practical limitations of budget, seasons, and geography. The acumen he developed was considerable: in addition to managing relationships among the kitchen servants and with suppliers, he had to be vigilant: against theft, spoilage, shortage, poison, uncleanliness, and above all disorder.

One food historian likens the "professional corps" of kitchen workers who were systematizing accounting and staffing practices to the military revolution of the time in which the "motley feudal army transformed into a uniformed, salaried, professional, and standing army."[60] The steward was the link between the physical and human resources and the upper court officers who, as nobles, were not to concern themselves with commerce or to keep house.[61] Therefore, the steward was essential for advancing the mission of control and discipline.

The foot soldier of this codification of court hierarchies and practices, however, was the position right below the steward, the kitchen clerk. The related departments of the cellar and the silver chamber each had their own clerks who maintained their own accounts, adding to the large quantity of documentation of daily consumption.[62] The most illustrative way of exploring this position is perhaps not just through the life stories of the individuals, but through their work—as they are the only kitchen servants with significant written remains to analyze. Dozens of folio volumes of annual kitchen accounts exist from the Königsberg residence and provide a diachronic record of foods consumed, as well as the officers who submitted the records, and the objects inventoried in the kitchen. From these, one can trace the lifespan of cooking tools such as the wooden molds for the table sculptures (also called "subtleties") that, over time deteriorated from potent symbols of noble status to dusty, worm-eaten remnants of a vibrant Renaissance court culture.

The Königsberg kitchen clerk recorded the purchase of subtlety molds depicting various meaningful religious, dynastic, and hunting motifs, which he described as for *Schaweßen*, literally show food. One mold depicted the Elector's coat of arms, another a shield with ostrich feathers, two others a crucifix and a *Salvator*. Then, there are the animal figures: a pelican, a lion's face, four deer heads, a fallow deer, antlers, a running horse, a leaping deer without antlers, a swimming swan, a recumbent aurochs, a gemshorn, and a seahorse. One can imagine the various tableaus that could come to life with such evocative subtleties set among dishes for specifically themed meals, such as one heavy with game from a recent hunt or for Christian feast or fast days.

However, these wooden molds were not maintained. Between 1648 and 1659, eleven of them disappeared from the inventory. In 1670, the clerk annotated that the molds were "of no use." By 1677, a horse with four detachable feet was not only "partially unusable" but was also missing some body parts. From 1683 until Friedrich Wilhelm's death in 1688, the remaining molds were described as "chewed through by worms and no longer useful." Finally, in the last inventory in this format in 1690, there were no more subtlety molds of this kind, for which the clerk explained, "of the wooden molds: everything has been consumed by worms and is no longer around."[63] The long demise of these tools begs the question: why did the palace keep these unusable objects for decades?

Like human actors, objects have biographies. And, just as with biographies of people, biographies of things "can make salient what otherwise might remain obscure."[64] The clerks recorded the same objects over and over; many clearly gathering dust and falling into disrepair as the court visited Königsberg less frequently over the seventeenth century. Other goods were recast or purchased new as the court prepared for big events at that residence (including the fealty oaths by the Prussian estates in 1663 and at the 1681 wedding of the elector's son, Ludwig). This diachronic record suggests answers to the questions outlined by Igor Kopytoff in his foundational article "The Cultural Biography of Things." For instance, what is the career of the object, how does it move through the periods of its "life," and what happens when it reaches the end of its usefulness?[65]

The object-specific questions help answer more fundamental lines of inquiry into the early modern relationship with material goods. Material objects were difficult to come by and expensive in the early modern world, and used goods continued to carry a high enough value to prevent them being discarded or destroyed. This dynamic becomes more complicated when an object is part of a fashion that fades, as was the case with edible table sculptures when porcelain took the place of prominence on the table. The consumption of trendy objects with only short-term value was still rare in the seventeenth century, but mainstream in the eighteenth.[66] In Königsberg, however, the court clerks' contracts were quite clear that their job was to protect the objects from being sold. There was no defined process or agency for them to deaccession useless things.

Renata Ago, in her reading of Roman inventories of the seventeenth century, theorized that "objects gave material concreteness to the owner's presence in the world."[67] This is possibly what accounts for the persistence of unused or nonfunctional objects in the Königsberg palace. Perhaps the lingering objects projected the message that the ruler was present even in his physical absence, and, in theory, his Prussian residence needed to be ready to serve him at a moment's notice.

However, the act of inventorying these items reflected the concerns and values not only of their owners, but of the kitchen clerks who signed their names in these annual account books. None of the cooking or dining tools described in this chapter exist anymore. The only evidence that they ever existed are the records penned by the kitchen clerks. We are not looking at the actual objects, but at their descriptions of them. Giorgio Riello wrote of inventories as "forms of representation" and, as such, these Königsberg account books are interesting not just for their content but for *how* they recorded the objects.[68]

These molds, once functional and a part of the busy mechanisms of a large household kitchen, were all neglected by 1670. Dying a slow death, they ultimately became food for another species. It is the same wrenching drama of the velveteen rabbit, of the book by Margery Williams, who is made real by his usefulness to a small boy until he is deemed too ragged and the boy too old to play. This story could be a metaphor for the trajectory of human life. In the "real" story of the molds and other tools in Königsberg, the metaphor is the declining use of the palace there by the

Hohenzollern rulers as Elector Friedrich Wilhelm centralized his power in Brandenburg and devoted more of his funds and attention to his residences in Potsdam and Berlin. Through the moving descriptions of these objects as they lose limbs and are eaten away, the reader may suppose that this was a sad, forgotten palace.

A different picture emerges, though, when the clerks' rhetoric falls away and the entire inventory is viewed in a database covering the arrival and disappearance of objects over the elector's reign. When the inventories are viewed thus, it is apparent that new objects were still entering the court kitchen. Therefore, there was not a complete and steady demise of this kitchen, but rather an evolution into a kitchen that served a different purpose than it had in the sixteenth century. In 1677, ten different types of objects described as being "of sheet metal over tin," entered the inventory. In 1690, such objects were listed under the subheading "a service of sheet metal over tin in a wooden cupboard."[69] Tin can be used as a protective coat for other metals or in an alloy with copper known as pewter, which is likely what is being described here.[70] This would correspond with the increasing trend of matching dinnerware noted by Daniel Roche in *A Cultural History of Things.*[71]

Furthermore, with the addition of new lanterns and "room lights," the kitchens brightened, in line with the general trend in Europe of "conquering the dark."[72] Therefore, the kitchen evolved in response to different tastes and technologies: sugar sculptures were out (possibly because very few festival meals seem to have taken place there after the 1663 homage festivities), but pewter and lights were in. On one hand, the annotations to the inventory are evocative of a sad decline, to the point of overshadowing the actual renewal or evolution of the tools of the kitchen. A diachronic view of the inventory, on the other hand, makes apparent the new things that entered the kitchen.[73]

What can explain this renewal in the midst of a focus on decaying and worm-eaten tools? Perhaps the nature of the source offers an answer. Inventories are not "'snapshots of reality,' but the result of strategies, biases, and representational intentions."[74] Indeed, not everything that was in the kitchen was inventoried, which underscores that particular conventions and strategies went into the inventorying of kitchen goods. When seen from the context of other early modern kitchens (for example, the ideal kitchen arrangement recommended by the sixteenth-century chef Bartolomeo Scappi), it is clear that many tools were likely to be found in the kitchen but were not inventoried. For example, pieces of furniture or storage are absent from the inventories (except for a spice box in 1663 and 1664).[75] Things of low monetary value were not inventoried at all. Scappi recommended that a "proper" kitchen have rakes, shovels and mops to clean the ovens, but those are not mentioned in the Prussian inventory even though an expense record indeed notes that the kitchen purchased them.[76]

A brief prosopography of the kitchen clerks helps to explain the expectations for this role and to see the clerks as individuals deploying certain rhetorical strategies in their work. The accounts were compiled (in chronological order) by Johann Benzer (sometimes written "Hans Pentzer"), Christoph Augustin (sometimes "Augstin"), Gottfried Augustin, Günther Daniel, and Kaspar König. According to Günther Daniel's appointment contract, as clerk he was to "protect the inventory so that nothing is lost from the kitchen."[77] The clerk was provided a "clean" writing room near the kitchen to carry out his work: an apartment warmed by a green-tiled stove.[78] This entailed tallying daily, weekly, and annual expenses and communicating regularly with the steward to ensure that no outsiders were in the kitchen and none of the servants made off with anything from the kitchen, the slaughterhouse, and any of the other sites associated with food. Perhaps the hoarding of the molds was simply fulfilling this part of the contract not to remove anything (even useless things) from the kitchens.

The contract for Daniel also stipulates that he report any mistakes and not try to cover them up. As Daniel's contract was drawn up after the death of Gottfried Augustin in 1668, it might have been written thus as a reaction to accounting irregularities during Gottfried Augustin's tenure. Indeed, Augustin's accounts during the period of the great *Huldigung* feast in Königsberg were so convoluted that it took a commission from Potsdam years to sort them out (from 1684 into the reign of the next elector in 1688).[79] The confusion may have stemmed from the fact that Augustin paid many bills at once, but the commission was still looking for his heirs in 1688, possibly to track down missing money from the kitchen.[80]

Gottfried Augustin was not the only kitchen clerk under Friedrich Wilhelm to invite censure. His successor, Günther Daniel, was described as being "so culpable and irresponsible." He repeatedly got into trouble in the beer and wine taverns. Eventually, in 1672, he went to debtors' prison and was made to pay arrears for years afterward.[81] Kaspar König, who replaced Daniel, though, stayed in the position until he became too old to carry out his duties and was replaced by his son in 1703—loyal service could paid out dividends for generations.[82]

Along with such nepotism in the kitchens, there was room for professional advancement over the course of a career at court. Many of the clerks had performed other jobs before becoming kitchen clerks. Christoph Augustin held the position from May 3, 1638 (when he filled in for the sick Johann Benzer), until 1657, when Gottfried Augustin (possibly his son) replaced him. Christoph then became the clerk to the exchequer (*Rentschreiber*) and would have been responsible for the elector's broader finances.[83] There was also lateral movement between the electoral residences. Daniel Graupius was the scribe under Erdmann Schmoll in Cleves in 1652, then became travel kitchen scribe in Berlin in 1656, "with the prospect of becoming the steward in Königsberg."[84] He was indeed officially installed as steward in Königsberg in 1657 and was then called by the elector to be steward in Berlin when Erdman Schmoll died.[85] A person by the name Danail (possibly a relative of the errant Günther Daniel) was the scribe at the Mühlenhof in Berlin.[86]

What was at stake for the clerks when they provided the descriptions of the decline of the symbols of courtly power and virtue? Every year the inventory was submitted to the elector's treasury council in Prussia (the *Rentkammer*) and they reported to the elector on the needs of the Prussian government. The inventory, then, was an indirect path of communication between the kitchen and the ruler: potentially an outlet for voicing discontent from the periphery as court life was blossoming in Brandenburg. When the court was not in session at the clerks' location, they received only half pay with only a food allowance (much less valuable than the free meals they would have eaten when the court was present).[87] One way the clerks might have mitigated this loss of income might indeed have been to sell off old goods. It was not unusual for a court to discard old things like clothes and candle stubs by giving them to servants. The clerks' descriptions might have been a strategy to expedite their appropriation of things that might at least have value as firewood. Caspar König, who otherwise had a long and unremarkable tenure as kitchen clerk, would have had some cause for disappointment after spending most of his career at the shadow court in Königsberg on such reduced pay.

The exact descriptions of decrepit zoomorphic "subtlety" molds were perhaps a strategic rhetorical choice. It is not just the objects themselves that are telling, but the ways that their stories are conveyed. This shows how members up and down the court social ladder affected the information flowing to and from the residences. The clerks were the formal point of connection between the elector and the kitchens and therefore their work shaped the perception of the kitchen. The scribes shaped the biographies of the kitchen tools; they decided how these objects would be counted and remembered.

THE INVENTORIES do not relate when the objects stopped being used or, indeed, how they were used. That was handled by someone else in the kitchen—the cook. The cook bore the responsibility for turning those ingredients into dishes that would be pleasing to the stomach and the imagination. Although they were not creating the records, the cooks, too, can be traced in the archives. As their craft was more ephemeral, it is more difficult to see their output. But, their life stories illustrate the opportunities these craftspeople had to advance their personal interests and the political interests of the court.

One privy chef (*Mundkoch*), Adolf Wilcke (1616–1679), was a near age-peer of the elector, and his life trajectory paralleled that of the elector on a different social plane.[88] While Adolf Wilcke's story is interesting, it is not exceptional—many court servants can be similarly traced in the archives as individuals who worked both with and against the corporate interests of the court. Furthermore, Wilcke's case shows how servants, and specifically, those in the kitchen, used the privileges of court employment to their advantage and were, in turn, deployed to advance the position of the court vis-à-vis local subjects and among European peers.

The privy chef was, like his overseer the steward, between the high and low officers at court. The position carried some prestige because of the chef's daily proximity to the ruling family and his influence on their health. Although the privy chef performed a physically intensive job, he was valued for his knowledge—not just of cosmopolitan cooking techniques, but of the appropriate foods for different occasions, seasons, social classes, and physical temperaments. This focus on health mirrors what Max Rumpolt, the renowned court chef from the previous century, said about the privy chef's responsibility: "Many illnesses come from the ignorance of the cook, and that is why the great lords often hear from their chefs that the life and well-being of the lord lies in their hands."[89] The chef's rigorous training then, was likely both physical and theoretical.

Wilcke was part of Friedrich Wilhelm's court for most of his reign. He came from a Reformed Calvinist family in Eberswalde, fifty kilometers northwest of Berlin. His family likely had some stature there as his father was once mayor.[90] His title, *Meister*, denotes that he passed through the apprenticeship training and tests to be recognized as a master craftsman. His father might have been involved in the food trades as well. There is no record of when Wilcke began his employment with the court or how old he was when he joined Friedrich Wilhelm in Cleves. Had he accompanied the young electoral prince to the Netherlands? Did he train in the Hague in the kitchens of Friedrich Wilhelm's future father-in-law, the stadtholder Frederick Henry? He would not have been the only servant to bring the flavors of the elector and electress's youth in the Hague to their later palaces.[91]

Wilcke was responsible for cooking the dishes directly for Elector Friedrich Wilhelm and, when they ate together, the Electress Luise Henriette. Most of the records indicate he had his own two servants (*Mundkochknechte*) to assist him, in addition to one to three other chefs who cooked for lower court officers and servants. A typical day began in consultation with the steward and scribe about the *Tageszettel* or menus for the day and collecting the ingredients to prepare them.

Wilcke submitted multiple supplications to the elector, which signal that he felt it within his rights to advocate for himself and expected his concerns to be addressed by his lord. His first appearance in court records was in October of 1648 when he successfully petitioned the administrative chamber (*Amtskammer*) of Cleves to double his annual salary to 100 thalers "for his true and obedient service."[92] After Friedrich Wilhelm's ambitions were disappointed when he was not appointed to be his nephew's guardian (and *ipso facto* stadtholder of the United Provinces of the Netherlands) in 1652, Wilcke moved with the rest of the court to Berlin. It was a major pivot for the whole court and necessitated the transportation of a staggering quantity of material goods, which were carried in 304 pieces of baggage that traveled in the elector's caravan over land and water to establish a new era of Hohenzollern rule centered in the province of Brandenburg (first in the city of Berlin and later in Potsdam). In the move, the privy chamber president, Count George Friedrich von Waldeck (1620–1692), brought along forty-six pieces of luggage. The Dutch painter, Willem van Honthorst (1594–1666), whom Electress Luise Henriette employed from 1647–64, brought just one chest—an undersized reflection of his influence on the visual aesthetic and record of this court.

Our "M[eister] Adolphen, the privy chef" brought three chests on this journey as did the *Pastetenbecker* (responsible for the pies) and the confectioner (*Konditor*). The rest of the kitchen servants together brought an additional three cases. There are no inventories of what their luggage actually contained. Perhaps Wilcke brought specialty items to make Dutch comfort foods such as waffles—we know that a waffle iron was later used by a "Dutch woman [named] Bent" to make waffles for the electoral prince Ludwig.[93] Whatever was in those crates, the move was a turning point from the westward-looking objectives of Friedrich Wilhelm's early reign in Cleves in the Netherlands to the Brandenburg-centric court of the rest of the Hohenzollern rule. The painter, the chef, the baker, the confectioner, and yes, the privy councilor all played their part in bridging the westward-oriented court in Cleves with the new court culture in Berlin.

By 1656, Wilcke was earning a high salary of 200 thalers, which was supposed to be reduced to a previous salary when a "new chef came from France." There is no evidence that that French chef ever did come as there was only one chef during Friedrich Wilhelm's reign with a French name and that was the "old master servant Jean" who is listed as Pomeranian in other records anyway.[94] This is a tiny detail, but it is the only indication that, though unsuccessful, Friedrich Wilhelm might have sought French culinary fashion on his table, just as Georg Wilhelm of Celle and other German princes. Instead, the strongest traceable outside cultural influence on the Berlin court, as other scholars have noted, was that of the Dutch during their golden age.[95]

There were 344 members of the court on the payroll along with Wilcke in 1656 (twenty-two of whom worked in the kitchens).[96] That year, he was spared the duties of the watch.[97] Another privy chef, Hans (or Johann) Goldschmidt, joined him in Berlin from Königsberg, which was probably a good thing because Wilcke was pensioned in October 1658 for the unspecified "weakness" that had excused him from the watch in 1656.[98] It is not known whether Wilcke's pensioning was related to injury from the dangerous work of cooking over an open hearth. His impairment was likely temporary, though, because Goldschmidt was the only chef in 1664 (with a salary of 120 thalers). Wicke was listed again in 1665 and was still working in 1668 when his *Deputat,* or payments in kind, were increased.[99]

Wilcke had at least one other food service venture beyond the palace walls and he, too, made an impact in developing a new section of Berlin. In 1660, he was building a beer and wine locale (*Gastwirtschaft*) on a corner of the "wide Kreuzgasse" in the neighborhood of Friedrichswerde, which was under construction at the time and populated mainly by court

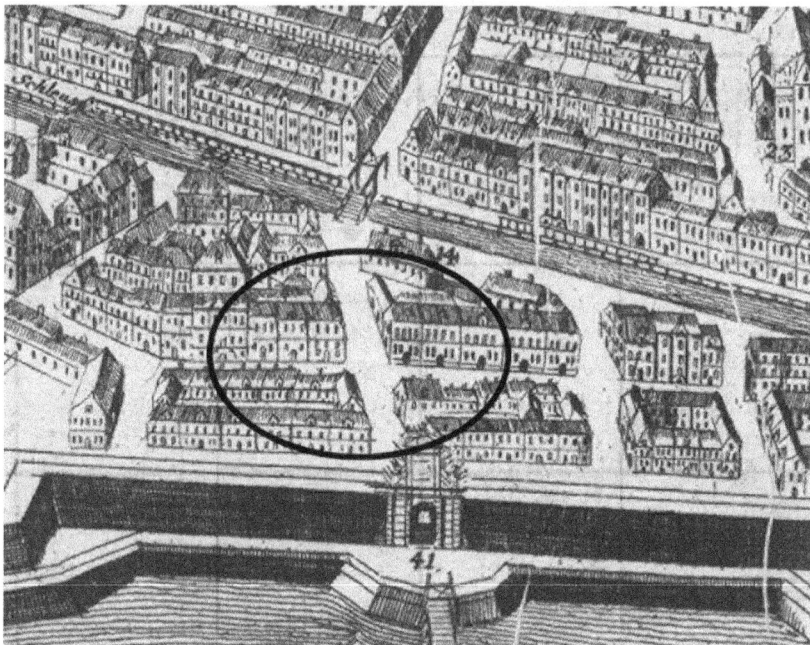

Likely location of Adolf Wilcke's *Gastwirtschaft* on the corner of Kreuzgasse and Kurstraße between the Jungfernbrücke and Leipzigertor in Friedrichswerder. Detail showing neighborhood in proximity to electoral residence from Johann B. Schultz's 1688 map, *Residentia Electoralis Brandenburgica*. (Staatsbibliothek zu Berlin; http://resolver .staatsbibliothek-berlin.de/SBB0001C3BC00000000)

officers.[100] The elector granted him the right to do so with the stipulation that he sell only local beers—in fact so local that they could only be purchased from the brewery of the palace captain (*Schloßhauptman*), Zacharias Friedrich von Götz (d. 1682) and his wife, Elizabeth.[101]

In the wider network of court officers in the urban fold, the von Götze family maintained that monopolistic privilege to brew beer and fortified wine (*Brennwein*) and to sell wine in Friedrichswerder until other citizens complained in 1669.[102] An additional mark of favor on the von Götze family was that Friedrich Wilhelm granted them all of the materials for their brewery and home for free from the court's resources.[103] Other kitchen servants, too, were given plots of land and/or privileges on the island of Freidrichswerder: the confectioner (*Hof-Konditor*), Johann Teigel, received permission not only to build, but also to sell spices, horse medicines, house paint, and wines.[104] The horse supplies and house paints were likely used for further construction in Friedrichswerder.[105]

By 1666, there were ninety-two houses in Friedrichwerder, forty-seven of which belonged to court servants.[106] Noteworthy court servants to receive land or housing in the neighborhood included the palace gardner, Michael Hanff; the personal physician to the elector, Otto Bötticher; the apothecary Christoph Fahrenholtz (who also received the privilege to have an apothecary and spice shop there); the butler Johann George Thorman; the hunting clerk (*Jagdschreiber*) George Wilhelm Wolff; and another privy cook named simply Hieronomy.[107] The Dutch engineer Johann Gregor Memhardt (1607–1678), who had been tapped by Friedrich Wilhelm to rebuild the palace island of Cölln, surveyed and administered all of these plots. Eventually, Memhardt became the mayor of Friedrichswerder. The court, therefore, incentivized its (often, nonnative) members to invest in Berlin suburbs where they, in turn, were well placed to profit from the development. Furthermore, they were connection nodes between the ruler and local subjects. While Wilcke and the von Götzes were taking advantage of opportunities for Friedrich Wilhelm's sponsored developments in Berlin after the Thirty Years War, these efforts were not without criticism from other Berliners.

Wilcke is not mentioned again in the archival record for almost twenty years, when they mark his decline and replacement in the kitchens. In 1678, Jacob Troschke, who had worked his way up the ranks as *Meister Knecht* (the head of the menial servants), took over as privy chef from Wilcke, who was deemed "too old" for the work. Troschke's appointment contract provides reference for Wilcke's duties. The first part of it explains the chain of command: the privy chef answered (in descending order) to the court and chamber of ministers (the *Hoff und Ambts Cammer*), the marshal, the palace captain (*Schloßhauptman*), and the steward (*Hoffküchen Meister*) and the kitchen clerk. Next, Troschke was charged to make healthful food for the elector's wife and children. He was to monitor the food, spices, and especially the valuable meat, to ensure nothing was stolen; he was not to give food to anyone without the knowledge of the officers above him and he was to make sure his servants and any outsiders did the same. When he cooked, he was to use ingredients sparingly ("only take what was necessary"). Likewise, he was to monitor the kitchen tools and report any that were missing. Once he took his oath to carry out these duties "cleanly and honestly" and follow the stipulated court order

(*Hofordnung*), Troschke was to receive 120 thalers a year, a livery, rye and barley, and a daily allotment of Brandenburg wine.[108]

Wilcke died the year Troschke was promoted to the position, and as Hans Goldschmidt was now the senior privy chef, he petitioned to receive the deceased Wilcke's former *Deputat* of half an ox, four mutton, four *Achtels* of butter (about 13 kilograms), a *Scheffel* of salt (about 55 liters), and a pig as *he* was now the senior cook.[109] Like many servants in the kitchen, the archival record for Adolf Wilcke stretches for many decades—an entire career in the service of one lord. The benefits of secure employment, the proximity to the elector, and the protections that it provided outweighed the disadvantages of inconsistent pay and antagonism from jealous burghers.

THIS SAMPLING of kitchen servants' biographies brings to light shared interests and trends, yet it also introduces a set of individuals with their own ventures, duties, kinship networks, and modes of expression. As in any corporate structure, the people nominally in charge were not free to dictate their wishes and see them done: in the web of court and city life, various members influenced each other and their work. Friedrich Wilhelm, too, was held to reciprocal bonds of loyalty to respond to the material needs of his servants. The magic of courtly dining was orchestrated by people with a range of ages, duties, status, and backgrounds, yet they were in a network with one another that might have multiple connection points in and beyond the palace. While they dined together in the palace, they might have intermarried and contracted business with each other outside of it.

The low attrition of kitchen workers—as evidenced by the ability to track them over decades in the archives—signals that even menial court employment had its benefits. This was not always without conflict, but even so, servants remained on the payment rolls and advocated for themselves through written means (and possibly other, undocumented means). Feeding the court required that its boundaries were permeable and connections with the court mattered in urban life outside of the palace. The number and titles of kitchen servants expanded and contracted with financial circumstances and the Great Elector may have given fewer resources to his kitchens than peer courts. But even so, the kitchens and the people who worked in them performed critical labor for representative politics through their mastery of material tasks.

An *Alltagsgeschichte* (history of everyday life) approach to the history of the court of Friedrich Wilhelm means that this is not another biography of "the founder of Prussia" but rather a study of how the court *functioned*. Food history allows us to decenter the story from the rulers and big names of the administration to consider these actors in the relational and material contexts in which they worked, lived, struggled, ruled, advocated, and failed. Instead of a dichotomous concept of rule presented in "histories from below," here, daily choices tell a bigger story about the dynamic web of relationships at court.[110] Just as the wooden molds themselves were empty frames of something ephemeral that once was, so too, the archives hold only the outlines of past lives.

These traces expose the entangled relationships, up and down the social ladder, of this early modern society. Senior officers and low kitchen servants were shaping the written records of court order—showing a desire to account for their resources, their world, and their place in it. If the court meals were a ritualized way of reifying social order, recording the meals was likewise a part of early modern statecraft. The kitchen records demystify the production of the awe-inspiring premodern feasts and draw attention to the actors who created them, yet they also highlight the quotidian material concerns of court life. The other material component of the task of feeding a court of hundreds was *procuring* food, both from within the palace walls and far beyond. This too, as will be seen in the next chapter, was a social exercise with far-reaching consequences.

3

The Field and Forest and River Richly Provide

THE REGIONAL FOOD SYSTEM

IN THE middle of the Thirty Years War, during the reign of the Great Elector's father, Georg Wilhelm (r. 1619–40), the Mark Brandenburg and its ruler were at the mercy of foreign troops for survival. Imperial forces claimed taxes from the natives of the Altmark region, Danish troops held parts of the northern Mark Brandenburg, and Cossacks controlled parts of the Neumark. Then, in the summer of 1630, King Gustov Adolph of Sweden (r. 1611–32) marched his army into Georg Wilhelm's land demanding support against the Holy Roman Emperor, Ferdinand III (r. 1637–57). Brandenburg was a sitting duck. In November of that year, Georg Wilhelm and his court were residing at the fortress in Küstrin, a safe distance from the foreign troops stationed in his territories. But, from that outpost, how would Georg Wilhelm feed himself and the court?

To do so, the elector tried to mobilize resources from the various dominions under his personal union and ordered food and lighting from his residence in Königsberg, Prussia, about three hundred miles away. Georg Wilhelm, however, was to be disappointed: as the report of the Königsberg equerry, Richard Ficklend, made clear, the supply chain between the elector's holdings was not able to overcome the challenges of war, disease, and climate. On November 9, 1630, Ficklend reported:

> I have gathered the requested 100 oxen (and they could be sent off within hours), as well as the twenty tons of butter, the wax, and the tallow. The dried and salted salmon, though, cannot be gotten because the Swedes took it first and now have the salmon fisheries in their control. As for the oats, we have collected fifty *Last*,[1] but there is not a single *Scheffel* of barley to be had in Königsberg because of the great plague in Poland and Lithuania. The chief councilors [*Oberräte*] are endeavoring with all

diligence to obtain the requested grains. But they report that it will still be impossible to deliver them. We would send the available butter, wax, tallow, and oats by water through the fort of Stettin, but there is no boat in Königsberg that will depart so late in the year as a hard frost has already set in. The risk would be high because any ship that could be had now would be very expensive, and because the goods are expensive to come by and cost us much effort to gather, the chief counselors suggest land transport by horse and sleigh to Marienwerder. I await your command through this post rider.[2]

A few days after Ficklend wrote this, the high councilors in Königsberg sent their own report to the Berlin officers in which they elaborated on some of the problems mentioned by Ficklend. Namely, there were no ships to send to get the needed grains in the trading centers of Hamburg, Stettin, or Lübeck, and prices were too high that autumn anyway. They reported that they would wait to ship the grains until the spring thaw, but would send the tallow and wax by horse-drawn sleigh (even though, as they wrote, they did not know how they would gather the needed horses). They promised to send the one hundred oxen immediately, but added the feeble sentiment, "Hopefully, they will be delivered to you at court."[3]

Ficklend and the Berlin privy officers had only the barest hope that the required supplies would reach the court.[4] There is no surviving record detailing how Georg Wilhelm, his court, and the guard at the fortress castle in Küstrin fared that winter. What is clear is that on the ground and in the general chaos of war, the personal union of the Hohenzollerns's different territories meant little more than their having the same ruler. There were few cultural similarities and even less coordinated administration of resources across the disparate territories. The metaphor of food production was also employed by a contemporary political theorist to describe the failed unification of another composite state, Spain. As he put it, "Valencia grows oranges but not chestnuts, and Vizcaya chestnuts but not oranges, and that is how God made them."[5] While describing core divisions in the territories, his statement also hints at the symbiotic exchange of food that was possible in culturally diverse, but politically connected states.

A few decades after Ficklend's desperate efforts, Georg Wilhelm's heir, Friedrich Wilhelm, commanded a more effective interterritorial food system. His lordship over multiple territories enabled resources to be mobilized from distant places when the local food supply was insufficient.

Eventually, the diversity of agricultural products provided a critical political advantage. Under Friedrich Wilhelm, even in wartime, the food-ways were more passable between the elector's residences.

As was true of Britain, France, and Spain (the most prominent composite monarchies of Europe at the time), "new territorial acquisitions meant enhanced prestige and potentially valuable new sources of wealth."[6] Composite states were not easy to rule, however: each one had its own entrenched systems of governance. Friedrich Wilhelm struggled to negotiate with the enclave in Cleves, the estates in Brandenburg, and Ducal Prussia. However, the wider reach for regional food resources was a critical component of financial stability as his court recovered from the Thirty Years War. This chapter follows this supply chain as administrators normalized the movement of food across the diverse territories.

Indeed, food from the elector's own territories made up the largest source of food for his court (even though it did not carry the same prestige as the expensive foods that were purchased from abroad). The electors of Brandenburg-Prussia could lay claim to this produce because of the coercive peasant labor system in place. Brandenburg and Prussia lay to the east of the Elbe River; they were regions described by economic historians as practicing seigniorial (*Gutsherrschaft*) farming in the seventeenth century.[7] This system of agriculture (as opposed to the *Grund-herrschaft* system, which developed to the west of the Elbe) was nominally controlled by the nobility, who consolidated their control over the peasantry in the area in the sixteenth century and maintained forced *corvée* labor there.[8] This exchange relationship between peasants and lords was the main driver behind production in this region, not the market. And, although the village farmers still might have had rights to possess and exchange property, the landlords had some influence on crop choice.[9] However, the importance of local climate and farming traditions were also presumably factors in that decision.

Somewhat surprisingly, the decline in population (and therefore people to work the fields) due to the Thirty Years War led not to a reduction but rather to an increase in the demesne system. The Hohenzollern profited from the misfortunes of their own subjects in this regard, as they were able to increase their landholdings around Berlin when abandoned farms could be acquired very cheaply. This was the condition that enabled the elector to buy fields and pastureland in Wedding between 1635 and 1648. Otherwise, the loss of particularly the peasant population and the subsequent rise in grain prices hurt both the rural peasant farmers and the lower nobles who had previously relied on their labor to work their lands.[10] In the demesne system, the ruler—in this case, the elector—laid claim to a certain amount of natural wares from the inhabitants of his territory.[11] Along with duties and tolls, local farms delivered their produce to the elector as a tax—a large portion of which directly fed the court. In other words, the main currency for paying taxes was food, a further reminder of the place of food in the history of Prussian bureaucracy. The Berlin Office of Domains (Amtskammer zu Cölln an der Spree) managed all such income-in-kind from the administrative districts (*Ämter*) of Brandenburg, which was the most dependable source of income for the court.[12] The Brandenburg *Amtskammer* became the model for resource administration in the elector's other dominions. Furthermore, over the course of the seventeenth century, the power of the Amtskammer expanded to include the administration of the domains in Cleves and Prussia as well, another point of connection between resource management and the larger process of centralization.

The taxes arrived and were accounted for at the Mühlenhof domain before being processed for consumption by the court. The administrative evolution of the Mühlenhof was piecemeal and in response to *ad hoc* needs. It had little to do with a rational, planned bureaucratic system. Mühlenhof began as a mill and granary on one of the oldest sites in Berlin: the Mühlendamm bridge, which connects Cölln to Berlin at the southeast corner of the palace island.[13] In the sixteenth century, the resources and profits of the mill were split between the elector and the mill master (*Mühlenhauptmann*). This *Mühlenhauptmann* eventually oversaw all water mills in the city. As his responsibilities grew, his title changed to *Amtshauptmann* or *Amtshauptmann auf den Mühlenhoff*.[14] Likely due to its convenient location directly by the palace, the functions at the Mühlenhof continued to expand and it was the collection and dispersal point of tolls and duties from the ten other Berlin domains.[15]

Members of the ruling family took an interest in agriculture in both a broad sense for governing the territory and more locally in the running of their own estates. Some of the produce from these estates fed the court and may have influenced farming practices more broadly in Brandenburg. Much has been made, in particular, of Electress Luise Henriette's personal influence on regional farming via her work at her estate in Oranienburg, just to the north of Berlin.[16] Friedrich Wilhelm had purchased the estate of Bützow for his wife in 1650 and acknowledged her family of birth in renaming it Oranienburg. The flat landscape was reminiscent of Luise Henriette's homeland, and the Dutch-trained architect and engineer Johann Gregor Memhardt designed her Dutch-style, water palace renovations.

Agricultural historians have claimed that technological innovation was limited in central and eastern Europe in the early modern period. However, Dutch farmers were recognized agricultural innovators of the period; they developed polder technology (a method of diking that had increased arable land in the Netherlands) and followed a new, efficient crop rotation. At the same time, dairy farming increased in the Netherlands, and new breeds of cattle produced more and better milk.[17] Luise Henriette reportedly imported some of the agricultural innovations of her native Holland to Oranienburg.[18] The story that has been repeated in histories over centuries is that in her attempt to strengthen the economy and to repopulate Brandenburg, Luise Henriette encouraged Dutch farmers to settle her estates, imported and husbanded Holstein Friesian dairy cows (bred in the Netherlands), and promoted some of the Dutch farming advancements listed above. Is it contested how successful these resettlement efforts were, however.[19] Only two of her estate notebooks survive, which provide scant evidence of her prolonged involvement in Brandenburg farming. In these, she sporadically recorded, in Dutch, the income and expenses from her estates in both Oranienburg and Strahnsdorf (to the southwest of Berlin, near Potsdam).[20]

Nonetheless, the records bear out that Luise Henriette's connection to the court in Berlin helped promote the financial success of Oranienburg. In 1656, Friedrich Wilhelm's first minister, Otto von Schwerin, instructed the steward Erdman Schmoll to purchase butter and cheese from Oranienburg.[21] Perhaps this preferment was due to Luise Henriette's personal sway, or perhaps it was because her estate offered a better price or tastier butter than previous external suppliers (as Schwerin attested in his order). In any case, Luise Henriette had a secure market for Oranienburg's produce of grain and butter. Multiple actors at the top of the court hierarchy benefited from food expenses being kept in the family.

Beyond the personal estates of the ruling family, the different territories of Brandenburg-Prussia had their own particular growing conditions and agricultural traditions, which enabled the production of different foods. The Mark Brandenburg has notably poor, sandy soil and a cool climate, which make agriculture difficult. The "Little Ice Age" of the seventeenth century additionally limited crop yields and, consequently, what could be delivered from the region to the Brandenburg residences. Furthermore, the manorial system there discouraged agricultural innovation so that Brandenburg produced less grain in the seventeenth and eighteenth century than other central European territories.[22] It is, after all, because of the otherwise poor growing conditions that potatoes would be so quick to catch on in Brandenburg in the eighteenth century. But in the seventeenth century, hearty rye was the most cultivated and consumed grain in the region and this was true at the Berlin palace as well.

Although the farms around Berlin provided grains, meat, dairy (cheese and butter), eggs, and honey to the court, they never supplied enough to meet the court's entire need.[23] It was therefore standard practice to get resources from elsewhere. At the end of the Michaelmas harvest in 1673, for instance, the court's need was so great that grain was brought to Berlin from the dispersed areas of the Neumark, the Mittelmark, and Prussia.[24] The region of Mittelmark, which surrounded Berlin, and Neumark (to the east of the Mittelmark) supplied some amount of wheat, rye, barley, malt, oats, and, in the case of Mittelmark, peas. Prussia sent only two kinds of grain to the court in Berlin, but supplied more than half of the amounts of them (55 percent of the rye and 63 percent of the barley).

As the above statistics confirm, Prussia was much more productive agriculturally than Brandenburg; as opposed to being the "sandbox" of Europe (as Brandenburg was called), Prussia was considered its breadbasket.[25] Supplying the Prussian residential palace in the city of Königsberg was, therefore, a much easier task than supplying the Berlin palace. Robert Bargrave, an English traveler to Königsberg in 1640, described the abundance of Königsberg in poetically flattering terms:

> Here is the greatest trade For oake timber that I thinck is in all those Countries. . . . Itt commeth downe From the Country, where are vast woods off oaks, pine, etts. This place affoards allsoe greatt store off hemp, Flax. . . . I never in my life att once saw greater quantity off any sort off Fowle as here were of wild ducks alongst the shoare by the Naring afforesaid, Their seeming to Fill the aire and cover the sea thereaboutts. . . . Allsoe a wonderful Number of Tame geese beetweene Dantzig and Elbing, it beeing a trade, by report, in these Countries For many to keepe thousands of them For their proffitt, as with us Flockes of sheepe, as the

one For their Flesh and wool, soe the other For Food and Feathers, both having keepers and both Feeding on grasse. Soe Farre they may bee compared together, butt nott any way in the benefitt and service For the use of Man, the Former not to bee regarded in respect of the latter.[26]

The foreigner's impression of plentitude stemmed from Prussia's particular topography, climate, trade position, and development history. Königsberg's position on the southeastern corner of the Baltic Sea meant that fresh fish was readily available. The Hanseatic and Dutch trade routes that connected the Baltic region with the rest of Europe put Königsberg in a convenient position to obtain goods from outside the region as well. Furthermore, Prussia enjoyed rich resources from its old-growth forests. The deforestation that had spread from the Italian peninsula north to the rest of Europe reached Prussia relatively late. Earlier deforestation in Bradenburg had reduced the plants and animals available for human consumption. However, the dense growth of the oak and beech hardwoods in Prussia provided big game and profitable building materials. Animals that were no longer found, or only seldom found, wild in the rest of Europe, such as bison and possibly even the aurochs, still lived in the Prussian forests and were hunted and consumed at the Königsberg palace.[27] All in all, these old-growth forests, the good conditions for rye farming, and its position as a Baltic port city made the Königsberg palace much easier to provision than the palace in Berlin, which explains why foodstuffs more often moved from the former to the latter. Prussian resources helped feed Berlin's rise to become the representative residential city of the Hohenzollerns.

Butter and even live cattle came to Berlin from Prussia as well.[28] In contrast to the belabored attempt of Richard Ficklend to move twenty tons of butter during the Thirty Years War, during a different war in 1672, food was successfully transported between territories. Butter and sides of bacon made it the six hundred miles from Königsberg, through Berlin, to supply the elector in the village of Hornberg where his army was camped en route to aid the United Provinces against the army Louis XIV.[29] By the 1680s, it was a regular occurrence for Prussian butter to supply the court in Berlin. Friedrich Wilhelm's orders for butter or dairy cows from the Prussian chamberlain, Friedrich Knyern, exist for the years 1680, 1681, and 1682.[30]

Not just any butter would do for the elector, either. Even from a great distance, Friedrich Wilhelm attempted to control the quality of butter he received. In 1680, he wrote to Chamberlain Knyern from Potsdam with instructions to ensure the quality of butter shipped to him there. Friedrich Wilhelm instructed that each vat was to be labeled with the name of its maker and its point of origin, as well as the names of those who handled the butter and where while it was in transit. That way, Friedrich Wilhelm wrote, if the butter was found to be "*untüchtig*," (unsuitable) it could be returned and the appropriate parties be held accountable.[31] A similar order two years later evidences additional attempts for getting butter safely to Berlin or Potsdam.[32] Food transport was increasingly normalized.

Slightly surprising, considering that Brandenburg produced far fewer edible goods than Prussia, is the reverse of this supply system (when foodstuffs were sent from Brandenburg to supply the court residing in Königsberg). When the cellar master requested twelve tons of Brandenburg land wine be sent to Königsberg, his wish was fulfilled by multiple local Brandenburg suppliers. Organizing the transport of the wine motivated administrators to bridge the disparate landholdings of the elector, and the *Amtskammer* sent the wine over water through Friedrich Wilhelm's fort town of Küstrin.[33] In this way, Friedrich Wilhelm was able to leverage the personal union as a material advantage by leapfrogging goods across his different lands.

Revisionist scholarship has determined that Friedrich Wilhelm had limited success at centralizing and rationalizing the administration across the dispersed domains under his personal union.[34] However, sharing food resources across the different realms demonstrates collaboration and communication that predated other administrative streamlining. As can be seen in the example of the transport of butter, under Friedrich Wilhelm, infrastructure and tighter administration of agricultural resources increased the court's access to the food resources of all of the elector's domains, regardless of where the court was in residence. This is an important facet of the character of the Prussian state: it did not rise simply from an imposing military ethos; it grew from disjointed and diverse parts that were gradually and incompletely linked over the seventeenth and eighteenth centuries. More effective administration of food provisions demonstrated a capability to coordinate resources across the elector's territories.

While the vast majority of the food consumed at court was produced in the elector's dominions, some desired foods simply could not be produced locally. To procure these exotic goods, the court turned to markets

and merchants. The Hohenzollerns' ability to procure faraway specialties was a part of their representation of elite status. At the 1684 wedding of Friedrich Wilhelm's son and heir to Sophie Charlotte, duchess
of Braunschweig-Lüneburg, one dedicatory poem imagined the global
markets as part of the wished-for happiness in the union:

> You will want for nothing
> That field and forest and river richly provide,
> What the Rhine and Mosel Rivers send and Spain as well,
> The East and West, and Charcas and Peru,
> What luxuries Bantam, Malabar and China send,
> The spices disposed of in Goa,
> What Madagascar carries, Comagra, Manoa, Panama, Mozambique,
> Kilwa Kisiwana, and Soffola.
> Above all of these, the most excellent dish,
> Is what you yourselves bring,
> Your coming in history:
> A true princely heart and German well-being,
> And old-fashioned honesty that shines over all.[35]

Clearly, nothing exceeded the value of the couple's innate and simple
German qualities, but as the poem attests, it was appealing to command
the finest goods of the far reaches of the globe and to enjoy the stability
and abundance that resulted from access to so many food sources. This
allegorical expression of the court's interest in trade was borne out in the
elector's trade infrastructure projects even though these did not signifi-
cantly impact market availability yet in the late seventeenth century.

Consumption of foods from the Americas, particularly those introduced to Europe in the seventeenth century, is not evident even at the
elite level of the court. Instead, most of the luxury foods and drinks purchased by the court in the seventeenth century were produced *within*
Europe. Chapter 4 will chart American plants as they entered the palace gardens, but the story of trade during Friedrich Wilhelm's reign is
not that of Brandenburg-Prussia becoming a major player in new global
commercial networks. But, the infrastructure developments during
Friedrich Wilhelm's reign did lay the groundwork for new commodities
to catch on and be traded through Brandenburg and Prussia in subsequent generations.

Historians have noted the use of the luxury foodstuffs of tea, chocolate, and coffee toward the end of Friedrich Wilhelm's reign (a consumption habit possibly brought by Huguenot refugees to Brandenburg after Louis XIV's revocation of the Edict of Nantes in 1685).[36] And there is anecdotal evidence of consumption of these emblematic early modern commodities. Some contemporary witnesses and later historians blamed the sudden death of the electoral prince Ludwig in 1687 on his predilection for coffee, as its strong flavor might have masked poison.[37] Tobacco was cataloged in the Berlin palace garden in 1656, but may have been used to make a fermented drink rather than for smoking.[38] There were no instructions for smoking or sniffing tobacco, as was popular practice elsewhere and in later Prussia (most famously, in the "tobacco ministry" of Friedrich Wilhelm's grandson, King Friedrich Wilhelm I). The only one of these "new" commodities that Friedrich Wilhelm is recorded to have consumed is tea. Starting in 1684, his physicians prescribed him a regimen of tea drinking to treat his gout.[39] It is notable that this was per medical order, not for any recorded personal taste.

Otherwise, though, there is no record that confirms the purchase of these new commodities at Friedrich Wilhelm's court.[40] The Italian historian Gregorio Leti charged with boosting the reputation of the Hohenzollern in his Italian history of the family, *Ritratti Storici,* described the typical offering at the elector's table thus: "I say, the table of this serene elector could not be more nobly served, whether because of the variety of meats, the fruit, the sweets, the beer, or the excellent wines."[41] Leti praises only the wide variety and high quality of ingredients on the elector's table, not their novelty. One of Friedrich Wilhelm's physicians, Dr. Elsholtz, too, was aware of chocolate, tea, and coffee, but in his dietary manual, he noted that those products were not as commonly used in Berlin as they were in Amsterdam, London, and Paris.[42]

Although tea, chocolate, coffee, and tobacco are seen as hallmarks of seventeenth-century European culture, early modern Europe was diverse, and even elite European culture was heterogeneous. The scattered evidence for tea, chocolate, coffee, and tobacco consumption in Brandenburg-Prussia is not significant enough to signal a shift in taste or habit there at the end of the seventeenth century.

Imported foodstuffs were only a small percentage of the overall volume of food and drink consumed, but they had an outsized impact on the flavor of the dishes served. The menus from January 1652 (detailed in chapter 1) name imported ingredients in approximately a quarter of the dishes. These included cooked apples with raisins, mutton with rice, sauerbraten with raisins, prunes with wine and sugar, mutton with capers, boiled chicken with pine nuts, and rice tarts.[43] Spices and other foreign flavorings were likely present in some of the other dishes as well. For example, in the French cookbook Elsholtz appends to his dietary manual, olive oil is recommended in one recipe for pancakes; another recipe for a sweetened egg sauce for poultry called for lemon pieces, cinnamon, and pistachio; and many meat recipes used pepper, wine, and citrus peels.[44]

The selection of items purchased from abroad changed very little over the course of the seventeenth century. In 1601, a cargo ship carrying wares for the court from Hamburg became frozen in place en route. The reports from the incident present a grocery list of items left there that look similar to later merchant bills.[45] The court purchased spices, dried fruits, and otherwise preserved vegetables (such as capers in olive oil), and sometimes foreign cheeses. There were also ingredients such as isinglass (a collagen from fish guts) and juniper berry that were useful in making certain confections and dishes.[46] These ingredients were also purchased throughout Friedrich Wilhelm's reign at both the Königsberg and Berlin palaces.

Wine was grown within the limits of the city of Berlin; maps of the period indicate a vineyard on the site of the present-day Viktoriapark in Kreuzberg, and in 1670, the elector's second wife, Dorothea, began managing the vineyard in the Tiergarten.[47] The local "land wine" was distributed as part of daily food allowances for members of court. But, even if the court did produce a local version of a product, like wine or beer, foreign versions were also sought for variety and perceived higher quality. Indeed, the most esteemed wines were from abroad and purchased through mainly Jewish merchants, who could secure multiyear supply contracts.[48] Of these, the most highly regarded (and expensive, according to purchase records) were the wines from the Rhine and Mosel River regions, followed by wines from Franconia (southern Germany today) and then France. Additionally, wines were imported from Spain, Portugal, the Canary Islands, and Hungary.[49] Only one of the wines purchased by court might have come from Italy, the malvasia, which Dr. Elsholtz claimed originated in Crete.[50] These wines were traded through the long-standing Hanseatic routes.[51]

Some varieties of beer were considered worth importing from outside the elector's dominions. Along with most foreign wine orders and inventories, the cellar master usually recorded *Zebster* beer from the residence of the Zerbst-Anhalt princes less than ninety miles from Berlin.[52] This beer was famous, according to an eighteenth-century lexicographer, not just in Germany, but in the Netherlands, Denmark, Sweden, Poland, and even East India.[53] The high quality of Zerbst beer was attributed to its fresh water source on the Elbe River and was praised for medicinal properties, including the ability to cure dropsy.[54] The accounting practice of listing Zerbst beer with the foreign wines demonstrates its higher status compared to other beers at court. Zerbst beer cost four times as much as "table beer" in 1622 and accounted for only five of 954 barrels of beer consumed that year (around half a percent).[55] In 1628–29, the percentage of Zerbst beer was slightly more (67 of 1044 barrels, or around 5 percent). A new dining regulation of 1673–74 designated a ton (or half a barrel) of Zerbst beer for the princely tables, compared to six barrels of "common" beer.[56]

Like Zerbst beer, other luxury goods from further afield maintained their reputations for high quality for an extended period, too. Many of the products purchased by the court carried geographical appellations in the account records including Westphalian ham, mortadella from Bologna (recorded as *sausice de Bologne*), and Edam cheese. Parmesan cheese was purchased at least twice by the court under different reigns in 1602 and 1652, and in 1684, Elsholtz deemed it the best cheese (followed by Edam).[57] In other words, food did not have to be novel or from the Far East or the "New World" to be considered luxurious, and the perception of their quality was stable. Friedrich Wilhelm is not associated with luxury consumption, but courtiers were eating and drinking some of the best European goods on the market.

While Brandenburg and Prussia did not purchase "new" commodities on the scale of other parts of Europe at the time, Friedrich Wilhelm's infrastructure initiatives laid the groundwork for such markets later. Under Friedrich Wilhelm, Berlin established a new stock exchange, new warehouses, and quays that helped it become a regional trading center. More importantly, waterways were dredged and extended to connect Hamburg and Leipzig through Brandenburg canals, and in the 1650s Friedrich Wilhelm had the Havel River dredged to support larger ships. Like the renovations to the palace gardens and work on the Oranienburg farm, these projects utilized modern technology and expert engineers, controversially again from abroad.[58] The most significant of these projects was the building of the Friedrich Wilhelm Canal, which connected the Spree with the Oder River over six miles away, thus linking Hamburg by water with markets farther east.[59]

In Prussia, Friedrich Wilhelm tried to wrest toll income from the Danes and the Swedes by improving overland routes that avoided the Danish Sound and the town of Stettin (then in Swedish possession in West Pomerania). Furthermore, in the 1680s, he ordered improvements to the Königsberg port to allow larger ships to dock there directly.[60] In addition, the Kolberg Harbor was improved for ships in 1660 and 1681–82. Since it was the only significant port in East Pomerania, this increased competition with the Danish and Swedish trade routes.

These changes to roads and waterways in Brandenburg and Prussia likely did not benefit the general population in the seventeenth century, but they set the Hohenzollern territories up to profit from increased commerce from Dutch shipping in the North and Baltic Seas. Berlin or Königsberg did not suddenly rival the booming centers of Amsterdam, London, and Paris because of these changes, however. In 1700, Berlin's population was not even a tenth of that of London. Moreover, the buying power of the average citizen in Brandenburg remained too low to participate in a global consumer culture. Although it was likely possible for Brandenburgers to acquire tea, chocolate, coffee, and tobacco at the end of Friedrich Wilhelm's reign, it is not evident that this was a considerable feature of dining culture. Nevertheless, the infrastructure set in place during Friedrich Wilhelm's reign enabled such commodities to reach new markets in the eighteenth century.

In sum, trade had an impact on the culinary culture in Brandenburg-Prussia, but it was not the type of trade described in general economic histories of the late seventeenth century, which dwell on what was new. Instead, the ingredients purchased for the kitchens from abroad came via trade routes that had been in place for over a century even if the merchants were increasingly Dutch. The biggest changes during the reign of Friedrich Wilhelm were the infrastructure projects that increased Berlin's importance as a regional trading center. In this area of northern Europe, such developments likely affected dining culture for Brandenburg-Prussia more widely in the eighteenth century. They increased revenue for the state through tolls and tariffs, and sped up communication and transportation throughout the elector's territories.

As the aphorism goes, what people eat is a reflection of their identity. However, *how* people acquire their food is also an expression of identity and aspirations.[61] The choices Friedrich Wilhelm's court made in order to access food show that the economy was just as important as (and tied to) representations of power. The integration of the disparate territories of Friedrich Wilhelm can be traced in other parts of daily administration, such as in the postal system, which enabled the various stadtholders to communicate directly and, for the most part, efficiently with the elector.[62] Here, though, the constant challenge of provisioning the court triggered administrators to collaborate across the elector's disparate territories.

Food choice not only expresses aspirations, it also reveals state formation as an everyday process that was deeply integrated with the household structure of the court. Much has been written about the administration of personal unions with a focus on financial and military integration as well as friction with local estates and parliaments.[63] J. H. Elliot wrote: "Multiple monarchies presented multiple opportunities as well as multiple constraints. The test of statesmanship for early modern rulers was whether they could realize the opportunities while remaining aware of the constraints."[64] In accessing butter and rye from Prussia in Berlin, court administrators took advantage of those opportunities.

In response to the powerlessness of the Brandenburg-Prussia ruling family in the Thirty Years War, the subsequent generation sought a food system that was, first and foremost, stable. While there were more luxurious, foreign foods that added to the prestige of the court, a consistent supply offered by food production of multiple territories, made that part of war recovery possible. While this chapter has explored the wider network of production feeding the court, the next chapter focuses on a food-production site much closer to home: the palace gardens. Although this site did not provide a large quantity of food, it was essential to the court's projection of power and knowledge. Nowhere is the striving for power and control seen more clearly than on the sliver of land in the Spree River on which the elector planted his garden.

4

Prince of the Living World

THE BERLIN PLEASURE GARDENS

In 1656, a physician wrote to the elector of Brandenburg-Prussia adver-
tising his services as a botanist to catalog the plants of the palace garden
in Berlin.[1] This Johann Sigismund Elsholtz (1623–1688) had made the
requisite academic peregrinations for the task: from Frankfurt an der
Oder to Leiden to Padua to Wittenberg. Elsholtz flattered the elector by
saying that "the fame of the garden had grown in so few years through
the elector's great care and expense" and that he could "add to the name
and reputation of the garden with a catalog to match those of the great
gardens of Copenhagen, Leiden, Paris, Montpellier, Padua, Pisa, and
Messina."[2] Friedrich Wilhelm enthusiastically accepted and ordered his
gardeners to assist Elsholtz in any way he might need.[3] Elsholtz completed the catalog within the promised year and was rewarded with a
permanent position at court.

By this point, Elector Friedrich Wilhelm had not yet gained the moniker "Great" from his success in battle against Louis XIV in the 1670s, and
Elsholtz had not yet secured his place in medical history as the first person to inject medicine intravenously. The thirty-somethings were merely
looking to build: one a position of stability and security in the Mark
Brandenburg, and the other to contribute knowledge in the Republic of
Letters, the informational scientific network of the day. Their goals con-
verged at the garden on the tiny island of Cölln, where local and exotic
plants grew in the service of state.

Elsholtz's offer appealed to the elector, who had prioritized rebuilding
the Berlin palace gardens even before returning to live in Berlin after the
Thirty Years War. Both the palace garden and the nearby hunting grounds
of the Tiergarten had fallen into disorder over the course of the war. But,
already in the winter of 1649 Friedrich Wilhelm engaged the services of
the Dutch-trained landscape architect Johann Gregor Memhardt (1607–
1678) to redesign Berlin palace grounds. He was even thinking about

Friedrich Wilhelm and
Dorothea as Apollo and
Diana over the Berlin palace
garden. Frontispiece of
Elsholtz's 1672 *Vom Garten-
Baw*. (Bayerische Staatsbibliothek München, 4 Oecon. 103
(p. [7]), urn:nbn:de:bvb:12-
bsb10228605–6)

specific plants for the garden as he ordered citrus trees for Berlin from
his seat in Cleves.[4]

Although the gardens supplied only a small percentage of overall food
consumed, they were a public canvas for court aspirations. Palace gardens, such as those in Königsberg in the sixteenth century and Berlin
in the seventeenth century, were "testaments of power and prestige" of
the ruler.[5] Displaying control over nature was a reminder of the justifica-
tion for divine rule and abundant foodstuffs from the garden confirmed
the ruler's paternalistic ability to provide for his court and thus acted as
a metaphor for the wider care of his people. For Friedrich Wilhelm, in
particular, renovating the garden was an expression of the yearning for
stability following the turbulent war-torn decades in Brandenburg.

Elector Friedrich Wilhelm and his officers brought the palace gardens
to new heights during his reign, but the gardens predated him by three-
quarters of a century.[6] It was Elector Johann Georg (r. 1571–98) who had
ordered the original building of a garden on the palace grounds in 1573.

Although it referred to the area as a "pleasure garden," the order stipulated that the garden's primary task was to supply the needs of the kitchen.[7] When the ruling family was largely absent during the Thirty Years War, the garden on the island of Cölln had been "reduced to the ground."[8] According to one biographer, only the kitchen garden remained, and it could not adequately provide the kitchens as fruit, cauliflower, and celery had to be purchased from Hamburg, Braunschweig, Erfurt, and Leipzig.[9] Under Friedrich Wilhelm, the kitchen gardens still served a practical purpose, but the ornamental flower beds took increasing pride of place. Friedrich Wilhelm prioritized the gardens his entire reign and even near the end of his life he paid dearly to replenish the fruit orchard with pomegranate trees from Italy.[10]

The garden renovations under Friedrich Wilhelm mobilized a tremendous amount of labor and expert knowledge. Cölln was not a naturally fertile slice of land; only extensive and constant effort made it so. To counter the sandy soil, topsoil was hauled in and buffalo from the hunting park (*Tiergarten*) were paraded around the island to drop their nitrogen-rich dung.[11] Greenhouses were constructed with ovens in them so that nonnative plants (particularly citrus trees) would survive the gray and cold Brandenburg winters. In 1648, a storm destroyed one of these (the Pomeranzehaus). At a time when the court was struggling to cover other expenses, the Pomeranzehaus was important enough to rebuild immediately and replacement citrus trees were purchased from Dresden and Leipzig.[12] In December 1655, a fire in the ovens destroyed the Pomeranzehaus and killed three gardeners. Again, the elector ordered it rebuilt and purchased replacement trees within the year.[13] These efforts underscore how edible produce from these gardens, referred to in court documents as "*naturalia*," was anything but natural. Instead, it was the result of desire, persistence, and elite resources—demonstrating the significance of homegrown foods for the elector in his self-fashioning as a ruler.

Each member of the design and gardening team brought his or her expertise and tastes to bear on the content and layout of the Cölln palace garden. The first member of the team was Friedrich Wilhelm, who had studied in Leiden, home of the famous university botanical garden completed in 1594. Electress Luise Henriette brought plants and agricultural methods to Berlin from her native Holland, then experiencing its "tulip mania."[14] Michael Hanff (1619–1678) was named head gardener sometime in the early 1640s and transferred from Prussia to Berlin.[15] Hanff's father had worked as a court gardener in Prussia, and Michael's education was sanctioned and likely funded by Elector Georg Wilhelm (1595–1640). Hanff studied in Hessen with the famous royal gardener Johann Royer and spent three years studying in Holland.[16] The garden's architect, Johann Gregor Memhardt (1607–1678), though born in Austria, also studied in the Netherlands, where he became an expert in hydroengineering.[17] Finally, Johann Sigismund Elsholtz, the Prussian-born physician, was hired as court botanist and physician (roles he held until his death in 1688).[18]

Considering the background of its builders, it is not surprising that the garden's most prominent features drew on Dutch technology and style. With training in the wet landscape of the Netherlands, Memhardt was able to create dramatic waterworks in the Cölln garden, where many plant beds were meant to be surrounded by water. A fishpond and numerous fountains were integrated into the design. Memhardt's designs also extended the island of Cölln into the Spree River to increase the size of the garden.[19] The Neptune fountain sculpture in the middle of a flower bed was a copy from Luise Henriette's father's garden at Huis ter Nieuwburg in Holland, and tulips featured prominently in the Cölln flower beds.[20]

Like most palace gardens in early modern Europe, though, the basic form of the garden derived from Italian design, inspired by humanist ideology (Elsholtz's humanist education in Padua, therefore, added to his appeal as court botanist). The Renaissance garden was perceived as a place where one could practice the humanist value of self-cultivation through the cultivation of plants.[21] These gardens contained a paradoxical "collaboration of art and nature" in which the most characteristic feature was strict geometry, both in the arrangement of the flower beds and the linear axes of paths through the beds. Gardens of this style typically featured water elements, such as fountains. Along with the natural order of the geometric patterns, water elements signified the perfection of God's creation. The ability to replicate the natural world in miniature emphasized the garden creator's divinely ordained privilege. Garden design was closely tied to architecture, and gardens had building-like features such as individuated rooms divided by steps and terraces, as well as hallway-like paths. In line with other humanistic impulses, most gardens contained classical references (usually sculptural), which allegorically extolled the noble virtues of the family that placed them there.

Cataloging garden flora was a standard practice of natural observation that accompanied this humanist self-cultivation.[22] Such a catalog was a definitive tally of what the garden contained, but also might serve to broadcast the magnificence of the garden on behalf of the ruler. Curiously though, Elsholtz never published his catalog. Only recently was any part of his manuscript catalog published: in 2010, two different sets of scholars translated and edited book 1 of Elsholtz's *Horta Berolinensis,* which describes the layout of the garden.[23] Book 2, however, which consists of the actual plant catalog, is still only available in the original manuscript.[24] After he completed this *Horta Berolinensis,* Elsholtz began an illustrated plant catalog, titled *Plantae Singulares Horti Electoralis Brandenburgici Coloniensis pro Eystettensis.*[25] He did eventually publish a popular vernacular gardening manual for the entire region of the Mark Brandenburg, which elaborated on the plants cataloged for Friedrich Wilhelm in the 1650s for a wider readership.[26]

As described in *Horta Berolinensis,* book 1, the new Berlin garden contained many of the typical components of Renaissance gardens. Memhardt's design was heavily geometrical, similar to the garden in Leiden and other Renaissance gardens.[27] His plan (never fully completed) included a water garden with islands of plant beds connected by bridges, which can be seen in a 1652 design. In keeping with the Renaissance desire to order nature, the garden, as Elsholtz described it, was divided into different types of plants: those that were useful, those only prized for their beauty, and those with an ability to instill wonder in nature.[28] The beds closest to the palace on the south side contained expensive tulips (of which there were nineteen varieties in 1656).[29] These four square beds had a wide center axis bordered by fruit and nut trees and interspersed with trellised paths and sculptures. Continuing northward to the tip of the Cölln island was the fruit garden (*pomarium*), which Elsholtz claimed was not fully used because there were enough fruit and kitchen gardens outside of the city to supply the kitchen.[30] To the west of the flower garden was an area for a planned hydraulic fish pond, which was likely never realized.

Beyond this to the north were medicinal herb beds (the *hortus medicus*), and opposite those, a bridge leading to the kitchen and vegetable garden (*hortus culinarius dive olitorius*). The first part of the herb/vegetable garden was long and divided into multiple beds, and the second part was made up of a circle of eight triangular beds with a square in the center and three additional beds outside of the circle. Most of this description from Elsholtz fits with Memhardt's 1652 plan. The other formal elements in the garden included an Italianate grotto, the hothouses for

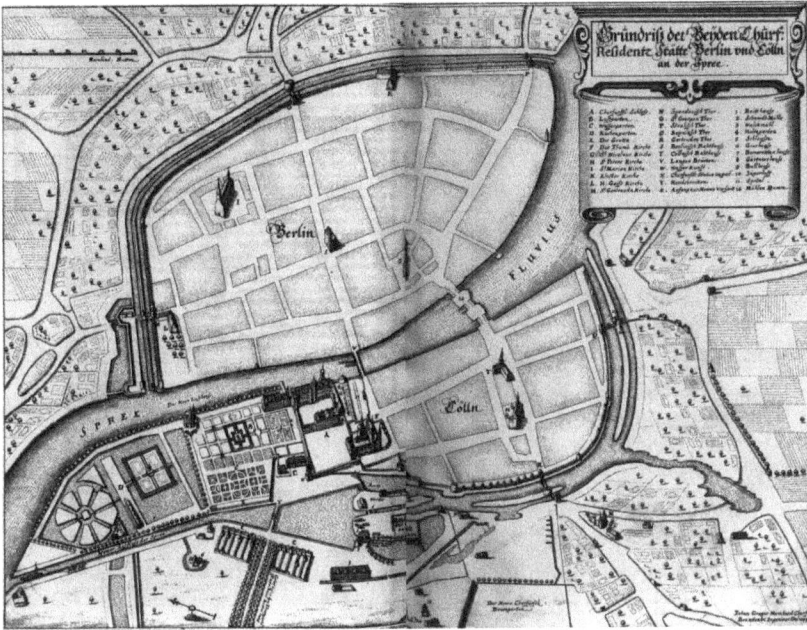

Johann Gregor Memhardt's 1652 design for the Berlin palace gardens. (Bayerische Staatsbibliothek München—Hbks/E 29–7 (pp. [74–75]. urn:nbn:de:bvb:12-bsb10802320-3)

growing foreign fruit trees, a birdhouse, and fountains. Clear axes guided the eye north from the palace out through the garden to the Spree River and west along a long alley of linden and nut trees (brought from Holland) that led to the elector's hunting park (the present-day Unter den Linden boulevard).

Following the description of the gardens, book 2 of *Hortus Berolinensis* listed the plants actually growing in 1656. The 172-page manuscript, *Catalogus plantarum ordine alphabetico digestus,* contained approximately 1,350 specific plant species by their seventeenth-century Latin name (the natural nomenclature was very much in flux at the time) and usually a German common name and short description in German and Latin. The catalog of so many plants from so many parts of the world gives the impression of an encyclopedic collection of plants creating an ordered microcosm of the natural world under the dominion of Friedrich Wilhelm. Of these circa 1,350 plants, slightly more than 15 percent were edible.[31] This catalog is a near complete snapshot of the naturalia available for use by the court kitchen and provides a concrete manifestation of court aspirations.

Indeed, not all of the potentially edible plants in the garden were meant for consumption, a fact that highlights the symbolic function of the garden in addition to its practical purpose. All common European cereals were grown there, but most of the grains eaten at court were sourced from elsewhere. Eggplant was present in 1656, but not for consumption: Elsholtz called it "an unhealthy food: although the Italians do not hesitate to eat it, instead, they slice it and eat it as a cooling salad with oil, vinegar, and salt."[32] Although he recognized it could be edible, Elsholtz categorized eggplant as a "summer ornamental" plant and did not mention it in his later dietary manual.[33] His disdain for eggplant may have stemmed from its belonging to the nightshade family, which has some poisonous species. Possibly, the eggplant was simply unfamiliar; Elsholtz did not even have an established name for it. He called it "long *Dolläpffel* or *Mala insana,* not because it is tasty but because it is an unhealthy food."[34]

Elsholtz did not show such disdain for another newly arrived nightshade plant, the potato. Because potatoes were so important in history of the later Prussian kingdom, previous scholars have been interested in when the potato arrived in Brandenburg and whether it was consumed in the seventeenth century or merely cultivated for its delicate white flowers.[35] Elsholtz's catalog is the earliest record of the food that would become a staple of the Prussian diet in subsequent centuries, and his writings definitively show that it was eaten in the seventeenth century. As with eggplant, he had no common German name for the potato in the 1656 catalog, but called it "nightshade with tuberous roots *that is useful as a food,* also known as Grublinger earth pears, and Tartuffoli."[36] By the time he published *Vom Garten-Baw* a decade later, he had settled on the name *Tartuffeln* and described four ways to cook them.[37] Elsholtz's writing, then, evidences an increasing familiarity with plants native to the Americas.[38]

Other American plants, such as cactus, were cataloged by Elsholtz but not connected with culinary purposes. Although Elsholtz called the cactus a "large Indian fig" in the catalog, he made no mention of its edibility in *Vom Garten-Baw* (as he did with the potato, for instance).[39] Likewise, he categorized chili peppers, avocados, and tomatoes as "ornamental summer plants" and did not mention culinary uses.[40] Curiously, other important American foods were not recorded at the Berlin court at all, such as wild rice, quinoa, chia, peanuts, and manioc.

Pumpkins, however—likely due to their similarity to cucumbers, melons, and other squash—were more quickly adopted into Brandenburg cuisine. There are six varieties of *Cucurbita* in the 1656 *Hortus* catalog, including one described as "large, round, with yellow flowers and intact leaves with hairy cracks," with a Latin alternative name of *Cucurbita indiea,* indicating Elsholtz's awareness of its American origin.[41] In the *Dieateticon* he noted that there were many shapes and sizes of pumpkins, but only five sorts that are grown "by us for the kitchen"; he described multiple means of cooking them, including the "usual way," of boiling with milk and butter, and some ways described in the appended *French Cook,* and he noted that their seeds have pharmacological uses.[42] There is, again, confusion between gourds from Africa and pumpkins from the Americas because Elsholtz quotes the ancients, Galen and Dioscorides, on the temperaments of pumpkins, of which they would have been ignorant.

Beans had also made their way into the garden in Berlin, where there were five American varities (genus *Phaseolus*). Across Europe, beans were generally easily and quickly integrated into cuisine after the Iberian encounter with the Americas.[43] The names Elsholtz gives these five—large garden bean, small garden bean, small Italian bean, Egyptian garden bean, and Indian bean—show some confusion about their origin and reflect variously their familiarity or exoticness in Brandenburg.

Possessing a nonnative edible plant did not guarantee that it would provide food for the court; sometimes climate got in the way. Elsholtz recorded pistachios, pine nuts, and capers in the 1656 garden, which did not typically grow in the Brandenburg climate. "Pistachio trees," he wrote, "grow in forests in Syria, Arabia, Egypt, and Africa where large numbers of the fruits are gathered and shipped to Tripoli and from there are traded by the seafaring English and Dutch."[44] Keeping pistachio trees in Brandenburg, Elsholtz lamented, took great effort and resulted in no fruit.[45] Capers, according to Elsholtz, did fruit in Brandenburg, but "as even the common man knows, the preserved kind and the type with closed buds come from distant lands."[46] This explanation of the sources for pistachios and capers is confirmed by court purchasing receipts.[47]

Although there is no discernible reason why some new plants were adopted in the Brandenburg court cuisine and others not, it is clear in Elsholtz's descriptions that it was not their novelty that made American native plants attractive, but rather that they fit into the encyclopedic aims of the Berlin garden. Elsholtz's objective in his decades of experimentation, cataloging, and writing about the gardens was to understand how to make plants thrive in Brandenburg—to ensure that gardeners would have the best chance of creating order and abundance from the Brandenburg land. In this goal, Elsholtz's scholarly interests aligned with the interests of the state in promoting the growth of the population and a return to order and stable provisioning. This is what the "Great" Elector promised his subjects and what Elsholtz promised the elector.

In addition to Elsholtz's descriptions, court household records further evidence how *naturalia* were put to use in the kitchens. The court confectioner (*Konditor*), for one, had a contractual claim to the fruits grown in the gardens for pastries and preserves. His employment contract stated: "It is promised that Johann Tiegeln receive as much wine and any type of fruit and plant he needs for confections from the country palaces (*Landhäuse*) and as much from the pleasure and herb gardens of the residences and administrative districts (*Ämtern*) in all our lands whenever he wants them."[48] Although the foods from the palace gardens were not monetized, they were still valuable. In the fall of 1656, someone "interfered" with the fruits, vineyards and other fruit farms that supplied the court. The elector responded to reports of missing fruit from faraway Königsberg and reiterated that only the confectioner had the right of access to these fruits (thus ensuring their availability for the court when it returned to Berlin).[49] The following summer, the elector stated even more emphatically that Konditor Tiegeln needed Borsdorfer, Rostocker, Rosenhäger, and Scheib apples as well as pears, quinces, cherries, and currants.[50] Friedrich Wilhelm ordered that these should be supplied from the palace gardens and local administrative districts, not purchased with cash, as they had been recently.[51] Clearly, edible plants were appreciated as financial assets in addition to their recreational, scholarly, and symbolic functions.

THE GREAT EFFORTS of Friedrich Wilhelm's team of gardeners, designers, and botanists did not bear fruit for long. In 1713, the palace gardens (in Potsdam as well as in Berlin) were razed for a military parade ground by Friedrich Wilhelm's grandson, King Friedrich Wilhelm I (r. 1713–40), known as the "Soldier King." Jutting out into the Spree River, the island of Cölln was a stage for exhibiting different ruling priorities from generation to generation. Although Elector Friedrich Wilhelm's military legacy obscures other aspects of his reign, tellingly, soldiers were once marshaled to work in the pleasure gardens.[52] His garden project manifested the stable presence of the ruler in the region and was as an oasis of pleasure instead of a testament to war. In the preface of his Mark Brandenburg gardening manual, Elsholtz elaborated on this sentiment: "Yes, it is heartily to be wished that the Almighty will allow the inhabitants of this land, who have endured so much trouble, to enjoy a long period of peace, so that they have the chance to recover from the suffered losses and so this Mark Brandenburg, that does not lack in natural fertility, will grow into a blessed garden of the Lord."[53] The fact that the garden served a practical as well as symbolic role in the court culture (or as Elsholtz called it, "*Lust und Nutz*") indicates the integration of these two aspects of food culture. The garden was the showpiece of the royal palace to the outside world and the prominent vista seen from the palace itself. That the garden also supplied actual need demonstrates the court was not only concerned with an empty show of wealth or fashion, but that it valued economy and practicality in expressions of power. This duality is also seen in the dining practices of the court, both in festival dining and at everyday meals.

5

Feasts and Everyday Dining

ON THE MORNING OF October 18, 1663, fifty carriages rode out from the gates of Königsberg, Prussia, to greet and escort foreign dignitaries on their ceremonial entry into the city. The occasion for such a grand reception was the pledging of fealty (*Huldigung*) that the Prussian estates had agreed to swear to Friedrich Wilhelm as their sovereign ruler. This elevation of status resulted both from the elector's calculated alliance shifts between Poland and Sweden during the Second Northern War (1655–60) and from two years of fraught parliamentary debate. No longer did Friedrich Wilhelm, as duke of Prussia, have to pay feudal tribute to the Polish king. Thousands of burghers participated in the main event of the *Huldigung* at the palace square. That day, before Friedrich Wilhelm and representatives of the king of Poland, the city councilors, the noble estates, the knights and representatives from other cities and towns of Prussia recognized Friedrich Wilhelm as their hereditary and sovereign ruler.

The ceremony concluded with a banquet at which those present toasted the good health of the elector and made merry. Inside the palace, the new status was confirmed in the manner of the meal: the elector ate at the center of a table on a raised dias with the royal Polish dignitaries to his left and an envoy from Spain to his right. Beneath them, the knights and nobility were "fed in a magnificent and stately style."[1] Out in the palace courtyard, red and white wine flowed from a painted Teutonic eagle for four hours. This so delighted the burghers that some reportedly came away with bloody faces from their attempts to reach the free wine. According to scholars studying a later festival in 1701 to mark the self-coronation of Friedrich Wilhelm's son, the contrast between the orderly meal inside and the disorderly jubilation outside was an important representation of the "disciplining power" of the ruler.[2]

No other meal of Friedrich Wilhelm's life was so well publicized or as sumptuous as that which marked his rise as sovereign ruler of Prussia. When compared to an everyday meal at Friedrich Wilhelm's court, at first glance, there seem to be few similarities. According to a court order from September 1665, an everyday meal was supposed to proceed thus: trumpeters would play for half an hour at lunch and dinner while diners arranged themselves at their assigned tables and rooms. Then, three court officers would make the rounds to ensure first, that no outsiders were at the tables and, second, that no member of court who received only an allowance for food was sitting down to a free meal. The officers were to remove any illicit diners and regain order. When all permitted diners were seated (twelve to a table), the officers were to go to the kitchens and inform the steward, who would bring the meal to the correct places. Everything was to be done in a "respectable manner and in particular, without neglecting the prayer."[3]

The *Huldigung* meal was a public celebration with a thousand actors from as far away as Spain. It conveyed the elevated stature of the host, the position of ruler over subjects, and a confirmation of the newly established political relationships that emerged after the Great Northern War. The September 1665 meal filled the daily need to feed the immediate servants and members of the court household and was intended for their eyes only. These differences in scale, gestures, and participants, however, obscure that both meals served as performances that confirmed a particular social order, one on the European scale and the other within the contained cosmos of the three hundred or so members of the court.

This chapter argues that all meals at the court of Brandenburg-Prussia, both the celebratory and the quotidian, were governed by rules that reified the court social structures. The perceived differences between the two levels of dining ritual correspond to the dual nature of the early modern court as both the center of representational power and the physical space where people and animals lived, worked, ate, and slept.[4] However, regardless of the occasion, every meal at the court of Brandenburg-Prussia offered the ruler and his court a chance for self-fashioning, asserting a social hierarchy, and demonstrating belonging. Furthermore, commensality brought the permanent members of court together, up and down the social ladder, for twice daily monitoring, instruction, conversation, and sustenance.

Sociologists beginning with Georg Simmel have studied meals as a system of order: a way of building a community and defining its boundaries.[5] With the idea that food is a code that reflects social relationships, Mary Douglas took this line of inquiry in an anthropological direction to look into what specifically is happening at a meal. She posed the questions:

What makes a meal? What are its necessary components? For Douglas, the "repeated analogy" of a meal constructs the standard of the institution of a meal. The meaning of any particular meal is drawn from a comparison to all other meals.[6] For this reason, it is useful to study the festival meals in conjunction with the regular rituals of daily dining, even though the two concepts of *Alltagsgeschichte* and festival culture are held up as separate fields of historical study. By Douglas's reading, the extraordinary meal only makes sense if there is an ordinary one to distinguish it.

Speakers at the Third Symposium of the Residenz-Kommission attempted to answer the question of whether a history of everyday life was even possible for courts. In his introduction to the published talks, Werner Paravicini notes that the everyday and the festival are inseparable and should, therefore, also be studied together.[7] A relationship-based analysis of court dining that looks at multidirectional influence across social classes bridges the two subdisciplines of *Alltagsgeschichte* and court studies.[8]

Food is a natural subject for the historian of everyday life because, as Simmel pointed out, eating is common to all humans, but the details of how and what one eats distinguishes individuals and societies. A task of *Alltagsgeschichte* is to question if "the image of the 'grand contours' of historical life actually accord with the concrete experience."[9] While the *Alltagsgeschichte* approach at first focused exclusively on "history from below," a later generation of historians recognized that everyday life encompasses the intermingling of social orders.[10] This is particularly true in court history, where, although it is often overlooked, not all culture was elite; different classes mixed constantly and in close proximity.[11] The concrete experience and the rhetoric of court dining both played a role in the grand contours of state formation in Brandenburg-Prussia.

However, a meal is ephemeral. It is difficult to capture a single meal, let alone the repetition of similar meals that constitutes the dining culture of a given family or society. The records of everyday and festival meals in Brandenburg-Prussia are not true reflections of the meals, rather, they are aspirational fictions. In addition to the above juxtaposed examples of a banquet and an average meal at court, the following chapter explores the court's communication of its dining in a ceremonial book that put the Brandenburg-Prussian festival meals in a European festival vocabulary and in ten internal court orders from Friedrich Wilhelm's reign. The efforts to codify and control dining and its messages shows how important dining was to early modern statecraft.

Feasting at Court

Elector Friedrich Wilhelm is often portrayed as a spartan, militaristic ruler with little interest in ceremonial pomp (an assessment that originated with Friedrich Wilhelm's great-grandson, Frederick the Great, in the mid-eighteenth century that was perpetuated by nineteenth-century Prussian historians). But this characterization removes Elector Friedrich Wilhelm from the context of seventeenth-century Europe, when ceremony was an essential component of foreign policy. Rulers communicated through ceremonial displays that enacted social and political relationships as a central part of early modern diplomacy. Barbara Stollberg-Rilinger, a scholar of political culture, has inspired a new appreciation for the political function of court ceremony. She argues that ceremony participants did not simply perform empty gestures because tradition dictated them. Rather, they agreed to a certain relationship and performed the appropriate gestures to actualize that relationship or mark a milestone.[12] In spite of his later reputation, Friedrich Wilhelm necessarily participated in the political rituals required for his role as ruler.

In the particular case of the Hohenzollern, Stollberg-Rilinger points to the role that "ceremonial self-representation" played in the rise of Friedrich Wilhelm's son, Friedrich, to the rank of king in Prussia. Only when a representative of another royal court formally recognized Friedrich I as a fellow monarch was the royal ascent an actual fact. Although the self-coronation took place in 1701, such recognition by a European peer did not come until June 7, 1706, when the ambassador of the English king treated King Friedrich I as a royal peer. This set the precedent for other European monarchs to recognize Friedrich as a king. Thus, the political change was about rulers' relationships to one another as marked in their gestures.

A small book from 1699 and 1700 called the *Ceremoniale Brandenburgicum* addresses how this political ambition was reflected in court ceremony during the reign of Elector Friedrich Wilhelm. Although the book was published under the reign of his son, this work of festival literature describes some examples of ceremonial dining at the court of Elector Friedrich Wilhelm in a context with other historical European festival meals.[13] Festival books typically honor the courts or the city that was participating in a festival. Though they present a biased account of festivals, such books are valuable sources for understanding a ruler's desired perception.[14] In its 187 pages, the *Ceremoniale Brandenburgicum* acts as a *Fürstenspiegel,* or "mirror of princes" book, to educate those planning and orchestrating courtly festivals to understand appropriate gestures through precedence.

The *Ceremoniale Brandenburgicum* is divided into three sections: the first explains how the elector interacted with different members of the Holy Roman Empire at various official events (imperial coronations, diets, peace negotiations, etc.). The second section relates to how the elector interacted with various monarchs, from the king of England to the "*Tartar Cham.*" The final section describes his interactions with rulers of ecclesiastical and smaller secular states (such as the pope and the grand duke of Tuscany). The political ceremony described in the *Ceremoniale Brandenburgicum* included the correct pronunciation of titles and honorifics, the number of coaches and horses that would carry a ruler in a festival entry, and where in the palace the personage would be met by their host. The distance the host moved to greet their guest alluded to the prestige of the guest. The greatest honor was bestowed if the host met the guest at their coach in the courtyard. A lower dignitary, by contrast, might be made to wait a few days before being received by the host from their throne in the great hall. Like the description of the 1663 homage ceremony in Königsberg, the *Ceremoniale Brandenburgicum* helped to set the status of the Hohenzollern in relation to other European rulers.

Dining was particularly important for enacting political relationships, and when European rulers came together, meals were meticulously choreographed. For example, at his coronation banquet in 1612, Emperor Matthias dined precisely five steps above the seven electors, who themselves were seated at equally sized tables facing one another with the ecclesiastical electors (the prince-bishops) receiving the honor of sitting closest to the emperor. Even though the elector of Brandenburg was absent from this event, his place was still set among his peers so that his political standing was still recognized *in absentia.* The *Ceremoniale Brandenburgicum* describes the protocol for such a situation: "When an elector [at an imperial banquet] is absent, his table will still be set, however without food, just three empty covered bowls, which will be given to the elector's envoys to bring back with them."[15] An engraving of the event served to reify and broadcast the event and hierarchies played out in it.

The parts of *Ceremoniale Brandenburgicum* that pertain to dining are primarily concerned with seating order, the number and status of the servers, and who was expected to bear the cost of the meals of visiting

The 1612 imperial diet meal with tables set for all the electors (including the absent Elector Brandenburg). (Gothardus Arthusius, *Electio et Coronatio* [Frankfurt am Main]: Officina de Bry, [1612], 22. Deutsche Fotothek / SLUB / Dresdner Digitalisierungszentrum)

dignitaries. For example, a ducal envoy who presented his credentials to the elector would be served at the table by one page, would be seated beneath the carver (*Vorschneider*), and would not be presented with water (for ceremonial hand washing).[16] Similarly, an envoy from one elector to another elector would be seated at a table under the electoral prince. He would be served by one page, he would not have a *chaise à bras* (armchair), and he would also not be presented with any water.[17] The *Ceremoniale Brandenburgicum* describes three occasions when this type of reception took place: in 1661, 1670, and 1671. Undoubtedly, the diners were aware of ceremonial precedent (just like the author of *Ceremoniale Brandenburgicum*) and therefore monitored the manner of their service at a meal and policed their own behavior to deliver the intended message.

When seen in the context of the royal ambitions of Friedrich Wilhelm's son, this small volume is quite controversial and its authorship somewhat murky. It was published anonymously, and even by 1761, when Johann Oelrich's *Beyträge zur Brandenburgischen Geschichte* devoted an article to it, the author remained unknown. Oelrich speculated that the author must have been in the inner circle of the Brandenburg court and he postulated two likely authors: Johann Magirus, the electoral councilor and archive secretary, and Zacharias Zwantzig, a "famous publicist" of the court and member of the privy council in Berlin under Friedrich III/I.[18] In current library catalog records, another name has been attached to the work: that of Johann Friedrich von Besser, the court ceremony master in Brandenburg under Friedrich Wilhelm and Friedrich III/I. The possibility that the book was written by a high-ranking member (or members) of the household of Friedrich III/I is even more intriguing when one learns that Friedrich banned this book shortly after its publication.[19]

The official reason for the book's censure was that it was "full of errors *in iure & facto* and presented personal opinions on public figures without permission or proper censorship."[20] But more likely, the ban was due to the recent change of status of Brandenburg-Prussia. Whereas before the coronation in 1701, it might have been advantageous to broadcast the elector's status as a prince elector, after 1701, Friedrich III/I likely wanted to distance himself from his previous title and reinvent his ceremonial traditions as a member of the most elite set of European rulers: monarchs. Reminding readers of historical precedents might have hindered reception suitable to his new status. For instance, the *Ceremoniale Brandenburgicum* describes how the Elector Brandenburg would be treated as an equal with the other secular prince electors of the Holy Roman Empire: "After the emperor, came these most important and dignified members of the Holy Roman Empire. All people and nations legally acknowledge them as equal to royalty. They also have a king among them [the king of Bohemia], who follows the ecclesiastical electors in rank. They do not bow down to foreign kings during *Solennien* in the empire. And, when they are together, they treat one another as kings."[21] The elector of Brandenburg, in this instance, sits beneath the emperor, the three ecclesiastical electors, *and* the king of Bohemia. As newly a king himself, Friedrich might have been hoping to be on par with the king of Bohemia and distinguished from the three remaining secular prince electors.

The descriptions in the *Ceremoniale Brandenburgicum* convey which components of a banquet would have been meaningful for planners, participants, and those who read about the event afterward. The references in *Ceremoniale Brandenburgicum* to particular festivals confirm that Brandenburg-Prussia was a full participant in the ritualized political culture of the seventeenth century. A festival meal was a means of communicating status, and the Hohenzollern were fluent in the semiotics of ceremonial dining.

Everyday Dining

While festival meals were part of foreign relations and meant to be widely broadcast in literature, in image, and via diplomats, everyday meals were largely confined to members of court. Yet everyday dining was also im-bued with meaning about social status within and beyond the court. Everyday dining ritual was not explicitly agreed upon, as were public ban-quets. Instead, it developed over time through routine and in response to particular situations, such as financial hardship or court expansion.

Mealtimes set the daily rhythm at the Brandenburg-Prussia residences. The elector attended to official business in solitude between his 6 a.m. beer soup (or, toward the end of his reign, tea) and the 11 a.m. midday meal.[22] Meiselman argues that in the eighteenth century, breakfast was not con-sidered a meal because it lacked meat. Another reason the morning beer soup might not have qualified as a meal is that it was consumed alone, without any companions, or people with whom one breaks bread.[23]After lunch, the royal family typically spent the time until the evening meal in outdoor exercise of hunting or riding. So, the meals, considered as such, were only at midday and in the evening, which was, not surprisingly, also the number of meals recommended for good health by the court physi-cian, Johann Sigismund Elsholtz.[24] The midday meal was the more sub-stantial of the two; if members of the electoral family were in the same city, they ate this meal together. The rest of the court, too, would be pulled from their other tasks to meet for the meals.

No images and few descriptions of everyday meals at court remain. But manuscript court orders detail the expectations and participants in these meals. Court orders were standard for early modern court admin-istration as administrators attempted to codify behaviors and relation-ships.[25] A new order might have been written, for example, as often as a ruler changed residences.[26] Other common reasons for drawing up a new order were regime changes or setting up an ancillary household for a widow or prince.[27] As court orders were often part of reform measures (either during wartime hardship or other upheaval), they indicate dining habits in flux, not the status quo, and can be read as aspirational fictions.

The approximately ten court orders pertaining to dining during Fried-rich Wilhelm's reign provide a diachronic picture of dining regulation as the court contracted and expanded and habits evolved.[28] The surviv-ing orders from the reign of Friedrich Wilhelm generally coincide with overhauls of the entire financial administration of the court, specifically in 1650–52, 1664, 1673, and 1682.[29] Over the course of the seventeenth century, the number of diners and tables increased but not in a constant upward trajectory because the court orders were sometimes made in an attempt to reduce costs, not increase prestige.

These dining orders typically indicate the participants, the number of tables, the number of dishes for each table and who cooked the dishes. Additional, but not standard, elements include an estimate of how much beer, bread, and/or wine each person or table would consume, a list of people who were given a food allowance instead of free board (and how many shillings or thalers they received), and, less often, where in the residence (or in the external properties, such as hunting lodges or grain warehouses) particular individuals dined. The first mark of belonging to the court was whether one received board from the kitchens (*freie Tisch*) or was simply paid a food allowance (*Kostgeld*) to purchase provisions outside the court.

As was typical in all European houses up until the eighteenth century, there was no fixed space dedicated solely to dining. A historian of the court pages wrote that when no guests were present, the elector ate most of his meals "en serviette," meaning that the meal was brought to his apartments and laid out on a table that might have served other purposes at other times during the day.[30] As in the festivals, proximity to the ruler at everyday meals bestowed honor and status. Only the high court officers had the privilege of dining in the same space as the electoral family.[31] However, it was also a particular privilege of high court administrators to have their food brought to them at their own lodgings.[32] Lower-ranked court servants ate with other members of their office.

Diners sat at either a *Tafel* or a *Tisch*. The distinction between these two different words for table drew a line between the highest-ranking diners and all others. A *Tafel* was a larger, more substantial piece of furniture while a *Tisch* might have been something as simple and temporary as a board that diners set on their lap while eating. Elector Friedrich Wilhelm, his wife, and children and other high guests or officers ate at *Tafeln*, of which there were usually two or three per meal.[33] All the other members of court who received board as part of their employment contract ate at *Tische*.[34]

The food itself, both in type and quantity, was another means of social distinction stipulated in the court orders. Food for the less-prestigious

Tische was prepared by the less-prestigious "knight's cook," as opposed to the privy cook. Additionally, beer, wine, and bread were distributed according to status and function. Furthermore, as discussed in chapter 1, all members of the court ate bread daily, but the *types* of bread varied.[35] The three grades consumed at the court of Brandenburg-Prussia in this period were *Gesinde-* or *Junkerbrodt* (a rye bread consumed by high and low), *Semmel* (a white bread made from finely ground, and therefore more expensive, wheat), and *Herrenbrod* (the most exclusive "lordly" bread, which might have been sweetened with sugar).[36] Those individuals who ate *Herrenbrod* also received some *Semmel* each day for breakfast, suggesting that *Herrenbrod* was perhaps too fine for even the most elite person to eat all the time.

Different types of beer (*Speisebier, Junkerbier, Herrenbier,* and then the especially fine, imported Brunswick *Mummebier, Bartensteinisch Halbander,* and *Zerbst* beers) were distributed on a similar basis, that is, according to the quality of the beer and perceived caloric need of the imbiber.[37] Wine gradations were even more specific. To begin with, not every member of the court received wine; there was, also, a larger variety of available wines, compared with the available beers. These wines included Hungarian, Alacant, Muscat, Spanish, Canarian, Malvasier, Port, and Franconian wines. The three most consumed wines at court were the Brandenburg land wine (naturally, the cheapest), French wine (more expensive), and Rhenish wine (most expensive, due to its rarity). In a 1647 order, the elector explicitly stated that the consumption of Rhenish wine be limited because of its expense. He ordered that only the princely table receive it. The other tables would receive "Franzen" wine.[38]

Along with status, taste and marks of favor also factored into the decisions of who drank which wines. In 1672, courtiers consumed a large amount of Franconian wine because "the land wine in the elector's cellar was too sour to consume with food."[39] For reasons of either taste or status, the wine distinction was so important that in 1682, the steward was ordered to ensure that no substitutions be made in the Rhenish wine for the elector and his sons.[40] The squires (*Junkers*), however, were forced to "make do" with land wine.[41] The table of the lord marshall (*Obermarschall*) also received Rhenish wine, due to the fact that high-ranking foreign guests and officers frequently ate there. But Friedrich Wilhelm did not mind treating his close servants periodically and wrote that "he would be happy if, every so often, his and his wife's chamber servants and the privy councilors—without abusing the privilege—received a quart or two of Rhenish wine." All other tables though were ordered to receive land wine.[42]

In one fall day in 1672, while the elector was away on military campaign, the amount of wine that his children and remaining household consumed was recorded. The list gives a sense at the specificity, quantity, and array of uses for wine on an average day. Two quarts of Hungarian wine went to a secretary named Müller (probably in payment for services rendered). Two quarts of Rhenish wine went to the royal princes' and princesses' table, an additional half-quart went to the young Prince Philip's soup and another half to the mistress of the robe (*Hoffmeisterin*). More than twice as much Franconian wine was consumed as Rhenish wine (eight quarts). One quart of Franconian wine each was given to the palace manager, the electoral prince Ludwig, the wife of the highest lieutenant, someone's mother (*Jänicken Mutter*), the princes "for washing," and the widow of a court officer. The court painter received two quarts. Other household servants (nurses, chamber maids, cooks and cellar laborers, etc.) consumed another twenty-two quarts of land wine that day. Two quarts went to the apothecary, while a quart and a half was used as a cooking ingredient in dishes for the princes and princesses.[43] On average, each person on this list received a quart of wine for the day, with distribution reflecting the status, duties, and age of the recipient.

Status at court also dictated when one would eat and how much choice one would have. The menu detailed in chapter 1 of this book was part of an intense period of court reform from December 1651 to January 1652.[44] As outlined in the four remaining menus and in the dining order drafts from that period, the elector's meals consisted of three loosely defined courses of twenty-six dishes with *service à la française*. The meal started with the *potages*—or mixed vegetable or meat dishes, then came the *entremets* and *Braten*—or side dishes and meat roasts—and it closed with sweets and pies. The sequence of courses was important for the rest of the diners as well because it dictated when they would get to eat. Only after the elector and the ladies' (*Frauenzimmer*) tables had finished their first course, could the pages "lift" their dishes and take them back to the kitchens to be refreshed, reheated, and brought to the next tables down the court hierarchy (in this particular case, the lord marshal and the *Junkern* tables).[45]

Leftovers were expected to nourish many people at court and were carefully monitored and controlled. Although the long procession of dishes was certainly part of a performance of "conspicuous consumption," they do not indicate the extravagant waste Veblen implied with that oft-used phrase.[46] In fact, administrators expected that the elector (and the others dining at his table) would be served such an abundance of dishes that even before a meal had taken place, they divvied up the leftovers and counted on serving them again to lower tables at the same meal.[47]

Indeed, the twenty-six (and sometimes even more) dishes that were served to the elector's table seem extravagant, but if this court was similar to other Renaissance courts, it is unlikely that the elector actually ate from all of the dishes on his table. During a *service à la française*, diners typically ate only from the dishes within their reach. In accordance with humanist ideas about health and diet, a wide variety of dishes were typical at Renaissance meals so that individuals could select the dishes best suited to their particular temperament.[48] This was also an intended purpose of the menu (*Tages-* or *Küchenzettel*) that the kitchen scribe made to list the dishes of every meal (see figure 2). According to the dictionary definition of *Küchenzettel*, the lord of the house received the menu before every meal to help him pick and choose the dishes he would consume.[49] This suggests that a number of dishes would have left the lord's table completely untouched.

Meals and their leftovers were opportunities for educating the electoral princes and the young pages and for demonstrating the social order of the court.[50] In his death year of 1640, the ailing Elector Georg Wilhelm issued a reduced dining order in response to depleted wartime finances. The new meal plan had clear guidelines for how leftovers should be distributed.[51] The leftovers from the twenty-six dishes served to the elector's table went to the pages who would then have to give up two of their meat dishes to the lackeys, in order to "keep the pages disciplined" (perhaps by modeling charity).[52] Sixteen dishes were served to the *Frauenzimmer,* who gave their leftovers to the chambermaids. The *Junkers* handed the leftovers from their fifteen dishes down to the lackeys (to supplement the two meat dishes the lackeys received from the pages). Next on the list, a table of servants from mixed departments (the barber, the travel apothecary, two chamber servants, and some clerks) sent leftovers from their eight dishes to their own servants and "the mute" (likely a person maintained by the court out of charity). Anything that the highest kitchen officers did not eat from their dishes went to the undercooks and kitchen boys.[53]

Was it uncomfortable for the undercooks, kitchen boys, lackeys, chambermaids, charity cases, and other lower servants to wait and watch their superiors eat the food they might have been eating themselves? Many of them had labored all morning with little more than beer and possibly a bit of bread. This method of distributing leftovers according to department seems a visceral reminder that lower servants were not to bite the hand that fed them. Perhaps, though, there was also a sense of honor in having access to the same food as those higher up (albeit with potentially less selection). Participation of the members of court implies a tacit acceptance of the daily policing that occurred during a meal. The limitation of choice down the social ladder was a metaphor for the general principle of rule: when one accepts a ruler or a group of rulers, choice and freedom is exchanged for protection. In the seventeenth century, in particular, the "search for stability" opened the door for consolidating rulers like Friedrich Wilhelm to wrest choice in many arenas, not just food.[54] The sequence of the communal meal suggests a particular experience of bodily discipline in which the pangs of hunger made the social order a physical and performative reality.

Much is communicated in the manner of a meal. Festival meals, by their nature, were a public ritual: their meaning was directed at parties *external* to the court. Certain festival elements from Friedrich Wilhelm's 1663 tribute day were mobilized later, when his son, Friedrich, crowned himself king *in* Prussia. Then too, wine flowed from fountains, and money was thrown into the crowds. Karin Friedrich and Sara Smart described the festival in this way: "The abstract idea of the 'state' contained little that could compare itself with the sensual experience of the masses in the presence of the ruler on the public stage, as the ceremonial events unfolded."[55] Indeed, the relationship between ruler and subject and the relationships between different rulers had to be felt, or even imbibed, in order to have been real. The everyday meal was still an expression of relationship, but the message was directed inward. Court dining was normative in that it bound members together, yet subtle differences in how one dined distinguished one's place in the court microcosm. The differences in scale and reach between the festival meal and the everyday meal are only apparent when the two are set up as foils to each other. Thus, the everyday practice bestows meaning on the grand events of history.

Food was also a tool of social control beyond the palace walls. As will be seen in the next chapter, impinging on local tastes and food traditions was one way that the elector gradually seized control over aspects of the local market in Königsberg. A court baker selling his baked goods to city inhabitants complicated the boundaries between palace and city life. Just as with dining, the actions of forgotten historical actors could have wide-reaching social implications.

6

The Northern War and
the Prussian Bread War

IN EARLY 1669, Martin Hones, the court baker in Königsberg, complained
to his lord, "The city bakers attacked my assistants on the street, man-
handled them, took my bread, and generally conducted themselves in a
rude manner."[1] By Hones's account, such harassment had been going on
since at least 1658, when the prince-elector first granted him the right to
sell his wares at a stall in front of the palace wall. Hones lamented: "If
the un-Christlike jealousy and resentment of the local bakers goes un-
checked, they will continue pursuing their ungrounded quarrel—as they
have done not just once, but many times; (causing me to involve Your
Highness!) because my bread is different. They make such trouble—not
just about my bread—but also about my pastries and biscuits. I cannot
believe they have carried on for so many years with their complaining,
which has damaged my livelihood."[2] As Hones's letter makes clear, the
city bakers' attack was part of a conflict that spanned decades. Hones
wrote lengthy appeals to Friedrich Wilhelm on three separate occasions,
submitting documentary evidence from 1657 to 1672. What is more, his
implicit confidence in the elector's interest was justified.[3] In the spring
of 1667, Friedrich Wilhelm was contemplating war with Louis XIV, ap-
prehensively following the progress of the Second Anglo-Dutch War and
applying the first excise tax in Brandenburg to fund the rebuilding of the
Berlin city palace. Yet he also found time to respond to Hones's supplication, by instructing his representatives in Königsberg to "firmly defend
the baking master's privileges in my name."[4]

Hones's supplications concerned his own personal disputes, but they
were also a reflection of the larger tensions created by Königsberg's reduced political autonomy as Friedrich Wilhelm imposed tighter control
on Ducal Prussia. There are two schools of thought about how Friedrich Wilhelm consolidated power in Prussia. The older school argues
that the emerging fiscal-military state enabled his army to subdue the

Prussian nobility with the threat of violence.[5] The other school, known as "the compromise theory," has been ascendant since the mid-twentieth century. This theory suggests that central power grew when the nobility abandoned the local interests that they shared with the lower estate because they increasingly saw their material interests allied with those of the elector.[6] Both camps developed their theories largely on the basis of institutional documents, which devoted little attention to the lived experience of governance. The quotidian aspects of state formation are visible when one reads the official decrees in conjunction with other sources, in this case, supplications.

Beyond Prussia, scholars of early modern European state formation have turned their attention to the negotiated qualities of power. William Beik and Sharon Kettering, foundationally, demonstrated that political power in France in this period relied on negotiations with local nobility and on entrenched networks of patronage.[7] This involved more than just debate between the estates and the ruler. The most recent historical perspective on state formation is that it was an "interactive process between centre and periphery with substantial input, if not impetus, from below."[8] These interactions were not monodirectional (in either direction), however.[9] To understand early modern state formation processes, historians must examine political culture as a whole, including the connections between political institutions, economic structures, cultural practices, and personal loyalties.[10]

This is where a particular case can elucidate macro processes.[11] The story of the baker Hones demonstrates that, on an everyday level in Prussia, Friedrich Wilhelm was not just concerned with raising taxes, winning battles, or convincing the estates to agree to his new sovereign status; he was also interested in dictating the rules of business. Bakers were among the wealthiest and most influential craftspeople in any early modern European city, and in Königsberg, where the craft guilds were accustomed to a high degree of political enfranchisement, the bakers were particularly powerful. As an immigrant in Königsberg, Hones stood at the nexus between these local bakers, who wanted to maintain their rights, and a prince-elector who was testing the practical limits of his new sovereignty in Prussia. Over the course of Hones's career, Friedrich Wilhelm repeatedly defended the baker and expanded his legal right to sell his goods in Königsberg. This simple act drew business and control away from the guild-sanctioned bakers. The sale of Hones's bread undermined the guild and contributed to Friedrich Wilhelm's seizure of power from traditional municipal institutions.

Beyond the parliamentary debates in Königsberg regarding Friedrich Wilhelm's capacity to rule, a parallel debate was taking place on the streets between the court and the city bakers. The Great Elector was personally entangled in dictating the terms of the sale of bread—the most basic nutritional necessity for Königsberg residents. The turmoil surrounding the court baker shows the balance of power tipping toward the foreign ruler and away from the guilds and city business elites. Hones was an instrument of this shift because he opened a new means for Friedrich Wilhelm to attack traditional city rule. The fight over bread exemplifies the way Friedrich Wilhelm's success in consolidating the Prussian state derived in part from quotidian negotiations. Hones is not in any history book on the rise of Prussia, but his story is that of Prussian state formation on the ground.

Martin Hones's Career in Context

Examining Martin Hones's career in the context of local and even international politics reveals how something as basic as bread aggravated the fault lines of commerce, confession, politics, and civic identity. The first mention of Martin Hones in Königsberg was during a tense moment in the autumn of 1657. Amid conflict with the local estates, Friedrich Wilhelm appointed Prince Bogislaw von Radziwill (1620–1669) stadtholder in Prussia to rule jointly with the *Oberräte* (the four highest officials of the Prussian estates). From the dating of the documents, it seems likely that Hones was hired to serve as Radziwill's personal baker (*Mundbecker*), a role he had previously performed for Electress Luise Henriette.[12] Radziwill, like Friedrich Wilhelm himself, was Calvinist and had been educated in the Netherlands.[13] If he acquired a taste for Dutch bread as a young man, he was probably pleased with the choice of Hones, who hailed from the region of Limburg and would bake familiar bread for him in the far eastern reaches of Europe.[14]

As a servant of the court, Hones had an express route to professional protections. He received his citizenship (*Bürgerrecht*) from the town hall in Kneiphof (one of the three towns that formed Königsberg) on 27 September 1657.[15] This document, which he called "expensive" at fifty thaler, granted him the right to "carry on with his baking of all types from wheat in butter and milk, pies, and all else that belongs to the pastry chef's art, including *Zuckerbrod* and *Leckkuchen,* as the *Los-* und *Festbäcker* make."[16]

A year after Hones purchased his citizenship, the elector instructed Radziwill to bestow a baking privilege on him and to order the city bakers to cease harassing him. The elector's order, sent from Berlin, stated that Hones was free to bake his "pastries and whatever else is part of the pastry chef's art including cakes, gingerbread, and other baked goods with wheat in butter and milk in the method that he learned it." The elector added that Hones and his heirs were allowed to sell these goods to the inhabitants of Königsberg as well as on the palace grounds (*Schloss Freiheit*). "No one," the decree continued, "but, particularly the city bakers, may hinder him—by unrelenting punishment (be it with words or other inimical means) from selling wheat, spices and whatever else he needs to sell to make his living." Friedrich Wilhelm hammered home his preference by freeing Hones from paying city taxes for four years.[17]

Hones's next court appointment coincided with another turbulent moment. In the middle of the spring of 1661, as nobles were gathering in opposition to the elector, Hones was promoted from *Mundbecker* to *Backmeister* (baking master) in the palace bakery.[18] The role of *Backmeister* was less physically demanding but carried the considerable responsibility of ensuring that the entire court got the bread that accounted for the majority of daily calories (depending on their social station). This included bread for members of the household, day laborers who received *Kostgeld* (food allowance), and all guests. In the decade before Hones's appointment, the position had changed hands at least twice.[19] In general, the high-ranking food servants had long careers at court. In Berlin, for example, there were only two head stewards over Friedrich Wilhelm's long reign, both of whom died in office.[20] The unusually high attrition rate of Königsberg baking masters in the 1650s therefore suggests that it was a fraught position.

Martin Hones's troubles emerged during a period of encroaching central power in Königsberg in the 1650s and 1660s. They also coincided with an economic crunch in the city: after several failed harvests, cereal prices reached new heights in 1660–62.[21] For bakers facing financial struggles and seeing fewer options for political expression, contesting Hones's privileges were a form of political protest.

This local unrest unfolded amid international conflict. The Northern War broke out in 1655, when King Charles X Gustav of Sweden (1622– 1660) invaded parts of Poland, Lithuania, and Russia. "Defending" against

Charles and the "Swedish Deluge" offered Friedrich Wilhelm the chance to wrest Pomerania from the Swedes, which would give Berlin and Brandenburg access to valuable ports on the Baltic Sea. During the war, Friedrich Wilhelm shifted his allegiance from Charles Gustav to King John Casimir of Poland (1609–1672).

Although he feared being rendered powerless between two more powerful rulers as he had been during the Thirty Years War, Friedrich Wilhelm was eventually able to negotiate for sovereignty in Ducal Prussia, which had formerly functioned as a fiefdom of Poland. The king of Sweden granted him Prussian sovereignty in the Treaty of Labiau on November 20, 1656, and the king of Poland promised the same concession in the Treaty of Wehlau on September 19, 1657.[22] When Friedrich Wilhelm first succeeded his father, he had been obliged (like all the Hohenzollern dukes of Prussia before him) to appeal to the king of Poland to confirm his title of duke. Military successes as well as these backroom negotiations released Friedrich Wilhelm and his heirs from that obligation and made them independent from the Polish king for their status.

The Northern War concluded with the Peace of Oliva in 1660—an agreement between rulers that did not take into account the Prussian estates. Many Prussians viewed their right to appeal to the king of Poland as a safeguard against the tyranny of their foreign duke, and they were not ready to accept the Hohenzollern unconditionally as their sovereign lords. Additionally, a number of Friedrich Wilhelm's wartime measures supplanted older governing practices, which increased their resentment. In October 1657 Friedrich Wilhelm replaced the former Polish court (*Hofgericht*) with his own upper court (*Oberappellationsgericht*), and later that month he installed newspaper and book censors.[23] Militarily, he asserted his power by building a new fort, where he left a permanent garrison and from which he could control the mercantile ports of Königsberg.[24] To businessmen of Königsberg, the new Fort Friedrichsburg was a "chain around their necks."[25] It did not help that the early commanders of the fort were foreigners: the first, a Dutchman named Gerhard von Belgum (d. 1670), and the second, a native of Hildesheim who was married to a Dutch woman and had served Friedrich Wilhelm in the Netherlands.[26]

On October 11, 1657, the three estates of Prussia presented a formal protest against the quartering of Friedrich Wilhelm's soldiers, the imposition of excise taxes to pay for the army and new fort, and the installation of foreign officers. All three estates could agree on this final point because Königsberg citizens of all social levels were being displaced by people—usually Calvinists—who were loyal to Friedrich Wilhelm. The protest named military officers, such as the governors of the forts at Pillau and Mümmel, as well as court servants.

After the estates' 1657 objection to foreign officers, Friedrich Wilhelm continued to promote his agenda of building a Calvinist presence, establishing a standing army and entrusting the running of Prussia to those loyal to him. The Prussians had previously controlled their own commercial regulations, and their resentment of the elector—and those, like Hones, who benefited from his new authority—was bound to erupt. Friction built until 1661, when the Königsbergers finally forced Friedrich Wilhelm to call parliament.

On February 11, 1661, two hundred noblemen assembled in the town hall of the old city (*Altstadt*). Over the next few days, they drafted a petition and presented it to the highest city officials (*Oberräte*). This was a problem for Friedrich Wilhelm. Before the Peace of Oliva could be ratified, the Prussian estates had to perform a ceremony (*Huldigung*) at which they publicly acknowledged Friedrich Wilhelm as their sovereign ruler. Now awake to the extent of the opposition against his *Huldigung*, the elector was ready to talk. He called a parliament on May 3, 1661, to negotiate the terms of government in Prussia. This meeting dragged on for over two years and became known as the Great Parliament (*der grosse Landtag*).

Friedrich Wilhelm's detractors also set their sights on court servants such as Martin Hones. In many ways, Hones worked in a separate world from that of the rest of Königsberg bakers. His work was part of a food system that was integrated into the very architecture of the palace. Chickens were kept in the bridge over the deep moat, and the grounds contained a slaughterhouse, a fishpond, and a garden with many varieties of herbs and fruit trees. Grain came from the local administrative districts (*Ämter*) but was processed in one of the three mills onsite. There was also a machine for cleaning cereals known as the *Putz-* or *Schleifmühle*.[27] The grain was stored in the main building of the palace quadrangle. As the traveler Caspar Stein put it in 1644, the palace building was "Bacchus, Mars, Jupiter, Venus and Ceres": the basement was a beer and wine cellar, the ground floor an armory, the next floor a church, the following a great hall for feasting, and the attic a grain storeroom.[28]

However, although the palace was set apart physically from the city, it was also a part of the city. This connection manifested itself in shared food traditions. In addition to his standard bread, Hones baked special pastries for important religious days. In the year of his promotion—which was also the year the Great Parliament began—Hones baked *Strützeln* for Easter and Pentecost.[29] This long wheat cake carried particular connotations in Königsberg, which regularly held a festival of the "long Prussian sausage" and the "eight groschen *Stritzel.*"[30] Throughout the medieval period and up to the early eighteenth century, this occasion ritualized the political relationships in the city and especially emphasized the city's guild (*Bruderzunft*) values.[31]

The account of the 1601 festivities illustrates how this festival wove the different members of Königsberg society together. Nineteen butchers worked for two days to make a *Wurst* from eighty-one hams, forty-five casings, one and a half tons of salt, 18¾ pounds of pepper, and one and a half tons of beer. After the church service on New Year's Day, the butchers marched with their sausage through the streets of the city, accompanied by trumpets and growing numbers of citizens. When they arrived at the palace, the sausage extended the entire length of the courtyard. A large piece was sliced off and taken to the palace kitchen as a gift for the duke. The procession then paraded back down the palace hill to the commons in the old town, where everyone received a slice of the *Wurst.*

The bakers were determined to provide an equally magnanimous offering of their craft. Six days after, on Three Kings' Day, the bakers of the three cities congregated to bake eight large *Strützeln* and six large *Kringel.*[32] The *Strützeln* baked by the town bakers were over three meters long.[33] Eight men baked for an entire day and night, during which they drank a full ton of beer and ate nine marks' worth of food. They made lion's heads, crowns, and stars of gingerbread, which were decorated with gold and with the bakers' seals. Altogether, their offerings valued 43 marks, 3 groschen. The festival was a performance of goodwill through a celebratory gift exchange between the two most important food trades of the city (the bakers and the butchers) and the duke. The revelers metaphorically tied together the three united towns of Königsberg as they wound through the streets. This was the power of the traditions Hones was tapping into when he baked *Strützel* for religious holidays.

Shared food traditions, however, were not enough to compensate for the threat that Hones and the elector posed to the commercial status quo. On July 12, 1661, the estates presented a forty-three-point objection to a proposal of the elector. Point eleven pertained to "profane" aspects of

Friedrich Wilhelm's rule and included a complaint by the cities of Königsberg against the craftspeople, caterers, and merchants whom the elector permitted to work in the unincorporated part of Königsberg near the palace, known as the *Schloss Freiheit*. "They come by the hundreds," lamented the Prussian estates, "so that there is no competing with them!"[34] Hones was one of these hundreds selling his wares in direct competition with the native, licensed bakers.

Not long after that petition, on August 20, parliament was suspended. Plague was cited as the official reason, but it is likely that Friedrich Wilhelm's officers were merely fed up with the stubbornness of the estates. But, while the official debates about power and commerce in Königsberg stalled, the encroachment of Friedrich Wilhelm's sovereignty was contested by craftsmen in the city streets. Two days after the suspension of parliament, the Prussian ruler issued a decree reinforcing Hones's right to bake and sell "white and rye bread (using wood and flour he purchased himself) in front of the city palace as well as for weddings, baptisms and holidays."[35] The decree was in response to another appeal from Hones, who claimed the city bakers were mistreating him.

The Cause of the Bread Wars

A privilege to sell wares outside the walls of the city palace was not unprecedented for a palace baker. Writing *Freibriefe* and other tax and guild exemptions was a regular activity for early modern rulers. Local craftsmen and merchants usually accepted them as a minor annoyance.[36] But the privileges granted to Hones provoked violent resistance. Practicing his trade under the aegis of the new sovereign, Hones became a target for everyday forms of resistance to the elector's intrusion on local authority.[37] What was it about Hones that so angered the Königsberg bakers?

Partly, it was a matter of taste. Hones repeatedly wrote that the Königsberg bakers were "jealous" because he baked in a "different way."[38] Bakers in the city used rye and water, but Hones baked with "wheat in butter and milk."[39] Butter and milk were used in the breads of his hometown of Maastricht in Limburg. Like most of the rest of northern Europe, the Dutch grew few grains of their own, importing their cereals from the "breadbasket of Europe" in the Baltic region, which included Prussia. The wet, grassy Netherlands were more suited to raising livestock, specifically cattle, and Dutch dairy farming made tremendous advances in the seventeenth century, when the prolific Holstein breed was developed. Because dairy products in the Netherlands were fresh and abundant, they naturally made up a large part of the Dutch diet. The milk and butter in Hones's bread, then, were pungent reminders of the expanding Dutch influence in Prussian society.

Yet the ingredients were merely the most visible part of a conflict that stemmed from many sources and was rooted in the same concerns that fed parliamentary opposition to Friedrich Wilhelm. These concerns included political disenfranchisement and the loss of control of city commerce and production. The bakers believed Hones was undermining the regulations that had given the baking guilds a monopoly on protecting bread consumers, educating new bakers and selling bread.

The primary regulations that Hones challenged as he persisted in baking his buttery bread were the municipal baking ordinances. In theory, these regulations on bread weight and quality protected consumers as well as bakers. Consumers could trust that they were paying a fair price for bread, and bakers enjoyed the patronage ensured by a safe reputation. The regulations were meant to mitigate a distrust of bakers dating back to antiquity, even though (or perhaps because) they were essential to any bread-eating society. The first baker in the Bible was Cain, who murdered his brother, lied to God, and introduced weights and measures to the world. This need for weights and measures had been interpreted as a sign of distrust.[40] An eighteenth-century dictionary of fraud listed the many ways that bakers could cheat customers, including selling moldy, worm-eaten, bad-tasting, hackneyed, or black-flour bread as expensive bread; disregarding weight regulations; puffing the bread up or pumping it with holes so that it appeared larger; substituting barley for wheat and passing the result off as good wheat bread, just to name a few.[41] The Prussian stadtholder even once sent a bread roll filled with plaster and other indigestible ingredients to Berlin as evidence of the bad state of the economy.[42] The eighteenth-century lexicographer Johann Krünitz warned that "great precaution is necessary to avoid being deceived by the baker."[43] Clearly, consumers had cause for suspicion when it came to their bread.

The primary safeguard against such deception, Krünitz advised, was a municipal baking ordinance. Municipal baking ordinances involved contentious and drawn-out negotiations; it might take decades to agree on the terms.[44] The guild developed as the corporate body representing the bakers in these negotiations, and its role in monitoring prices helped secure its authority in the town. Guild responsibilities included random weight inspections with city officials as well as an annual baking exam to test adherence to the baking ordinances. In Berlin, for example, a new baking ordinance from 1626 was created to help contain the exploding price of bread after years of bad harvests and other effects of the Thirty Years War. The components of such a document included a chart of the cost and weight of a loaf of bread relative to the type and amount of grain used and then stipulated the unit price of both rye and wheat bread on a sliding scale based on the price of raw grain. For instance, if a *Scheffel* of wheat cost six Brandenburg groschen, then a one-pound loaf would cost one old pfennig. The whole regulating endeavor was tied to Judeo-Christian tradition and morality: "You must have accurate and honest weights and measures, so that you may live long in the land the Lord your God is giving you" (Deut. 25.1).[45]

Bread regulations, therefore, had deep social and political significance in early modern cities. Hones's seemingly innocuous breads and cakes posed a serious threat to those in place in Königsberg and, by extension, to the guild bakers who were held to them. His wheat bread with milk and butter would have had a different density than bread baked with rye and water, making it impossible for him to be held to the same standards as the other bakers. In fact, he wrote, "Now, with wheat, butter, and milk, I cannot deliver such a heavy and large piece of bread as the bakers who bake from pure rye or wheat with only water."[46] With its different ingredients and weights, his bread undermined the corporate trust that the bakers' guild in Königsberg had developed over centuries.[47]

Hones also threatened the guilds' monopoly on craft training, which was another means that the guilds justified their exclusive privileges. As Hones had presumably learned his art in the Netherlands, baking knowledge was clearly not exclusive to the Königsberg bakers. According to Hones, one of the bakers' complaints was that he employed "a lot of boys and servants" in baking and used widows and maids to deliver his wares.[48] This suggests that he employed nonguild labor while also acting as the master or instructor of young bakers. One of the prime functions of any guild was to limit the number of craftspeople in a city in order to guarantee work for its members. Without its roles as gatekeeper to the craft, arbiter of consumer protection and sole source of training for younger bakers, the bakers' guild in Königsberg had little to offer its members; if the guilds could not claim the exclusive right to perform their craft, they had no reason to exist.

Finally, Hones's Dutch origins carried significance in seventeenth-century Königsberg beyond his style of baking. Wheat bread with milk and butter may have been an affront to local palates, but antagonism toward Hones became enmeshed in the wider debate about immigration. Coinciding with Hones's likely arrival in the fall of 1657, the estates named the Dutch, in particular, as a problem: "The cities complain that many Dutch and Scottish have been granted citizenship regardless of nation and religion, causing great detriment to their livelihoods and traditions."[49] This anti-Calvinist enmity was in part a response to Friedrich Wilhelm's replacement of local, oppositional Lutheran city officers with imported, loyal Calvinists (like Hones, presumably).

While the immigration issue was political and religious, it also had economic significance. Since 1565, during the reign of the first duke of Prussia, Albrecht (r. 1525–68), native Königsberg merchants had held an exclusive privilege that all wares going to be sold elsewhere in Prussia or passing through Prussia (on the way to Danzig) had to be traded first in Königsberg. Other Prussian towns tried to chip away at this monopoly by gaining their own privileges, which Königsberg's merchants always protested. The rhetoric behind this regulatory protectionism was aimed at preventing foreigners from peddling wares in Königsberg both on the street and at the yearly market. The "expensive" citizenship that Hones purchased in 1657 was supposed to have conferred the right to sell in the city, but clearly his purchased citizenship did not convince Königsberg's merchants that he was one of them. Instead, Hones's commercial activity was construed by his fellow bakers as an imposition on their ancient privilege.

This privilege was cited in the terms of the resolution of the Great Parliament, published on May 1, 1663. Like the agreement on taxation that formed the majority of the document, the resolution about electoral *Freibriefe* contained a loophole that left the fundamental problem unresolved.[50] In a nod to the local business concerns, Friedrich Wilhelm declared that all *Freibriefe* signed by him were void, but he then stipulated that "since the palace baker made different things than the wheat and rye bakers [*Los- und Festbäcker*], there should be no conflict and nothing to upset them about the palace baker in the future."[51] This vague statement did not satisfy the local bakers, and Hones continued to complain of their harassment for another decade.

Conflict within the Palace and with Hones's Heirs

The nature of Hones's job changed after the resolution of the Great Parliament, leading to conflicts for him within the palace as well. Following the *Huldigung* (held in October 1663), Friedrich Wilhelm spent less time in Königsberg and reduced the size of the court there. In 1642 the court numbered four hundred people, but this number dropped to just seventy in 1666.[52] Thanks to his "many years of service," Hones retained his position even though Friedrich Wilhelm no longer thought it necessary to keep a *Backmeister* in Königsberg.[53] Still, Hones's responsibilities were eventually reduced to save money. In his revised contract of August 1669, he was instructed to "only bake for the prisoners in the palace jail, the members of the hunting lodge, and the soldiers at the fort."[54] But, these new orders were not strictly followed: in December, Hones was still allocated money for milk and yeast to bake *Strützel* and *Putterkuchen* for Christmas.[55]

Furthermore, Hones continued to bake for others at court. This was no longer part of his salaried job, so he gave out bread on credit. He claimed he fell into debt because those debts were never paid. He later lamented that when he tried to collect his debt from the *Landhofmeister*, not only was he not repaid, he was insulted "with many swear words."[56] Hones appealed to the elector to cover the expenses he incurred baking for members of court and particularly cited a holiday *Strützel* and *Kringel* in 1670 for which he had never been paid.[57] Perhaps to distract attention from their debts for Hones's bread, those at court who were eating it complained bitterly about its poor quality, going so far as to report to the elector in Berlin that it was "so bad, even the dogs would not eat it."[58]

In the face of potentially well-founded complaints from his highest officers in Königsberg, Friedrich Wilhelm himself penned a forceful and thorough reply that defended Hones and—in a remarkable testament to Friedrich Wilhelm's assiduity—referred by date to the previous occasions on which he had interjected for Hones. Friedrich Wilhelm even gave Hones money to cover his debts so that he could continue baking.[59] Hones not only had the ear of the elector, but his support against his most trusted advisors.

While relations with other members of the palace deteriorated, clashes with the city bakers continued as well. Hones devoted the second half of his letter about unpaid debts to affronts from other bakers in Königsberg.

First, he reported, they ignored the rights granted by his privileges and citizenship and subjected him to various secret baking tests. In one test against a baker from the town of Angerburg in East Prussia, Hones recounted, the bread he baked was heavier than the other baker's. "When the baker from Angerburg was asked whether he couldn't get more out of a *Scheffel* [of flour], he answered no and was sent to the *Kücke*."[60] In addition, the steward (*Landhofmeister*) secretly took one of Hones's "hardest and burnt breads" to a city official. Hones continued: "Not only have they attacked the women working for me (with swear and smear words), they have stolen my wares on numerous occasions. What can I—poor harried man—do against such a large group? I cannot proceed with such people. Please give me financial assistance once again so that I finally get the respect of these city bakers and earn *my piece of bread* in the future."[61] In May 1667 and January 1669 the city bakers were again ordered to back down.[62]

In their August 1673 report on Hones, the four *Oberräte* in Königsberg noted the poor quality of his bread for the palace workers and related the complaints of local bakers that he had unfair advantages in firewood, his rent-free bakery, and the cheap labor he employed. "He had so many women working for him that he could go out daily with his baked bread in the city and the *Schloss Freiheit* and make a marked impact on their livelihood."[63]

The summer of 1673 was the last time Hones was mentioned in the court archive during his lifetime. Even death, though, could not silence the Hones name. After Martin Hones died in December 1683, his wife and son continued to invite controversy. Securing a replacement for Hones became a problem that dragged on into the reign of the next ruler. On December 10, 1683, Stadtholder von Croy wrote to Friedrich Wilhelm about filling Hones's position. Another baker had already petitioned von Croy to let his son have the job, but von Croy thought Hones's widow was doing a fine job baking the bread at the palace: "At this time, it is wholly unnecessary to install another baking master because the widow of the deceased court baker performs the job just as well, if not better, than when her spouse was still living. Furthermore, the rest of the *Oberräte* and I are happy with her baking and would gladly see that we do not cast her out. Instead, as she is a foreigner from Brabant, we should maintain her and if it suits your lordship, when we find a suitable replacement, perhaps they can marry."[64] Von Croy's fond hopes for Hones's widow did not come to pass. She eventually remarried, but not before Christian

Nolte arrived and took the position of baking master from her. In 1685 she wrote to the elector to announce her marriage and to complain that Christian Nolte was preventing her from earning her "piece of bread."[65] Nolte, she claimed, was doing the job of baking master without pay.

It is surprising that Nolte would do for free a job that once paid Hones 200 thalers a year, as the Königsberg bakers were experiencing a period of diminished economic opportunity. Moreover, Friedrich Wilhelm had long questioned whether a baking master was necessary in Königsberg since the court was so rarely in residence.[66] Nolte's willingness to bake for free demonstrates something that was also true during Hones's tenure: unlike any other baker, a court baking master had the opportunity to make a much higher profit than bakers paying for fuel, space, and equipment. Furthermore, the protection of the elector and his advisors brought with it important political and economic advantages.

Von Croy again sided with Hones's widow. As a testament to the import of the Hones name, she never used any other moniker even after she remarried. Her new husband, Heinrich Zoll, was also a baker who had spent some time at the Swedish court.[67] Von Croy reported that the chamberlain, Herr Kupner, had put Zoll and Nolte to a baking test. Zoll had done "respectably" while Nolte had failed.[68] That fall, however, the widow was fired for "excesses" in the bakery.[69] The *Oberräte* in Königsberg reported to the elector that "she and her current husband have begun such a gratuitous, evil trade, and they have led such an obscene life at our residence, that they have been cited and sentenced by a criminal court. We cannot suffer her presence any longer; she must be thrown out immediately."[70]

But such was the power of either the Hones name or of the court privileges attached to it that the position of baking master was still held open for Martin Hones's other heirs. His son, Christoff, was abroad at the time, learning his trade.[71] In the meantime, the court permitted the heirs to select a temporary replacement. They named Georg Berovsky, a baker who had learned his craft from Martin Hones himself.[72] This plan worked well for two and a half years, until Christoff Hones returned to Königsberg to claim his inheritance. The court felt beholden to Berovsky, who had "carried himself well in Königsberg and did the work capably." The *Oberräte* claimed that Berovsky, who had just married, had no other way to support his family. As Friedrich Wilhelm was on his deathbed in Berlin in April 1688, a compromise was reached in Königsberg: Berovsky paid three thalers for the right to sell his wares in the *Schloss Freiheit,* while Christoff Hones paid eight thalers to secure the position of baking master.[73]

Like his parents, Christoff Hones eventually found himself in serious trouble at the court. In 1690 the *Oberräte* in Königsberg reported to Friedrich Wilhelm's successor, Friedrich III/I (1657–1713), that Christoff was "not just guilty in matters relating to bread baking, but also participated in many other excesses." The report continued, "He was even involved in the murder of a person killed at night and was imprisoned for a number of weeks."[74] The *Oberräte* recommended firing Christoff and hiring another baker who had done well on the baking exams and would correct the "Hones mistake."[75] Yet Christoff's career survived even this denunciation, which testifies to the inscrutable codes of loyalty at court. A full year later, Friedrich III/I was still weighing what rights and privileges he owed to the Hones family.[76] This leaves the question open as to what relationship Friedrich III/I, who later crowned himself in Königsberg, had with the local business practices. It is clear, however, that the Hohenzollern defended the Hones family through an unusually high number of confrontations with local and palace authorities.

MARTIN HONES'S CAREER at court spanned more than three decades, during which he stirred up conflict time and time again: conflict with the soldiers and courtiers at the Königsberg palace over the poor quality of his bread; conflict with the privy councilors in Berlin over his pay and baking budget; and finally, conflict with the local bakers' guilds in Königsberg for selling foreign bread in the city. In response to these frequent skirmishes, Hones appealed to the elector to protect his baking privilege or to support him materially. He deemed it right to supplicate when he felt he was being wronged. Remarkably, the elector responded—often in his own hand.

The story of Martin Hones comes down to us through the numerous records of his conflicts: the complaints made against him as well as his various protests and defenses. Hones's long paper trail confirms what the historian Thomas Robisheaux has noted: subjects in the Holy Roman Empire formed relationships with their princes that entitled them to directly pursue their own rights and interests.[77] While the elector was subduing the Königsberg parliament and fighting wars with Sweden and France, he was also fulfilling his responsibility to listen and respond to the petitions of his servants. The conflicts surrounding the baker Hones, however, not only demonstrate the mode of expression open to him, but also express the larger transformation in the landscape of Prussian politics. Hones repeatedly drew Friedrich Wilhelm's attention to the currents of local power and gave the elector openings to confront the more elusive forms of resistance to his sovereignty. Political changes in every state are predicated on microdecisions that correspond to the social, historical, physical, religious, and economic particularities of each locality.

Reading the correspondences relating to Hones, it is impossible to ignore Friedrich Wilhelm's intense involvement in and understanding of local issues in Königsberg. Just weeks before his own death, as he suffered from gout and kidney stones, Friedrich Wilhelm personally penned responses to Königsberg councilors regarding the Hones family. In numerous other letters in his own hand between 1658 and 1688, he cited previous exchanges with Hones, indicating his acumen for the minutiae of government and his clear concern about a single court servant's situation.[78] Why did Friedrich Wilhelm care? He cared because the dispute over his Dutch baker formed part of his wider negotiations with the city of Königsberg. Everyday acts that undermined the previous order of business in Königsberg were just as important as formal declarations of support and subjugation in securing Friedrich Wilhelm's sovereignty in the city.

Yes, Hones was attacked for baking different bread. But it was not just the ingredients that left a bad taste in the city bakers' mouths: paired with the standing garrisons of foreign, Calvinist officers and changes in governance, Hones and his buttery bread were intolerable. By repeatedly intervening in the dispute, Friedrich Wilhelm demonstrated that these disputes went beyond the town-crown conflicts and protests over guild privileges common throughout early modern Europe. The bread wars became an opportunity to set himself as the arbiter of urban business. According to the records of Hones's heirs, however, this was a cold war that with an absentee ruler was not decisively won.

The on-the-ground perspective on the growth of the Prussian state challenges the clear periodization of Friedrich Wilhelm's supposed subjugation of the Prussian nobility. According to that periodization, Friedrich Wilhelm disarmed the local estates for the last time in early 1674. As General Görtzke and Stadtholder von Croy occupied Königsberg with the elector's army, the *Junkers* quickly folded and abandoned the cause of the town. Beyond this ruler versus nobility narrative, there is another story. A figure such as Hones, who bridged social classes and embodied many of the points of conflict, elucidates the multilayered changes taking place in the state. This change affected and involved more than just the ruler and the estates: craftspeople also played a role in that history (and not always on the same side!). It was not just the threat of violence or the interests of the nobility that characterize Friedrich Wilhelm's expansion of power, but regular interventions in daily life. Like the court servants in Berlin discussed in chapter 2, Martin Hones leaves a narrative of an individual who pursued his own interests while advancing the elector's increasing dominion over the cities of Brandenburg-Prussia. However, Hones's story takes its meaning from its Prussian context of particular liberties and a custom of local autonomy. Hones was an intermediate node between the elector and the Prussian subjects and his personal interests and actions brought the fault lines of Königsberg politics to the surface.

As the story of Martin Hones came to a close, so, too, did Friedrich Wilhelm's reign. The Prussian estates and guilds were no longer a pressing concern, and Friedrich Wilhelm did not spend much time in Königsberg after 1669 and never returned again after 1679. His final decade was plagued with health problems related to gout and heart failure, and with an expectation of impending death, the elector focused on shaping his legacy. In Berlin, he fostered an atmosphere of scholarly pursuits that tied together practical and performative aspects of rule. The final publication of the court physician, Dr. Elsholtz, was a work that combined botany, medicine, and diet and brought into sharp relief a court culture in which medical research, tradition, and representative cuisine intersected.

7

The Great Elector's Legacy

FOLLOWING HIS SUCCESS on the battlefield against Louis XIV in the Dutch Wars of the 1670s, Friedrich Wilhelm's reign settled into a period of tenuous calm. Internal political conflicts with the estates in Cleves, Brandenburg, and Prussia were relatively subdued and the elector had time to attempt some financial reforms and get his affairs in order. The 1680s was not a decade of military campaigns or large building projects; rather, it was the time for legacy building. Multiple historians, including the jurist and political philosopher Samuel von Pufendorf (1632–1694), were called to court to write dynastic histories and biographies of Friedrich Wilhelm with the intent to solidify his place in history.[1]

The Science of Nutrition

Friedrich Wilhelm could not fully enjoy the relative peace, because gouty inflammation left him bedridden for weeks at a time.[2] His health problems were exacerbated as he had, as one British diplomat put it, "grown quite corpulent."[3] This was a serious matter of state because, as his physician put it, the "well-being of the whole republic relied on the health of the ruler."[4] Friedrich Wilhelm's health problems might have stemmed from a diet high in protein and alcohol (especially beer) and fittingly, the treatment his physicians recommended was also dietary. His four *Leibärzte*, or privy physicians, conferred and prescribed a regimen of tea drinking to ameliorate the debilitating flare ups of gout.[5] According to the privy council president, Friedrich Wilhelm's attacks became less frequent once he started drinking thirty to forty cups of tea every morning.[6]

In the context of a medical philosophy that saw diet as a key component of good health, it is not surprising that in this same period, another one of the court physicians, Johann Sigismund Elsholtz, published a treatise on the correct foods for good health. By 1682, the year of publication of Dr. Elsholtz's *Diaeteticon*, the food offerings in Berlin far exceeded what they had been during the dire subsistence crises of the Thirty Years

Late portrait of Friedrich
Wilhelm by S[amuel]
Blesendorf. (Bildarchiv und
Grafiksammlung, Austrian
National Library)

War. As an age-peer of Friedrich Wilhelm who came to court in the immediate postwar rebuilding period, Elsholtz had experienced the changes
in court culture through the different phases of Friedrich Wilhelm's reign.
    Elsholtz and Friedrich Wilhelm spent their adult years in each other's
orbit and died within months of each other. The *Diaeteticon* is the cul-
mination of Elsholtz's three decades observing and participating in court
intellectual culture. From collaborating with the elector in rebuilding and
promoting the palace gardens to contributing to burgeoning knowledge of
the natural world through scholarly networks and publications, Elsholtz
exemplified the characteristics of the seventeenth-century natural philosopher. His *Diaeteticon* is an artifact of a world in which court patronage
went hand-in-hand with developments in the medical profession.
    The book extolls the habits and resources in Brandenburg and pro-
motes Berlin as the fertile ground for such scholarly output, thus imbuing
the city with the cultural cachet attached to other great intellectual capi-
tals of the age. Furthermore, the dietary recommendations themselves,
are informed by existing consumption habits in Berlin. Thus, the court
setting shaped medical knowledge. Like Pufendorf's biography, Elsholtz's

Diaeteticon was part of the legacy building at the close of Friedrich Wilhelm's reign with lasting influence on dietary thought.

A look at Dr. Elsholtz's education and career explains the particularities of this vernacular dietary manual. After a short exploration of Elsholtz's life in the context of the Brandenburg-Prussian scholarly culture at court, this chapter analyzes the content of the *Diaeteticon* in comparison to other early modern nutritional advice books. While Elsholtz's nutritional theory was shaped by the local culture in Brandenburg, it was also informed by his Renaissance humanist education and by the developing experimental practices of the late seventeenth century. Finally, this chapter considers the curious addition of a French cookbook at the end of the *Diaeteticon* and argues that Elsholtz included it not for the obvious reason that he loved French cooking, but rather for other objectives it fulfilled for him.

Elsholtz was an intellectual of his time: a man who embodied the transition from the humoral medicine of the Renaissance to the empirical medicine of the Enlightenment. His early background and education account for his humanist tendencies and his professional activities demonstrate his participation in the New Science of the seventeenth century. Elsholtz was likely born in Frankfurt an der Oder where his father served as the city's secretary. His mother's family came from Berlin where her father was a member of the council chamber (*Ratskammer*).[7] Elsholtz matriculated at the Brandenburg state university in Frankfurt an der Oder when he was eleven years old. He followed the traditional *ars liberalis* curriculum before specializing in medicine.[8]

Like many erudite scholars of his day, he traveled around Europe to pursue his education. He studied at Wittemberg, Leiden, and possibly in France before heading to Italy in 1652.[9] There, he followed a common path for German medical students and finished his doctorate with the renowned medical faculty in Padua.[10]

Working as he did in a predisciplinary age, Elsholtz's scholarly interests spanned many topics. His dissertation on the measurements of the body (*Anthropometrie*) combined mathematics and anatomy in a work that, in proper Renaissance fashion, was addressed to physicians and artists alike.[11] He dedicated the published dissertation to Elector Friedrich Wilhelm, possibly an indication he was looking for professional opportunities that would bring him home. He also published treatises on distillation, minerals, and phosphorus.[12]

Since early modern medical therapies consisted for the most part of herbal treatments, botany was an integral part of his medical studies. Elsholtz's interest in botany, however, went much deeper than what was needed to practice medicine and he had a passion for collecting rare plants. His botanical interests had deep roots, as his paternal grandfather had been the court gardener at the Brandenburg fortress city of Küstrin.[13] As was discussed in chapter 4, his catalog of the plants in the Berlin palace garden provided his entrée to court employment in 1656. In that same year, he also inserted himself into Berlin society in his personal life through his marriage to Anna Guttwill (1630–1663), the widow of an electoral physician and daughter of the Brandenburg bursar (*Rentmeister*).[14]

Scientific Research and Medicine at the Court

In other ways, too, Elsholtz was participating in the scholarly trends of the late seventeenth-century. He had a wide intellectual network and participated in the new research institutions and scholarly associations. As an early member of the Collegium Naturae Curiosorum, later known as the Leopoldina, he contributed twenty articles to their *Miscellanea curiosa,* considered the first scientific journal.[15] In his scientific writings, Elsholtz demonstrated that he kept abreast of experiments and findings from around Europe. He was also a collector of "rarities" and curiosities such as a piece of unicorn fossil, eagle skin, and a piece of crystal with gold on one side, supposedly taken from the Temple of Diana in Athens.[16]

Although Berlin was not a recognized center of European scientific activity in the seventeenth century, Elsholtz found a conducive and collaborative environment for his work in natural philosophy. Indeed, the elector had sought to increase the number and reputation of scholars in Brandenburg over the course of his reign.[17] His efforts included the founding of a library in 1661 (the precursor to the Prussian State Library), an (ultimately unsuccessful) attempt to found a new university in Brandenburg, and the recruitment of prominent doctors and other scholars to create a learned medical community in Berlin.

Most famously, Friedrich Wilhelm called the "greatest chemist of the age," Johann Kunkel (1630–1703) to the court in Berlin in 1678.[18] Friedrich Wilhelm was so eager for him to carry out experiments related to his gold-ruby glass, that he set him up on his own island on the outskirts of the city to allow him to work without distractions and in complete secrecy. While Kunkel's experiments were supported in the hopes they would lead to a lucrative manufacturing venture, other scholarly projects contributed to the prestige of the court in less tangible ways. All leveraged knowledge in the pursuit of status and vice versa.

Unsurprisingly, given his personal interest in botany, Friedrich Wilhelm attracted a number of specialists in the study of plants and other *materia medica*. Like Elsholtz's work, these physicians' publications advertised Brandenburg as a favorable setting for natural philosophers. Thomas Panckow (1622–1665) published his *Herbarium Portatile* in 1654, the same year he was installed as a court physician. He dedicated this index of over thirteen hundred mostly native Brandenburg plants to the elector. Christian Mentzel (1622–1701), another Brandenburg native, received his doctorate from the University of Padua with Elsholtz.[19] He published on plants from Asia and the Americas, and both he and Elsholtz performed experiments in natural philosophy while employed by Friedrich Wilhelm.[20] Mentzel, too, was a contributing member of the Leopoldina and published on the phosphorus demonstrations at court in its *Miscellanea*.

Five court doctors, including Panckow, Mentzel, and Elsholz, lobbied the elector for decades for stronger medical regulation in Berlin, indicating that they practiced, or at least, monitored medicine beyond the palace walls. In their 1661 plea, they asked the elector to establish a *collegium medicum* of respected, formally educated physicians to be the medical authority in the city. As such, they advocated for the *collegium medicum* to be the regulating authority over Berlin's lay medical practitioners (apothecaries, barbers, bathers, occultists, midwives, etc.). This was, they argued, a safeguard from these "menaces to society with their uneducated mistakes."[21] The elector finally approved a medical edict in 1685 that formally called for establishment of a collegium medicum electorale. The body was led by court physicians or professors at state-sponsored university at Frankfurt an der Oder. The 1685 edict additionally set prices for drugs, instituted a register of apothecaries, surgeons, and midwives and regulated their practice. In this way, the court physicians' connections helped them standardize medical care to their advantage.

It was in this setting that Elsholtz developed the natural philosophy that informed his *Diaeteticon*. As Elsholtz spent his career navigating both scientific and courtly circles, he was aware of the social realities

Anonymous eighteenth-
century oil portrait of Johann
Sigismund Elsholtz. (Herzog
August Library Wolfenbüttel:
B 42)

underpinning scientific exploration. He dedicated the second edition of his most famous medical contribution, *Clysmatica Nova* (1667), to the highest-ranking court administrator, Raban von Canstein (1617–1680).[22] Von Canstein was responsible for the elector's finances and reforms after the Thirty Years War and dedicating this groundbreaking work to him showed Elsholtz recognized that power was diffuse across multiple people at court.

Furthermore, the court context impacted the actual experiments described in *Clystmatica Nova*. These experiments involved intravenous injection and were inspired by similar experiments elsewhere in Europe and the theory of blood circulation by a fellow Padua alumnus, William Harvey.[23] Most of the experiments described in *Clysmatica Nova* used dogs to test intravenous injection of medicines that otherwise would have been administered orally. But on one occasion, Elsholtz tested on human subjects. The subjects were three sick privates in the elector's bodyguard. Elsholtz also coached the lead surgeon of the bodyguards in performing intravenous injection. Not only does this indicate a close exchange between these two different professions in the medical field—surgery and internal medicine—which were traditionally separate, it shows how servants in different departments and levels of the court collaborated in medical research. Scholar physicians were fully integrated into social and

Intravenous injection, from
Dr. Elsholtz's *Clysmatica Nova*
of 1667, p. [38]. (Staatsbibliothek zu Berlin)

cultural life of the court and they mixed constantly with people in other
positions around the electoral residences.

The *Clysmatica Nova* is also significant in the culinary history of the
court for another reason: it reflects an openness to a new philosophy of
diet and medicine. The humoral theory of the body, in which Elsholtz
had been trained and which informed much of the content of the *Diaeteticon,* advocated for treating patients based on their individual habits and temperament. The experiments in the *Clysmatica Nova,* instead,
treated a nutritional deficiency medicinally.[24] Elsholtz diagnosed one of
the bodyguards with a "scorbutic impurity in his veins from improper
food," meaning he had scurvy.[25] For treatment, Elsholtz prescribed blood-
letting, an ancient procedure intended to release bad humors from the

body. After he deemed enough blood had been released, however, he did something quite revolutionary: he injected *acqua cochleariae* (a distillation of scurvy-grass) into the bloodstream to treat the scurvy.

These experiments heralded a shift in the relationship between diet and medical treatment. As the prescription of tea-drinking for Friedrich Wilhelm shows, however, this was not an abrupt break from Galenic medicine. While in England at the time, a debate was raging between humoral medicine that treated the individual, and "new medicine" that treated the disease, in Berlin the dichotomy was not so stark.[26] The two philosophies of health and nutrition, which seem contradictory in retrospect, blended in Elsholtz's writings and experiments. For him, conducting experiments in intravenous injection and writing on diet from a humanist medical perspective were not incompatible.[27] This is a mixing of the old and new found in all aspects of the court food culture.

Berlin was, of course, one of many courts nurturing experimentation and natural observation in the seventeenth century. It did not yet have the reputation as an intellectual center that it would gain under Friedrich Wilhelm's future daughter-in-law, Sophie Charlotte of Hanover (1668–1705). Still, cultivating a learned milieu at court was an important part of Friedrich Wilhelm's legacy. It was in this climate of court-sanctioned scholarship, that Elsholtz developed his wide-ranging scientific interests and produced a dietary text that had an impact beyond the court.

A Dietary Manual for Berlin

Elsholtz's wider career at court explains the particularities of the *Diaeteticon*. The first edition of the book is a 466-page quarto volume packed with food anecdotes from various ancient, medieval, Renaissance, and seventeenth-century physicians, naturalists, and other authors. The work presented a lay audience with the vocabulary for educated discourse about food. Elsholtz dedicated it to the electoral prince Friedrich and his first wife, Elisabeth Henriette (1661–1683). Prince Friedrich had already taken over some of the duties of rule from his ailing father and as heir apparent at this point was considered the "greatest threat to Friedrich Wilhelm's authority."[28]

Elsholtz may have been hedging a bet on the electoral prince's camp in his choice of dedicatee or just making the natural assumption that, considering the elector's health, he would not remain elector for long. As there was suspicion on both sides between Friedrich Wilhelm and Electoral Prince Friedrich (and even suspicion that the elector's second wife, Dorothea, was poisoning Friedrich and Elisabeth Henriette), it is noteworthy that Elsholtz refers to Friedrich Wilhelm in his dedication as "our pugnacious David" and says that since God has crowned him with a long and happy reign, we hope the same for you.[29] In any case, Elsholtz considers Friedrich Wilhelm's diet a lost cause because he writes that the purpose of his book is that "Friedrich and Elisabeth Henriette (and all the other people of Brandenburg) would follow it and enjoy good health."[30]

The book is organized into three sections. The main body describes individual foods by type: plants, four-legged animals, birds, fish, and drinks. This sequence of food types adhered to that of the first printed dietary manual, Bartolomeo Platina's *De honesta voluptate* (Rome, 1474). Platina's work set the standard in all learned dietary treatises of the Renaissance. Elsholtz's section on diet concludes with his expert answers to questions about proper diet (*Einige Tisch-Fragen*). Again, this *Questiones* format derived from earlier medical treatises, but in Elsholtz's version, it is not directed to physicians, but to lay readers. The final third of the book is not Elsholtz's own work, but a translation of a French cookbook, thus bridging theory and practice.

Elsholtz's *Diaeteticon* comes after the initial wave of Renaissance dietary treatises surveyed by Ken Albala.[31] Furthermore, it differs from the last phase of Renaissance dietary manuals in its court context, royal dedication, and in its acceptance of foods that would have been considered luxurious at the time, such as pastries, citrus fruits, and spices. However, in most ways, Elsholtz's dietary manual was very similar to others in the genre: even its name was not unique. Two prominent works with the title *Diaeteticon Polyhistoricum* had been published, one by Joseph Duchesne in 1614 and translated into German in 1625, and the other by Ludovicus Nonnius in 1627. The closest dietary manual, in terms of time and place, to Elsholtz's was Baldassaris Timaei von Güldenklee's *Responsa medica, et diaeteticon*. Von Güldenklee (1600–1667) had been a physician to Elector Georg Wilhelm of Brandenburg during the Thirty Years War before leaving in 1648 to serve his sister, Maria Leonora of Brandenburg (King Gustav Adolph's widow) in Sweden. He dedicated his work to the relatively new Elector Friedrich Wilhelm and the 1677 edition named von Güldenklee as an "electoral physician."[32] Therefore, there was precedence for Elsholtz's *Diaeteticon* even within Friedrich Wilhelm's court and a long-standing interest there in dietary theory. Von Güldenklee's one-thousand-page tome, though, was limited to a Latin-literate audience and, whereas von Güldenklee provided strict rules for healthy consumption, Elsholtz's dietary recommendations were more flexible.

Nonetheless, although Elsholtz enlivens his text for a popular audience with jokes and references to biblical, fictional, and ancient mythological stories, he still fashions himself a classically trained authority. Throughout his assessment of the various food groups, he refers to an astonishing number of ancient, medieval, Arabic, and Renaissance figures—in total, about 188 sources. His citations encompass works of medicine, botany, horticulture, viticulture, natural history, travel, philosophy, and theology. The most frequently quoted authors are the ancient physician Galen (born 130 CE), the naturalist Ulisse Aldrovandi (1522–1605), the German Helius Eobanus (1488–1540), Jean-Baptiste Bruyerin (1500s), and Baptiste Fiera (ca. 1460–ca. 1540). The majority of references are early modern and Renaissance (53 percent). Twenty-nine percent are ancient, 6 percent medieval, 3 percent literary, biblical or mythological, and 10 percent unknown or untraceable. While citations show a humanist's proclivity for Italian scholarship, they also include North African, Middle Eastern, and other European sources; 14 percent of the authors he cites are of German origin.[33]

Elsholtz certainly signals familiarity with his Renaissance humanist precedents, but he deviates from them by writing in German rather than Latin. That is to say that the *Diaeteticon* was more a popular advice book than a medical treatise. Indeed, it went through multiple editions and was extensively excerpted. A second edition was printed in 1715 in Leipzig as part of a volume combined with his popular gardening manual, *Vom Garten-Baw*. This second printing was recommended reading by the Hamburg periodical, *Der Patriot*, in 1724.[34] Furthermore, it is heavily quoted from in two reference works: Thomas Marperger's 1716 kitchen and cellar dictionary and in the *Curieuses und Reales Natur-Kunst-Berg-Gewerck-und Handlungs Lexicon* of 1746.[35] The *Tisch-fragen* were also reprinted in a 1712 cookbook of Susanne Eger.[36] Although it is not known how many copies were printed and sold, as of 2022, twenty-nine copies of the original 1682 edition existed in modern libraries (not including the four copies at the Prussian State Library that were lost in World War II). There are two known copies of the 1715 printing (one in the Czech Republic and one in Jena).[37]

Even if the form of the *Diaeteticon* was familiar and many of Elsholtz's sources had been worked over for centuries, he also includes new research and descriptions from contemporary travel and natural observations. He quotes from works published as recently as 1670, which positions the *Diaeteticon* in a specifically late seventeenth-century discourse.[38] Furthermore, although he respected his predecessors and contemporary colleagues, Elsholtz did not simply parrot their works. Drawing on his own observations from practicing medicine and on contemporary local habits, he expounds on foods like the sweet potato or chocolate, which were unknown to the ancients.

Ken Albala also found that while dietary manual authors might have generally aligned with humoral medicine, there remained a wide variety of interpretations on the particulars.[39]

This is borne out in Elsholtz's food assessments. In his description of pistachios, for instance, he synthesizes the opinions of others. Avicenna, Rhazes, and Serapio all thought the nuts had a very hot temperament while the sixteenth-century Fleming Rembert Dodoens and the twelfth-century Moroccan Averroes thought that pistachios were moderately warm and moist. But then, Elsholtz asserts his judgment: when ripe, pistachios are temperate.[40] According to Elsholtz, the other authorities were judging pistachios at the wrong time: only when old and rancid did pistachios become hot and dry. Thus, Elsholtz brings physicians from different times and places into discourse with one another and inserts himself into the conversation as part of a borderless, timeless medical republic of letters.[41]

Elsholtz's *Diaeteticon* has a unique geographic focus on the Mark Brandenburg and much of his nutritional advice makes concessions for local habits. For example, he writes that "*our* work habits differ from the ancients, so [whereas they ate two equal meals] we need to eat a stronger midday meal." Further, he adds, "the question cannot be answered otherwise, the way in this land is to eat a larger midday meal."[42] Elsholtz makes the local practice seem natural by claiming that the proper time to eat is when one is hungry, which for an average, healthy adult, he claims, should be twice a day, around midday and again in the evening with the midday meal being larger.[43] These recommendations suited the dining patterns indicated in court dining regulations where, at least toward the end of Friedrich Wilhelm's reign, there is evidence that the midday meal was the larger of the two meals.[44]

Elsholtz does not recommend breakfast except for certain people, although a liquid breakfast was fine, or something with bread, or even lettuce with spices and sugar(!).[45] And, he claims the beer soup breakfast (described as the elector's usual breakfast in chapter 1) was "fine for the common man."[46] Again, this recommendation aligns with the archival record, which indicates that many people at court, including the princes and princesses received bread and wine for breakfast.[47]

In his description of venison, Elsholtz defends local habit against received wisdom that it was unhealthy. Galen, Simeon Sethi, and the medieval Salernitan medical school had recommended that the hard-to-digest meat be avoided. However, in Berlin, where transplanted fallow deer were "thriving in the Tiergarten" and hunting was a popular activity for courtiers, Elsholtz diplomatically describes ways that venison could be healthy.[48] He specifies that it was really only very old deer that were harmful and wild newborn deer and yearlings could even be quite healthy: "Partly due to their youth and partly thanks to their constant movement, wild calves are tender and easy to digest and belong on the tables of the great lords."[49] As if that was not enough to recommend them, Elsholtz goes on to explain how the manner of cooking and the season of the year could improve the nutritional benefits of venison. In other words, it was unlikely that a health concern would override the established taste for the deer at the Berlin banqueting table.

On the other hand, Elsholtz draws connections between local, current food culture and ancient Mediterranean food culture to imply an illustrious heritage by association. In his description of swans, for instance, he notes that the third-century Roman scholar Solinus wrote about a River Eurotas in Sparta where many swans floated. "We can say [the same] about our Spree River," Elsholtz writes, "particularly between Berlin and Spandau."[50] There is scattered evidence, that indeed, swans were consumed at the court in Berlin and Königsberg.[51]

Local foods might even surpass what was common in the ancient Mediterranean. Elsholtz makes the case that butter (the most frequently used cooking fat in northern Europe) had a similar warm temperament to oil, but was even more nourishing and more useful in cooking. He describes the delicious flavor of butter at different times and in different dishes.[52] His preference for it, though, might have been due to the fact that only rancid olive oil ever reached a place as far from the Mediterranean as Berlin (even if Elsholtz himself would have been familiar with fresh olive oil from his time as a student in Padua). Similarly, sheep cheese—the customary cheese of Prussia—is judged as the easiest cheese to digest.[53] But, to be fair, Elsholtz lists Parmesan and Edam as the best cheeses to be had, and they were often the only imported cheeses purchased by the court kitchen.[54]

In these examples, Elsholtz directs his humanist education and experiences from his European travels toward promoting local products and
habits. But, the question remains, did the court have a healthy diet, according to Elsholtz's rules? The four remaining menus or *Kuchenzetteln*
from January 1652, provide some basis for judging whether court cuisine
aligned with Elsholtz's recommendations (or vice versa).[55] In terms of
cooking methods, the menus list beef and mutton prepared in three ways:
boiled with other ingredients, roasted, or baked into a pastry. In Elsholtz's
assessment, boiling meat was good for lean meats, pan frying dried the
meat and was not particularly recommended, and roasting was not wholly
bad as long as one was careful not to under- or overcook the meat.[56] The
suckling pig on the menu was considered to have an excessively moist
temperament, which Elsholtz says is, "why people with a sweet tooth
[*Schleck-mauler*] were particularly fond of it."[57] However, according to
Elsholtz, roasting it, as the court kitchens had done on January 7, removed
its harmful effects. He writes, "These days, one pays less attention to Apicius's strange way of cooking and instead considers roasting to be the best
means of removing the slimy moisture of the suckling pig."[58]

It is not surprising that much of Elsholtz's advice fit existing practice
at the court of his employer. Since we can assume that physicians would
not have been employed if they did not generally meet their patients' expectations for care, physicians' views on nutrition can also indicate the
patients' (or patrons') views.[59] This was even truer at court since rulers
could choose whom they deemed to be the very best physicians, which
has been traced at other early modern European courts too. For instance,
in looking at England in the same period, Harold Cook and Bruce Moran
found that the selection of privy physicians had political motivations and
an impact on medical practice more broadly.[60]

Beyond instructing the lay reader on the basics of the humanist dietary
theory, Elsholtz's descriptions accomplished two opposite objectives: they
associated Brandenburg-Prussia with an ancient cultural patrimony and
they praised the particularities and quality of local cuisine. Furthermore,
the *Diaeteticon* expresses both Elsholtz's personal erudition and the general cosmopolitanism of Berlin by referencing the practices of distant
cultures including Italians, Tartars, and Chinese. This manual, then, attempted to place Brandenburg cuisine on par with other notable cuisines

of the world. This pride of place, however, makes the addition of a French cookbook at the end of the *Diaeteticon* intriguing.

The French Influence on Food

After the first two sections of the *Diaeteticon* discussed above, Elsholtz transitions to a practical section with the following quote from Galen: "A physician should not be wholly inexperienced in the art of cooking since the foods that have a pleasant taste are much easier to digest than those that are just as healthy, but not prepared well."[61] It was not novel to include a cookbook component in a dietary treatise; the foundational work of the genre, Platina's *De honesta voluptate,* similarly included recipes (most of which came from a cookbook published a decade earlier by the chef known as the Maestro da Como). It is the precise choice of cookbook, however, that makes this addition so curious.

While it may seem obvious that the addition of a German translation of Nicolas de Bonnefons's *Les délices de la campagne* signals a prominent French influence on cuisine in late-seventeenth century Brandenburg, it is actually an unlikely reason for its inclusion.[62] In general, the influence of French haute cuisine in central Europe before the eighteenth century has been exaggerated for much of central Europe at the time. Paul Freedman touts the assessment of many other food historians when he writes, "In the era of Louis XIV, France was assuming the position of undisputed gastronomic leadership that would hold thereafter, or perhaps until just recently."[63] But a German traveler to France in the early eighteenth century still commented on the lack of spices there, suggesting that the cuisines were still quite distinct.[64] Likewise, Elizabeth Charlotte (Liselotte) von der Pfalz (1652–1722) famously derided the cuisine at Versailles writing that she "could not bear to eat a French ragout" and she credited herself with starting a "German fashion" at Versailles for game.[65]

The paramount influence of French cuisine also seems doubtful in the case of the *Diaeteticon*. Nowhere in the body of his text does Elsholtz suggest an affinity or admiration of French cuisine. Although one philologist has traced the French words that Elsholtz introduced into German through the *Diaeteticon,* these French words (for example, *délicatesse* and *confiture*) are only in the cookbook.[66] The foreign terms *tisane, bergamot,* and *limonade* that Elsholtz uses in his own text are just as likely to have been adopted from Italian or Latin as from French. In other words, Francophilia is not a theme of the *Diaeteticon*.

The choice of this cookbook may have been made through lack of alternatives. There was a break in cookbook printing in Europe during the wars of religion.[67] Due to the protracted effects of the Thirty Years War in central Europe, this trend persisted longer in the German-speaking lands than in France and no new cookbooks were printed in German between 1620 and 1670.[68] The numerous changes that Elsholtz made support the possibility that he chose this book out of necessity. Elsholtz copied the language of Georg Greflinger's 1665 translation verbatim, but he rearranged its order to match the sequence in the first part of his *Diaeteticon*, "From the Plant-Based Foods." Namely, dishes with root vegetable dishes came first, then those with fruits, and finally came breads and pies.

Greflinger and Elsholtz both made other editorial choices to suit their audiences. Neither of these Protestant authors include Bonnefons's second bread recipe of "bread to celebrate mass" (*pain à célébrer la Messe*).[69] Similarly, Greflinger and Elsholtz both edited Bonnefons's recipe for a rye bread to accompany venison. Bonnefons's description of rye bread is not wholly complementary. He writes, "This pastry is so hard that one cannot eat it. It is not even something to give to dogs because it would be too great a waste of salt."[70] This is incongruous with Elsholtz's earlier description of rye flour as "improved through acids, salts, and baking so that it makes a good and healthy bread."[71] When Greflinger and Elsholtz printed Bonnefons's recipe, they changed the title from "Brown bread for venison" to "A rye dough for all types of pastries from game," and omitted the negative comments in the recipe.[72] In a culture of predominately rye bread and abundant game, the changes to the cookbook are few, but telling.

Although alternatives were limited, Elsholtz's choice of Bonnefons's cookbook, was more likely connected to another of Elsholtz's expertise: botany. Bonnefons was an influential figure in the gardening craze among the aspiring new nobility who were building their estates in the suburbs of Paris in the late seventeenth century.[73] This fad was adopted from the Dutch, just as Friedrich Wilhelm's interest in gardens stemmed from his connections with the Netherlands.[74] *Les délices de la campagne* was a follow-up to Bonnefons's successful first book, *Le jardinier françois* of 1651.[75] *Le jardinier* was concerned with food cultivation and preservation, and *Les délices* complemented it by focusing more on food preparation and consumption.

Prior to the *Diaeteticon*, Elsholtz had primarily published works of natural philosophy in Latin for a specialized audience. The exception was his popular *Vom Garten-Baw* gardening manual, which was reprinted six times in various forms in the seventeenth and eighteenth centuries.[76] Elsholtz's implicit motivation for the *Diaeteticon*, then, may have been, like Bonnefons's, to promote the fashion for botany and gardening among rising urban elites. Remember, in one edition, *Vom Garten-Baw* and the *Diaeteticon* were even combined: the full title of the 1690 edition emphasizes the connection between the two as well as the vogue for gentleman gardeners who cultivated their own (sometimes exotic) collection of edible plants for home consumption:

> Medicine-Garden-and-Table book, or next installment of Horticulture. How one maintains plants, herbs, flowers, and roots created by God for the preservation of good health and maintains a long life through an orderly diet particularly through moderate consumption of foods and drinks: Both high and low (in particular the gardeners) [will find this book useful] because of the foreign plants, flowers, and herbs that are contained herein; and [this book] shows the right time to wait and to harvest these [foreign plants] in the German climate. Published in six books and with the necessary images as well as a full index with the *French Cook, Baker,* and *Confectioner.* With the privilege of the Holy Roman Emperor and the Electors of Saxony and Brandenburg.[77]

Bonnefons had already linked gardening and cooking in his oeuvre, but Elsholtz went step further by triangulating those with medicine.

Dietary treatises containing recipes were an established Renaissance genre. So, too, had popular books combining gardening and cooking been around for a few decades by the time the *Diaeteticon* was published. What Elsholtz introduced, though, was a hybrid of these two genres. The novelty of the format is not made explicit in the 1684 edition of the *Diaeteticon*, but it is consistent with Elsholtz's overall *oeuvre* that combined interests in many aspects of the natural world. From this context, Elsholtz's selection of Bonnefons makes sense: they share an interest in promoting foods from the garden.[78] Gardening was an important manifestation of the ethos of Friedrich Wilhelm and Elsholtz's generation and the *Diaeteticon*, again exposes the deep intertwining of natural, medical, culinary, and political interests.

WHEN ONE REFLECTS on the legacy of the Great Elector, botany is not the first thing that comes to mind. But Elsholtz's biography and the scholarly endeavors of Friedrich Wilhelm's court explain why a vernacular work such as the *Diaeteticon* was a product of the last decade of Friedrich Wilhelm and Elsholtz's lives. Elsholtz, whose father, grandfather, and father-in-law had held positions in city, court, and territorial administration adroitly navigated the social cosmos of the court. He used his skills and knowledge to influence culture in Berlin beyond the palace too. His work in political, popular, and scholarly arenas balanced novelty and tradition as well as local pride and cosmopolitanism. While his vernacular writings contained a multitude of practical advice, as a whole they benefited the representation of Friedrich Wilhelm's might. The *Diaeteticon* was the manifestation not only that Brandenburg food culture was honorable, but that Friedrich Wilhelm's court was a place in which the light of knowledge glimmered brightly. The *Diaeteticon* could only have come at this point in Elsholtz's career, at this moment of stability in Berlin, and in this age when experimentation and knowledge exchange were an integral part of political culture.

Conclusion

POWER AND VULNERABILITY AT THE TABLE

Up to this point, this book has explored food at the Brandenburg-Prussian court from many different angles—social, environmental, diplomatic, and so on–but always as a point of power, whether representational or material. However, food was also a ruler's greatest weakness. With every bite, a premodern ruler was susceptible to untraceable attacks by means of poisoning. Ironically, when a ruler's power increased, so too did this threat, because their household would expand in accordance with their stature, giving opportunity to more potential assassins. A case of suspected poisoning in the last year of the elector's life reveals how, in spite of all the gains he had made in status, territory, and economic stability, even just the fear of poisoning had the power to rewrite Friedrich Wilhelm's legacy and the course of Prussian history.

The alleged murder took place over Easter week in 1687 when the elector's second surviving son, twenty-year-old Prince Ludwig, margrave of Brandenburg, complained of stomach pains. He returned to Berlin from the city palace in Potsdam where the elector's personal physicians tended to him, but did not take his illness seriously. When he died a week after his first complaints, the doctors determined poison to be the cause of death. This diagnosis (and presumably the shock of the death of an otherwise healthy young person) led Friedrich Wilhelm to call a commission composed of his privy councilors in Potsdam and Berlin to investigate. Their examination of banal things provided a platform for courtiers to voice their prejudices and cast suspicion on their rivals. So began what the historian Johann Gustav Droysen called "sinister whispers" (*unheimische Flustern*) throughout the court.[1] All summer long, suspicion fell on a wide array of courtiers from a chambermaid to Friedrich Wilhelm's second wife, Electoress Dorothea herself, pushing the Hohenzollern into a succession crisis.[2]

The commission attempted to uncover the dangers in everyday court life by asking forty questions to nineteen of the courtiers in closest orbit around Prince Ludwig. Their resulting report (*Protocol*) presents the witnesses' detailed answers, which allow a reconstruction of Ludwig's last week and final illness. These and other contemporary accounts of the minutiae of court life during that dramatic week and its aftermath bring into relief the court culture of Brandenburg-Prussia at the end of the seventeenth century. While exposing the hidden actors in statecraft and the fault lines of the ruler's two bodies, this episode also touches on the other major theme of this book—the interconnectedness of medicine, food systems, economy, diplomacy, and court ceremony.

The Case Files

The story starts on Maundy Thursday, 1687, when witnesses reported that Ludwig seemed healthy although he ate nothing for breakfast. On Friday, he ate waffles in his wife's room, as he frequently did. They were prepared by a "Dutch woman," Frau Bent, who also prepared him coffee, either on Thursday or Friday. One witness, when asked if they held any suspicions, answered, "that Dutch woman," without further explanation.

The next day, Ludwig held an open table (*ordinair Taffel*) for lunch and dinner, which might have exposed him to poisoning by many people. Three witnesses reported that he started complaining of health problems on that day. One witness said that he reported feeling "off" (*wunderlich*) early in the day, improved after toileting but was sick again in the evening, and another witness heard something was off with his nighttime bathroom habits. Friday was also the night that the butler, Egidig Strupff, brought the prince oranges that had been sent by the steward Christoph Christian. No one saw him actually eat an orange until Saturday.

In the investigatory commission's *Protocol* and in the later historical narrative, Saturday is when the poisoning supposedly took place. Multiple witnesses reported that Ludwig ate an orange, then drank coffee and complained immediately afterward of stomach pains. Frau Bent may have made the coffee, but one witness said that a chambermaid brought the water and Ludwig himself made the coffee, which many people in the room drank (without becoming ill themselves).

On Easter morning, Frau Bent prepared Ludwig a breakfast soup and the duke of Holstein sent him scrambled eggs. Ludwig complained of poor sleep and feeling unwell. He took "sweet wine and rosemary elixir" for his stomach pains and after he came out from the first sermon of the day, he asked for his bed to be made if he did not have to attend church again in the afternoon.[3] By two accounts, Ludwig himself made the claim that the orange had made him sick.

That night, he called the physician Martin Willich to him and complained again of poor sleep. On Tuesday, he could hardly urinate without great pain (*vor großem Schriden*) and around that time the duke of Holstein was heard to have said it was poison. Eberhard Freiherr von Danckelmann (1643–1722), a young court officer who had been close with Ludwig his entire upbringing, visited him on Wednesday and brought the younger Dr. Weiß with him. At this point, Ludwig's body was bloated on his right side. The following day, the doctors gave him opium and Ludwig seemed to sleep but his pain did not decrease. On Saturday evening, blue and red spots appeared on his throat and his chest reddened. In the night, Ludwig started foaming at the mouth and breathing heavily (*singultus exeriret*).

None of the witnesses gave an account of Ludwig's passing at midday on Monday, but the French ambassador, François de Pas de Feuquères (1645–1695), comte de Rébénacq (hereafter, referred to as Rébénacq), described it in the most stirring account in his report to Louis XIV, dated April 12.[4] He claimed that the young prince was melancholy in general because he was mistreated by his father and that Ludwig had stated that his father would be the death of him. When he actually did fall ill, according to Rébénacq, the doctors had so little knowledge of Ludwig's illness that they told the elector he had just imagined it. The day before he died, Ludwig asked for his father to come and see him, "to kiss his hand one last time."[5] But the elector, convinced his illness was a chimera, reproached the young man for his weakness and did not attend him because he felt that if he visited, it would only strengthen Ludwig's belief that the illness was real and make him worse. An hour before Ludwig expired, the doctors entered the elector's room and joked that the prince was in such a fine condition, he could come himself to announce his death.[6]

So it was that Ludwig died three rooms away from the father who had refused to come say goodbye. Afterward, however, Friedrich Wilhelm displayed tremendous regret and grief; the shock of his passing likely added to the credibility of the poisoning diagnosis. Rébénacq, though, blamed the doctors for inciting the poison scare: to cover up their ignorance of Ludwig's illness, they rushed their autopsy and made their claim of poisoning without a surgeon or outside physician present. Furthermore, he believed that the elector himself fanned the flames of panic; if he had not given credence to the poisoning verdict, the rumors would have quickly dissipated.[7]

Multiple historians have described Rébénacq as an unbiased, third-party witness to the episode.[8] A closer look at this unstudied character reveals he was anything but. In fact, he was personally invested in down-playing the likelihood of poisoning in the account he gave to Louis XIV because just a few years earlier, his brother was one of the noblemen implicated in the notorious *Affaire de poisons*—a murder scandal and witch-hunt that sent elite Parisians into a panic from 1677 to 1682. That poison scare eventually resulted in the accusation of four hundred people and the execution of thirty-six. The investigation into occult practices was closed only once it came too close to the Louis XIV's inner circle with the accusation that his mistress, Madame de Montespan, was using love potions on the king.[9]

Rébénacq's brother, Antoine de Pas de Feuquières (1648–1711), marquis de Feuquières was an officer in Louis XIV's army and aide-de-camp to his cousin, the maréchal-duc de Luxembourg, a prominent French general and the marshal of France since 1675. Both men were named by one of the main suspects in the *Affaire* and accused of having sought to commune with the devil and possibly of poisoning the husband of Feuquières's mistress.[10] These were the two most prominent aristocrats to be implicated in the *Affaire* up to that point, and the accusations against them caused the investigation to ramp up and the minister of war to become involved.[11] Feuquières was interrogated in 1680 but was eventually discharged. Although he continued in his military career until 1701, he advanced no further than the rank of lieutenant general and nearing the end of his life, he complained that the king was displeased with him for his "sins."[12] The duc de Saint-Simon implied that Feuquières never recovered from the *Affaire de poisons*.[13]

Rébénacq was therefore well aware of the damage that accusations of poisoning could wreak on a family. Under such circumstances, it is understandable that he would try to deescalate fears of poisoning and emphasize the hysterical nature of the rumors that were pitting the party of the electoral prince against that of the electress. Rébénacq, though, was vastly outnumbered among the witnesses in not suspecting poisoning.

Like the doctors and the elector, some of the witnesses quoted in the *Protocol* also only suspected poisoning after Ludwig's death. But

Danckelmann claimed he suspected poisoning right away when he saw what he considered an unusual illness. He noted the doctors disagreed with him because they thought the fever would have been stronger. Only one, a Dr. Conis, considered poisoning as a cause, but he was contradicted by the other doctors. Danckelmann also related that Ludwig himself thought he was possibly poisoned but joked he was not "important enough" to be the target of an assassination.[14]

The mistress of the robe of Ludwig's wife, Luise Charlotte von Radziwill (1667–1695), claimed that she had not suspected anything until the illness lasted longer than three days. Other witnesses suspected poisoning, but shared no other information or likely suspects. A hunter, Friderich Hennerich, claimed he had actually warned the prince against eating the oranges, but Ludwig had called him a fool and responded, "They will do me no harm!" An equerry said he heard from someone he referred to as "the little Trockimsky" that others had eaten the oranges, implying that whatever ailed Ludwig was not caused by an orange.

Consultation with a twenty-first-century physician also confirms that poisoning was unlikely given the symptoms.[15] More likely causes of death are scarlet fever, typhus fever, a kidney stone that became a kidney blockage resulting in septicemia (a bacterial infection in the bloodstream), a ruptured appendix that became septic, a problem in the upper liver, or a blockage in the gallbladder that turned septic. If the prince was sick with typhus or one of these other ailments, eating and drinking acidic coffee or oranges would have caused a flare-up.

So much for conjecture. Without exhuming his body and performing a toxicology screening, it is impossible to know what (or who) killed Ludwig. The witnesses' testimonies, though, present a robust list of suspects and details that they found suspicious enough to report to officials. They name people they vigilantly monitored at court and thought had the opportunity and motive to poison the prince. Their suspicions drew from existing stereotypes and simmering conflicts, which makes the rumors historically revealing. So, who are the suspects and what made them so suspicious?

The Suspects

Suspicion fell on a number of people, but three, in particular, garnered the most attention in the *Protocol.* Foremost are the duke and duchess of

Holstein, who are mentioned either alone or together twenty-four times. Rébénacq, too, singles them out as suspects (although he clarifies that he did not suspect them himself). He wrote, "The people's suspicions are attached to two or three people, one falling directly on the electoress, by means of the princess of Holstein, her niece, who was recently in this court."[16] Mostly the Holsteins, and particularly the duchess, are named as confidants of Ludwig who dined with him frequently or otherwise spent a great deal of time with him.

The witnesses describe moments and places of opportunity to murder the prince. Two witnesses mention a "small staircase" or "small tower" that the prince would use to possibly visit the duke and duchess of Holstein away from the eyes of other courtiers. Witnesses noted the great care and attention that the duchess gave Ludwig during his last illness. The duke and duchess were both close relatives of Electoress Dorothea; Duchess Luise Charlotte (1658–1740) was the daughter of Dorothea's sister and another relative of theirs, Ernst Günther von Schleswig-Holstein-Sonderburg-Augustenburg (1609–1689).[17] She lived for a time with her aunt in Berlin, where she, too, wed a close cousin, Friedrich Ludwig von Schleswig-Holstein-Beck (1653–1728). The obvious motive for the pair was to help their aunt increase the inheritance of their cousins to the detriment of the elector's remaining children from his first marriage, Friedrich and Ludwig. Another motive was cited later, by the classic Prussian historian Eduoard Vehse, who claimed a poisoned orange was revenge for Ludwig spurning the duchess in marriage.[18] It could not have helped their case that the duke and duchess had already left Berlin for Denmark by the time of the investigation.[19]

The next most frequently named actor is a mysterious "Tristan," of whom little else is known. In the *Protocol*, it is revealed that he was a Frenchman and a Catholic who had been particularly close with Ludwig and, for unexplained reasons, had been banned from court. However, a page named Fürstenberg related that he had secretly fetched Tristan many times, and Ludwig had received many gifts from Tristan including a writing tablet, cheese, a chamber pot, sugar, a rapier, and ten thalers.[20] The valet Johannes Heßig, who gave one of the more detailed accounts in the *Protocol*, mentioned a frequent exchange of letters between Tristan and Ludwig as well as gifts of paintings and money that sometimes Heßig himself delivered, including six hundred thalers for a New Year's gift. According to Heßig, the correspondence ceased after Ludwig had a tiff (*brouillet*) with Tristan. Would this tiff have been enough to inspire murder?

Perhaps Tristan's illicit gifts to Prince Friedrich were soft diplomacy on behalf of the French, or perhaps they were tokens of an intimate, but forbidden, friendship. The butler Egidig Strumff corroborated the belief about soft diplomacy by vaguely noting, when asked if he had any suspicions, that "he just knew about the French that had come to beg favors of the prince." Heßig tied this specific suspicion to the French association with poisoning confirmed by the *Affaire des poisons* when he said, "The French were bad, they could make all kinds of poison that would last for one, two or ten years!"[21]

The third most often mentioned person was a Polish envoy who was named eight times in the *Protocol.* He had recently been hunting with Ludwig in Potsdam, where Ludwig had borrowed a sable from him and had taken a sip from his bottle of Hungarian wine. The hunter Hennerich mentioned that they often went hunting together. At the last hunt, many witnesses related that the party drank heavily, but Ludwig, who rarely drank to excess, did not.[22] What motive might the Polish ambassador have had? One theory is that he killed Prince Ludwig in order to free Ludwig's wealthy wife, Luise Charlotte, to marry the heir to the Polish throne and claim the valuable Radziwill holdings for the Polish crown.[23] The Poles had indeed attempted a marriage alliance before she had wed Ludwig, for which her Catholic relatives had advocated vociferously.[24] Poland had reportedly put many obstacles to the union between Ludwig and Luise Charlotte.[25] Notably, after Ludwig's passing, his half-brother, Philip, was put forward as a suitor for the newly widowed Luise Charlotte, a political misstep, which added credibility to the accusations that Electress Dorothea was an opportunist in her sons' interests.[26]

The Means

The orange and coffee are the two most frequently suspected means of administering poison to the prince. The orange brought to mind the association to the family of Friedrich Wilhelm's first wife, Luise Henriette of Orange-Nassau, thus connecting the alleged murder weapon with simmering tensions between the offspring of Friedrich Wilhelm's first marriage and his new family. The most sensationalized account of Ludwig's murder came from Carl Ludwig Freiherr von Pöllnitz (1692–1775), a courtier at the court of Frederick the Great. In his eighteenth-century telling, which he claimed came from stories he heard as a child from older courtiers, von Pöllnitz referred to a *Pomeranz*, or bitter orange, as the possible murder weapon. Almost every detail in Pöllnitz's account is wrong except for the detail about the orange. Contemporary witnesses, however, refer to a different citrus, a sweet orange, or *pomme de Chine*.[27]

The *pomme de Chine* is named seven times throughout the *Protocol*. As its name implies, it was considered exotic: not just with the indication of the Chinese origin, but also in the fact that they use a French term meaning "Chinese apple." A few years prior to this, the court physician and botanist Dr. Elsholtz mentioned that these fruits were fairly new and had initially entered Europe through Lisbon.[28] There and in Spain, they had been so skillfully planted that, at the time of Elsholtz's writing, they grew abundantly all over Iberia.

Such exotic fruit was only available to the upper echelons of early modern European society, and Friedrich Wilhelm had expended a great deal of effort and expense during his reign to ensure that oranges were available in his household.[29] Oranges signaled affluence and good times and were thus a regular part of festival dining. As a frequent subject of Dutch still lifes, they brought the marvels of the expanding trade routes of the seventeenth century to the cold and gray climate of northern Europe.[30] Friedrich Wilhelm's favorite son, Karl Emil (1655–1675), had a particular fondness for oranges and he had been the one to lay the cornerstone to the new *orangerie* at the Berlin palace on July 22, 1663. This is likely where Ludwig's oranges had grown over the winter before coming to his apartment that spring.[31]

The mentions in the *Protocol* of oranges and even the waffles from Frau Bent describe an aspect of court life that is not mentioned in other household records: snacking. While some may think that snacking is a modern phenomenon, it is difficult, but not impossible, to find mentions of it in early modern records.[32] For Ludwig's snacks, oranges were delivered from the kitchens and left out for over a day in his apartments, where he was free to eat them when he chose. Other mentions of oranges in the Brandenburg-Prussian records indicate that citrus was cooked into dishes of beef tongue, sheep organs, or a tough leg of mutton.[33] The food casually left out away from the kitchen, though, opened an unmonitored opportunity for tampering.

The next most cited consumable is coffee, another foreign and still novel item in Brandenburg-Prussia and, likewise, something prepared away from the regulations of the kitchen. Dr. Elsholtz describes coffee in his 1682 *Diaeteticon* and made note of the numerous public coffeehouses

Engraving of citrus fruits, including the bitter orange, or *Pomeranze*, from Elsholtz's *Dieateticon*, p. [99]. (Bayerische Staatsbibliothek)

in London, Paris, and Amsterdam, where they distributed advertisements lauding the many health benefits of coffee. But Elsholtz makes clear that this was not the case in Berlin: "[These advertisements] spread the usefulness of these coffee beverages much further than is currently done by us: which we let be put in its place."[34] Another account credits the Huguenots immigrants to Berlin after the Revocation of the Edict of Nantes in 1685 with spreading trendy new consumables in Berlin, specifically, coffee, tea, and chocolate.[35] Princes Ludwig and Friedrich, though, already owned a coffee service by 1673.[36]

In other European contexts, too, coffee was associated with poisoning because its strong taste could mask the taste of poison. Indeed coffee had already been a suspected means of administering poison when the Electoral Prince Friedrich had fallen ill suddenly on February 7, 1679. The diarist Dietrich von Buch (1646–1647) attributed this to the fact that Friedrich ate too much, but according to Vehse, Prince Friedrich suspected his stepmother, Dorothea, had tried to poison him with coffee.[37] Buch relates that Danckelmann had many antidotes at the ready at the time, which he gave to the electoral prince and thereby, "saved him."[38] This signals that the intergenerational distrust reached back to the 1670s, but with the death of Ludwig, as Gerd Heinrich put it, "the atmosphere at court had been poisoned."[39] It was poisoned so much that it shaped the future of Prussia.

The Aftermath

The *Protocol* does not pass judgment; it presents only the answers of the witnesses who were questioned. No further investigations followed. The only recorded action taken on the part of the elector was to order that the other young princes and princesses not host any foreign guests. Furthermore, all their food was to be prepared only by the butler (*Mundschenk*) and all drinks tasted by him personally before the electoral family consumed them.[40] This would, of course, have only protected the electoral family from external danger.

Prince Friedrich became ill right after his brother's death, and he feared that he, too, was being poisoned. He sought protection from foreign courts with strained political relations with Brandenburg, including those in Hanover, the Hague, and Vienna.[41] He fled Berlin for his aunt Hedwig Sophie's protection in Hesse-Kassel and, even more to the chagrin of his father, went with his pregnant wife to his in-laws, Friedrich Wilhelm's rivals for northern hegemony, the duke and duchess of Hanover. By midsummer, even Liselotte von der Pfalz, duchess of Orleans, was commenting on Friedrich's plight from Versailles. She wrote in her characteristically acerbic wit to her beloved aunt Sophie of Hanover that she would prefer to die from poison than live among people who wanted to kill her.[42]

Prince Friedrich stayed away until his father cut off his income and his confidant, Freiherr von Danckelmann, was able to negotiate a reconciliation. Throughout the summer of their disagreement, father and son were still corresponding. Letters from both sides show they were attempting to repair the relationship, but Prince Friedrich insisted he would not return to Berlin until his safety was assured.[43] He does not specify in those letters whether he saw the threat as coming from his mother-in-law, but others reported that while in Hanover, Friedrich spoke openly of his suspicions of her. Sophie of Hanover wrote in a letter about the "*poudre de succession,*" implying Dorothea was using poisoned powder to secure her own sons' inheritance at the expense of Friedrich's.[44]

These fears were not ungrounded: Friedrich Wilhelm had indeed revised his testament to divide the territories under his personal union among *all* his sons. This would have left Electoral Prince Friedrich only the core electoral holdings, a fate that would have destabilized the northern part of the Holy Roman Empire after a half a century of recovery from the Thirty Years War and the territorial and titular gains for the elector of Brandenburg-Prussia. As Friedrich Wilhelm's biographer wrote, the tensions between Elector Friedrich Wilhelm and Electoral Prince Friedrich were not political but they became political (and political on an international level at that).[45]

Unsurprisingly, this succession crisis is the aspect of the poisoning narrative that has been of most interest to historians of Prussia. However, the traditional Borussian narrative of the rise of Prussia has obscured succession crises like this one, which presented sustained threats to the authority of the "absolute" Hohenzollern ruler from their own dynasty. A more recent historical evaluation, though, has viewed this episode as more than merely anecdotal and, indeed, as evidence of "serious dynastic problems."[46] In contrast to how others, notably Friedrich the Great two generations later, judged the Great Elector and his immediate successor Friedrich, Elector Friedrich Wilhelm did not intend to be the founder of a consolidated Prussia. If his last testament had been followed: various parts of his personal union would have been divided among his many male heirs.[47] It was Elector (and later King) Friedrich who went against his father's wishes after he died and mounted a coup, with the help of the Holy Roman Emperor, to keep control of all the lands that would eventually grow together to form Prussia.[48]

Findings

In the saga of Prussian dynastic history, Prince Ludwig is famous for the effect his death had on relations between his father and the older brother who would eventually become elector and then king in Prussia. If the shock and suspicion caused by Ludwig's untimely death had not estranged the electoral prince and his father, Friedrich may never have moved to secure all of his inheritance that would become a consolidated Prussia. Beyond this controversy in the last year of the elector's life, little is known about Ludwig. The later myths about his death are more often quoted in books about Prussia than the archived report from his murder investigation. The poison scandal of 1687 has many further layers of meaning to be explored about generational relations, gender, disability, and the culture of Friedrich's own court when he succeeded his father in 1688 and eventually became king *in* Prussia in 1713. However, for the purposes of the present book, this episode complicates the neat narrative arc of growth of Prussia over the seventeenth century. Here, the relationship between food and statebuilding, as discussed in previous chapters, is inverted: depending on others for food (or, put in other terms, having the power to compel others into one's service) invites vulnerability.

This contradiction brings into relief this book's overarching arguments about early modern society. First of all, this story illustrates a "two bodies" problem for premodern rulers: they both had physical bodies prone to the same weaknesses of any creature, and they embodied the more abstract state.[49] Barbara Stollberg-Rilinger argued that every state is a collective fiction and institutional order rests on ritual embodiments and a shared belief in these fictions.[50] Even so, although it has been noted how the records relating to dining practices at this court (as discussed in chapters 2 and 5) indicate a concern with codification and documentation as a means to control hierarchies and justify rule, this murder investigation shows that much dining at court was informal and did not conform to the ideals stipulated in the dining orders.

Food is indicative of cultural change in this period of rapid recovery and expansion of state powers in Brandenburg-Prussia. Unlike the situation at the outset of Friedrich Wilhelm's reign, when the Berlin palace and dining culture were in poor condition, solvency was not the primary concern of a court that moved freely between opulent palaces in Potsdam and Berlin, as it did at the time of the death of Prince Ludwig. A wide array of luxury goods were at the fingertips of Friedrich Wilhelm's circle, but that did not make this ruler absolute, in fact, it robbed him of control of his legacy.

The culture of the court also enabled scholars and physicians not only to provide medical care for the court, but to advance their profession to the detriment of lay medical practitioners. Around the time of Ludwig's death, the Berlin Collegium Medicum (made up of many privy doctors of the elector) petitioned Friedrich Wilhelm for exclusive oversight of all health care in the city. However, their medical knowledge was not so advanced that they recognized or could heal the life-threatening illness of Prince Ludwig. Evidence from this chapter and the chapter on Dr. Elsholtz (chapter 7) suggests that the doctors responded to the desires of their patron while working to extend medical knowledge and standardize the profession.

A diverse and cosmopolitan set of servants populated the court who, as was seen in the murder investigation and the case of Martin Hones in chapter 6, facilitated political change and cultural exchange through food. In both instances, it is Dutch foods (bread and waffles) that made an impact in the palaces of Brandenburg-Prussia, and there is no evidence yet of a taste for French haute cuisine or a mimicking Versailles's dining culture. This French flavor would come later, during the reign of Friedrich III/I and throughout the eighteenth century. The court cuisine under Friedrich Wilhelm was a mixture of frugal comfort foods (beer soup and scrambled eggs) and exotic commodities (coffee, waffles, and oranges). With regard to why members of court chose the foods they did, this episode reveals the same currents discussed in chapter 1: while luxury, exotic foods were highly valued, so too were their opposites: native, traditional foods like the Teltower turnip, beer, and big game. The diet of the Hohenzollern reflected a mixture of cosmopolitanism and local heritage.

This court, with officers from Vienna, Poland, France and other European courts, were watching and speculating on minute actions and reactions. Just as in the court of Louis XIV at Versailles, there was a culture of vigilance within the walls of the palace and beyond that marks this as a premodern society concerned with appropriate behaviors. There was an awareness from high and low members of court of the backroom gift economy that might have influenced diplomatic decisions. Public and private life mixed fluidly, and all of the culture at court was political.

Prince Ludwig's death and the ensuing succession crisis is a dramatic final act to Friedrich Wilhelm's reign. As much as the Hohenzollern had gained in stature and resources, they could not escape the physical danger in every meal, sip, or bite. A paradox of increasing one's power and court was that more hands came in contact with the ruler's food and drink: increased privilege was marked with increased dependence and danger. The investigation into Ludwig's death scrutinized the chain of contact with food but still could not overcome the constant danger of poisoning, the fear of which grew amid ignorance of toxicology testing. Ignorance breeds fear and in this case, fear propelled a new generation to take control of the direction of Brandenburg-Prussia.

THERE ARE SOME UNIVERSAL LESSONS from a study of a single food culture. For one thing: food is a cultural product. This book expresses how and why the Brandenburg-Prussian court defined and ascribed value to its edible goods. Within that society, novel and exotic foods were attractive for their exclusivity while, inversely, certain homegrown specialties were valued for placemaking and identity construction. It is clear from inventories and procurement records that members of Friedrich Wilhelm's court consumed a wide variety of plant and animal foods. While they could not strictly control what was available, their flexibility in defining edibility and their wide reach across their various territories enabled a high degree of food security. The disruptions to the food system seen in the Thirty Years War (which led to widespread malnourishment, death, and disease) were compounded by climate shifts as the globe emerged from the Little Ice Age. In some ways, stories of innovation and resilience by early modern actors who survived such difficult times can be inspiring.[51] On the other hand, it is a wakeup call to the impending upheavals in food production expected with the greater climate changes ahead.

In any premodern society, food was the largest household expense. As we saw in the case of the large household at the court of Brandenburg-Prussia, food was closely monitored and leftovers were tracked in regular accounts. Furthermore, food handlers at court paid close attention to healthy environments for the plants and animals they depended on for sustenance and made sure, for instance, not to overfish or deforest hunting grounds. While abundant and expensive food was essential to representing lordship, waste was not. Good lordship was also tight resource management. Horticultural expertise included an awareness of how difficult it was to cull food from the earth, particularly in the climate and soils of Brandenburg. All parts of animals killed for food were used and only on rare occasions were foods too rotten to be used by a part of the court economy (even if rotted food only helped to fulfill a *noblesse oblige* to give alms to the poor).

The intertwining of statecraft and medical knowledge seen in Friedrich Wilhelm's court opens questions about the role of governments in personal health and well-being. Dr. Elsholtz's dietary advice book, the *Diaeteticon*, is early proof of the long-standing connection between governance and nutritional theory. Understanding of foodstuffs and the generalized effects their components have on the human body has progressed substantially since the seventeenth century, resulting in massive gains in comfort and longevity. The questions scientists ask about food and how they categorize and value it derive from historically specific human decisions. As knowledge builds on itself, it is important to trace the educational and communication standards from which that knowledge springs. Examining dietary guidelines as cultural artifacts helps us to recognize the many actors and factors influencing ideas about health and diet.

Dr. Elsholtz's legacy is wide reaching. As someone whose scholarship contributed to dialogues about plant propagation, anatomy, and the systematic observation of natural phenomena, he was part of the development of the scientific method. More negatively, though, as the first person to inject medicines intravenously, his legacy also includes enabling millions of illicit drug overdoses.[52] Elsholtz could not have imagined such an eventuality when he first injected scurvy water into the arm of the elector's bodyguard, and it is not known how many lives intravenous medicine has saved. But, beyond the connection between the food and the development of western science, Dr. Elsholtz's court career highlights the role of social networks and court patronage in state-sponsored public health initiatives.

Another facet of the food history of Brandenburg-Prussia is the agency of food laborers. Chapters 2, 3, 4, and 6 discuss the work of growing, acquiring and cooking food for the court. In the Berlin, Königsberg, and Cleves palaces, kitchen servants were advancing their own interests while also playing a part in the development of Prussia through daily interactions that reached beyond the walls of the palace. This included servants like Martin Hones, who upset local custom and guild regulations to bake Dutch bread in Königsberg, and the kitchen clerks who used the rhetorical devices open to them in the account books to imply neglect. The elector's correspondences concerning the baker Hones and other food workers reveal a particularly early modern dynamic between those in power and their servants who shared a relationship that, while unequal and even oppressive, required proximity and reciprocal obligation. The sights, smells, and sounds of early modern Europe made the high environmental and labor costs of food an inescapable reality for even the most elite diners.

The court of Brandenburg-Prussia was transformed over the course of the seventeenth century, and its resource management, and cooking and dining practices were both indicative and constitutive of that rise on the European political stage. This transformative moment in European history helps us see that while food is a universal concern, food choice is culturally and historically specific. Ultimately, the study of the food culture of an early modern court transcends the issue of the courtly household itself to remind us that eating is more than a physical need: it is a political act.

NOTES

INTRODUCTION

1. König, *Versuch einer Historischen Schilderung*, 2:32.
2. Beger, *Thesaurus Brandenburgicus Selectus*. See also Nicolai, *Beschreibung der königlichen Residenzstädte*, 93–94; and Duchhardt, "Anspruch und Architektur," 31–52.
3. Nicolai, *Beschreibung der königlichen Residenzstädte*, 44; Clark, *Iron Kingdom*, 35n44. Franz, *Der Dreißigjährige Krieg*, 17–21. Bairoch estimated the Berlin population at 55,000 in 1700 (twelve years after Friedrich Wilhelm's death). Bairoch, *La population des villes européennes*.
4. The Borussian or *kleindeutsch* school of history that developed in the nineteenth century busied itself with determining the roots of the Prussian Empire they were living in and therefore studied premodern Brandenburg-Prussian history with a progressive agenda. Leopold von Ranke (1795–1866) described the power vacuum in northern Europe at the end of the Thirty Years War that Friedrich Wilhelm adroitly filled. Ranke focused on the necessity of territorial unification, not just for Prussia but for all of Europe to maintain peace. The prolific Prussian historian Johann Gustav Droysen (1806–1884), who is considered the father of the Borussian historians, took this premise even further to argue that in building the Prussian kingdom, the Hohenzollern had done what the Habsburgs as Holy Roman emperors had failed to do amid competition from France and England and created a unified German nation. Both historians focused on what they considered political history, that is, the history of decrees and correspondences between estates and courtiers, things that looked "official" to the eyes of the nineteenth-century administrative historian. Ranke, *Memoirs of the House of Brandenburg*; Droysen, *Geschichte der preussischen Politik*. For more on Prussian historiography, see Neugebauer, *Preußische Geschichte als gesellschaftliche Veranstaltung*.
5. Rabb, *The Struggle for Stability in Early Modern Europe*. Rabb does not mention the significant global impact of the Little Ice Age on European society, but this is a recognized root of many disturbances of the seventeenth century and, of course, had a major impact on food security and foodways. Parker, *Global Crisis*, and Behringer, *A Cultural History of Climate*.
6. For more on composite states, see Elliott, "A Europe of Composite Monarchies," and Kaiser and Rohrschneider, *Membra unius capitis*.

7. Beat Kümin offers an appropriately expansive definition for the term "political culture," which is the dominant theme of "new political history," particularly of early modern Europe. His definition, derived from Peter Burke, among others, is that political culture is "all human values, interactions, and perceptions relating to the establishment of binding rules." Kümin, "Political Culture in the Holy Roman Empire."

8. The Prussian archivist Georg von Raumer the Younger, who opened the archives in the mid-nineteenth century in order to set the constitutional foundations for Prussia, separated domestic papers from state papers. For him and subsequent historians, dynastic and domestic aspects of the court were viewed as peripheral, at best, to the overall "political" events. Neugebauer, *Preußische Geschichte als gesellschaftliche Veranstaltung*, 242.

9. Bohstedt, *The Politics of Provision*.

10. These visualizations of consumption at the palace in Königsberg, Prussia, during Friedrich Wilhelm's reign can be seen on the Königsberg Foodstuffs Database, by Molly Taylor-Poleskey and Jason A. Heppler, at https://www.taylor-poleskey.net/koenigsbergfood.html, undated. Bloch, *Feudal Society*; and Braudel, *Civilization and Capitalism*.

11. Lévi-Strauss, *The Raw and the Cooked*; for more about the rituals of the meal, see Douglas, "Deciphering a Meal."

12. Simmel, "Soziologie der Mahlzeit"; and Symons, "Simmel's Gastronomic Sociology."

13. Elias, *The Civilizing Process*, and *The Court Society*.

14. Wheaton, *Savoring the Past*; Tannahill, *Food in History*; Flandrin, "Le goût et la nécessité."

15. Kaplan, *Bread, Politics and Political Economy in the Reign of Louis XV*; Kaplan, *The Bakers of Paris*; Kaplan, *Provisioning Paris*.

16. Atorf, *Der König und das Korn*.

17. Campbell, *At the First Table*.

18. Watanabe-O'Kelly and Simon, *Festivals and Ceremonies*; Mulryne et al., *Europa triumphans*; Strong, *Splendour at Court*.

19. Stollberg-Rilinger, *The Emperor's Old Clothes*.

20. Stollberg-Rilinger, "Höfische Öffentlichkeit," 149.

21. Reinhard, "Was ist europäische politische Kultur?"

22. Emich, "Frühneuzeitliche Staatsbildung und politische Kultur."

23. Rohrschneider, "Zusammengesetzte Staatlichkeit."

24. There are excellent explorations of Prussian women's history on different aspects of court culture, from death rituals to literature. Unfortunately, these less masculine accounts do not penetrate the mainline Prussian narrative or the entrenched institutions for the study of Prussian history. Sara

Smart, "Höfische Trauer und die Darstellung der fürstlichen Gemahlin," in *Theorie und Praxis der Kasualdichtung in der Frühen Neuzeit,* ed. Chloe Andreas Keller (Amsterdam; New York: Rodopi, 2010), 277–301; and Bepler, "Welfen und Hohenzollern vom 16. bis zum 18. Jahrhundert," for two good examples.

25. See, for example, Clark, *Iron Kingdom;* Neugebauer, *Die Hohenzollern;* and Luh, *Der grosse Kurfürst.*

26. For more on the negotiated quality of early modern states, see Asch and Freist, *Staatsbildung als kultureller Prozess;* and Beik, "The Absolutism of Louis XIV as Social Collaboration."

27. Two influential calls for studying interactions up and down the social scale at court are Steege et al., "The History of Everyday Life," 376; and Holenstein's introduction, "Empowering Interactions," in Blockmans, Holenstein, and Mathieu, *Empowering Interactions,* xxxiii.

28. Steege et al., "The History of Everyday Life."

29. Siraisi, "Medicine, 1450–1620"; Cook, "Living in Revolutionary Times"; and Moran, "Patronage and Institutions."

1. To Dine with the Great Elector

1. Most of Europe was by then exhausted by war, and the Holy Roman Emperor himself stepped in to mediate the situation to avoid any further conflict in the area. Ralf-Peter Fuchs, *Ein "Medium zum Frieden": die Normaljahrsregel und die Beendigung des Dreißigjährigen Krieges* (Munich: R. Oldenbourg, 2010), 317–18.

2. During December and January, the elector was contracting the handover of the palace in Bötow (outside Berlin) to his wife while also corresponding with his privy officers about establishing court protocol for dining and for administrative committees. See Müllenmeister, "Ein Bild der Schwanenburg zu Kleve"; George, "Die ersten Regierungsjahre des Großen Kurfürsten," 374–77; McKay, *The Great Elector,* 81, 31, 170–73; and Hessische Staatsarchiv Marburg (HSTAM), Bezeichnung 117 Nr. 89.

3. Elsholtz, *Diaeteticon,* 195.

4. Adamson, *Food in Medieval Times,* 35.

5. This menu is in the personal archive of Count Georg Friedrich von Waldeck, a privy councilor of Friedrich Wilhelm. The *Küchenzettel* for that day is archived with other documents relating to an attempt to reform dining practices, discussed in further detail in chapters 2 and 3. HSTAM, Bezeichnung 117.

6. Geheimes Staatsarchiv Preußischer Kulturbesitz (GStA PK), XX HA [20th Hauptabteilung] Ostpreussische Folianten 13093–122. For the full charts of

these six hundred foodstuffs, please visit the author's online visualizations at https://www.taylor-poleskey.net/koenigsbergfood.html.

7. GStA PK, XX HA Ostpr. Fol. 13557.

8. Elsholtz draws on Johann Neuhof's travel description from his journey to China (http://www.deutsche-biographie.de/sfz99319.html). Elsholtz, *Diaeteticon*, 13.

9. Melitta Adamson, "Medieval Germany," in *Regional Cuisines of Medieval Europe* (New York: Routledge, 2002), 164. Hermann Kaiser cites the change from a meat- to a grain-based diet in the sixteenth century. Kaiser and Ottenjann, *Das alltägliche Brot*, 9. This is taken from Hans Teuteberg's periodization scheme for nutritional development across ten millennia in central Europe. Teuteberg, "The Diet as an Object of Historical Analysis in Germany," 118–19, and "Periods and Turning-Points in the History of European Diet," 11–23.

10. GStA PK, I HA Rep. 36 Nr. 1105, 3 and I HA Rep. 36 Nr. 40, 23. Court dogs received about as much baked bread as most court servants. GStA PK, I HA Rep. 36 Nr 1080, 36.

11. Elsholtz, *Diaeteticon*, 9.

12. In one of many such examples from a different war, in 1674, men are described as starving, "because they had not had bread for four days." Orlich, *Geschichte des preussichen Staates im siebzehnten Jahrhundert*, 2:129.

13. GStA PK, XX HA Ostpr. Fol. In this account, peas were still classified as "grain legumes," an inheritance from the same Renaissance classification system that Elsholtz employed in his six categories of vegetables (in which *Frumenta & Legumina* make up the first category). Elsholtz, *Diaeteticon*, 9.

14. According to a 1622 bakery account, the court bakery used five times as much rye as wheat per week, revealing that the majority of the bread was rye or pumpernickel. GStA PK, I HA Rep. 36 Nr. 1074, 55. See also Kaiser and Ottenjann, *Das alltägliche Brot*, 9. Elsholtz talks about the different types of rye bread. Elsholtz, *Diaeteticon*, 96.

15. König, *Versuch einer Historischen Schilderung*, 2:347.

16. GStA PK, I HA Rep. 36 Nr. 775, 68; Nr. 919, 62; and Nr. 1074, 55.

17. Albala, *Eating Right in the Renaissance*.

18. Marperger, *Vollständiges Küch- und Keller-Dictionarium*, 356–57.

19. "Der gemeine Mann bedienet sich der Bier-Suppen; Da dann die aus Breyhan / Tuffsein / Kniesenack / Rummeldieß / und andern dergleichen Bieren gemachte / nicht zu tadeln seyn / und sonderlich der mit Gewürtz und eingeschlagenen Eyern zugerichtete und gantz heiß eingetrunckene Kniesenack / welcher so guten *Effect* als manche warme Wein-Suppe thut und eine stattlich Stärcke in den Gliedern giebet." Ibid.

20. See, for example, Beuys, *Der Große Kurfürst*, 135; Scharfenort, *Die Pagen am Brandenburg-Preussischen Hofe*, 22; Orlich, *Geschichte des preußischen Staates*, 1:525.

21. Max Weber, *The Protestant Ethic and the Spirit of Capitalism*, trans. Stephen Kalberg (New York: Oxford University Press, 2011, rev. ed. 1920).

22. This *Früh-Trank* or "early drink" was the counterpart to the *Frühstück* (the German word for breakfast). GStA PK, I HA Rep. 36 Nr. 780, 179, specified that the "young princes" receive a "*Stüberl*" of beer "mornings for their soup."

23. Carsten, *Origins of Prussia*, 219, and Orlich, *Geschichte des Preußischen Staates*, 3:360.

24. One seventeenth-century carving manual described the proper presentation and serving of different meat dishes for over a hundred pages. The serving of cakes, in contrast, had "no great art in it." Klett, *Neues Trenchir-Büchlein*, 93–94. See Krohn, *Staging the Table in Europe*.

25. Beyond the edible uses of animal carcases, animal parts like hides and horns were fashioned into useful and beautiful objects. Animal hides provided leather for clothing and other goods. Horns and bones were combined with other materials and transformed into goblets, hooks, and drinking horns; some of these are masterpieces of German Renaissance art and are now displayed in museums. Fat could be used to make candles and soap, to polish church bells and armor, and to grease carriage wheels. Lard was also a preservative: when slathered on meat, it created a barrier from the air.

26. Rumpolt, *Ein new Kochbuch*, 1604, 2.

27. Ibid., 10.

28. GStA PK, XX HA Ostpr. Fol. 13093.

29. Elias, *The Court Society*.

30. Montanari, *The Culture of Food*.

31. There were plenty of hardwoods, whose leaves, bark, and shoots provided valuable nutrients for game, as well as many grasses and herbs. Mast-bearing trees, such as oak, European beech, and wild fruit trees, as well as berry shrubs, other plants, and mushrooms sustained the diverse selection of game animals. Mager, *Der Wald in Altpreussen*, 1:282.

32. GStA PK XX HA Ostpr. Fols. 13093–122.

33. See Johann Georg Krünitz, "Auerochse," *Oekonomischen Encyklopädie oder allgemeines System der Staats- Stadt- Haus- und Landwirthschaft* (1773), http://kruenitz1.uni-trier.de/ and http:woerterbuchnetz.de.

34. Friedrich Mager credits the aforementioned biodiversity of the Prussian forests as the reason why certain animals that are now extinct in Europe, such as aurochs, wild horses, bison, bears, beavers, and elks, survived

longer in Prussia than elsewhere. Mager, *Der Wald in Altpreussen*. The last aurochs' horn was fashioned into a prized drinking vessel, now in the holdings of the Royal Armory in Sweden.

35. GStA PK, XX HA Ostpr. Fol. 13096, 23v. This was possibly the Berbersdorf, who was a Calvinist court counselor (*Hof- und Gerichtsrat*) of Friedrich Wilhelm. *Urkunden und Actenstücke*, vol. 16, pt. 2:707. There is no record of a purchase of this animal, leading to the conclusion that it was given to the court by von Berbersdorf. GStA PK, XX HA Ostpr. Fol. 13095. At least in Poland in the sixteenth and seventeenth centuries, there were strict prohibitions (on pain of death) against not just killing an aurochs, but disturbing it in any way. It is a mystery how von Berbersdorf had access to the animal (dead or alive).

36. GStA PK, XX HA Ostpr. Fol. 13095.

37. This is a feature of Renaissance dining culture (particularly banqueting culture) according to Monika Bachtler, Dirk Syndram, and Ulrike Weinhold, *Die Faszination des Sammelns: Meisterwerke der Goldschmiedekunst aus der Sammlung Rudolf-August Oetker* (Munich: Hirmer, 2011).

38. This was the wedding of Elector Johann Sigismund (1572–1619) and Anna of Prussia (1576–1625) in Königsberg. Mager, *Der Wald in Altpreussen*, 1:286. The parade of celebratory foods included three *Auer* along with 20 elks, 10 red deer, 22 does, 36 wild boars, 29 boar piglets, 2 bear, 48 roe deer, 272 rabbits, 5 wild swans, 123 capercaillies, 279 black grouses, 433 hazel grouses, 47 gray partridges, and 413 wild ducks.

39. A sugar mold of a reclining aurochs was inventoried in the kitchen from 1631 to 1648. GStA PK, XX HA Ostpr. Fols. 13091–97.

40. Paul Freedman employs this formula to explain the popularity of spices in European cuisine. Freedman, *Out of the East*, 224.

41. This included capercaillies, grouses, partridges, bustards, geese, doves, and ducks.

42. Schubert, *Essen und Trinken im Mittelalter*, 127.

43. This expense report excludes bread, wine, beer, vinegar and vegetables. GStA PK, I HA Rep. 36 Nr. 1066, [101–4]. The numbers in brackets represent hand-counted page numbers in a document with unnumbered pages.

44. Esholtz, *Diaeteticon*, 194.

45. Kissane, *Food, Religion and Communities in Early Modern Europe*.

46. Hugo Landwehr, "Das Kirchenregiment des großen Kurfürsten," in *Forschungen zur brandenburgischen und preussischen Geschichte* (Berlin: Duncker & Humblot, 1889), 2:600–610; and J. J. Herzog, Albert Hauck, and Hermann Caselmann, *Realencyklopädie für protestantische Theologie und Kirche* (Leipzig: J. H. Hinrichs, 1896), 593.

47. Ibid.

48. Orlich, *Geschichte des preußischen Staates,* 1:586.

49. See also Albala, "Ludovicus Nonnius and the Elegance of Fish."

50. The butter would have been fresh or preserved with salt and was stored in the cool of the underground beer cellar at Königsberg, likely in wooden tubs. GStA PK, XX HA Ostpr. Fols. 13117 and 13107. Lydia Petranova, "From Traditional to Industrial Milk Processing," in *Food and Material Culture: Proceedings of the Fourth Symposium of the International Commission for Research into European Food History* (East Linton, UK: Tuckwell Press, 1998), 272.

51. For a ratio comparison, the other foods consumed that day were: 1 quarter of beef, 8¾ sheep, 2 turkeys, 13 chickens, 100 eggs, 2 sides of bacon, 1 bratwurst, 2 sides of pickled ham, 8 lemons, 13 pounds of dried cod (*Stockfisch*), 140 plaice, 22 pounds of plums, 1 dried salmon, 2 quarters of deer calf, 3 quarters of roe deer, and 4 partridges. HSTAM Bezeichnung 117 Nr. 2170.

52. Marperger, *Vollständiges Küch- und Keller-Dictionarium,* 185.

53. GStA PK, XX HA Ostpr. Fols. 13069, 13094, 13102-9.

54. Elsholtz was personally aware of the difference between the olive oil in Italy (where he studied) and the olive oil available in Berlin.

55. In all court accounting records, it is listed among the other exotic, imported condiments, such as capers, olives, and prunes. GStA PK, I HA, Rep. 36 Nr. 775, 61-64, and Nr. 1066, [15-22]; XX HA EM 50a Nrs. 57 and 160, Ostpr. Fol. 13091-122.

56. Elsholtz, *Diaeteticon,* 259.

57. Ibid.

58. Butter was made in Prussia and transported to electoral residences in other lands: for example, in 1672 to Berlin (GStA PK, I, HA Rep. 36 1066 [118]) and in 1680 to Potsdam (GStA PK, XX HA EM 50a Nrs. 71 and 96) and Berlin (GStA PK, I HA Rep. 36 Nr. 1109 [4]).

59. For more on the sources for butter and other foods, see chapter 4 on the court food supply system, GStA PK, I HA Rep. 21 13b 1, Fasc. 3, Blatt 1 [55].

60. GStA PK, XX HA Ostpr. Fol. 13099.

61. Ibid., Fol. 13096, for example.

62. Furthermore, Grefflinger advised that cheese and butter not be put on the same plate; "Some people may want just one and not the other. As cheese and butter have different temperaments, it might disgust the diner to have them touch each other." Grefflinger, *Ethica Complementoria,* 128.

63. GStA PK, I HA Rep. 36 Nr. 775, 62v-63.

64. "In unsern Nordländern brauchen wir die Butter nicht allein al seine Arzney / und Condiment: sondern auch gar al seine Speise: herggeben in den heissen Ländern halt man sie mehr für eine Medicin / oder machete

nur einige gewisse Speisen damit ab." Elsholtz, *Diaeteticon*, 133. Marperger noted that "in some places, they are still in the habit of eating butter for dessert, which they present at the table molded in forms such as lions, sheep, fish, birds and flowers." *Vollständiges Küch- und Keller-Dictionarium*, 185.

65. The Königsberg annual kitchen ledger for 1641 noted that the high table ate thirteen wheels of Edamer, the pastry chef took three wheels of cheese for a journey, Lord Leuchtmar received one wheel for a picnic (*auf die kalte Küche*), and an envoy to Warsaw took twenty wheels as provisions (potentially to be used as gifts to the king of Poland). GStA PK, XX HA Ostpr. Fol. 13093. There are other recorded instances of cheese given as a diplomatic gift. For example, the Medici were known to have sent Parmesan, mozzarella, and other Italian foodstuffs to foreign allies. Cassidy-Geiger, *Fragile Diplomacy*, 9.

66. Valenze, *Milk*, 83.

67. De Vries, *Dutch Rural Economy*.

68. The court also imported cheeses from England, Sweden (Limburg), and Italy (Parmesan). GStA PK, I HA Rep. 36 Nr. 1083, 5; HSTAM Bezeichnung 117 Nr. 2170.

69. GStA PK, XX HA Ostpr. Fol. 13093. In 1641 in Königsberg, the electoral table consumed 22 pieces of "big" sheep cheese (2 pieces fell on the ground and were ruined) and 1,101 pieces of "small" sheep cheese went to the kitchen (164 additional pieces were ruined and eaten by rats). My research has not uncovered what the terms "big" and "small" cheese meant (although they appear repeatedly in kitchen accounts). I am hedging a guess that they mean aged and fresh cheese.

70. See the GStA PK, XX, HA Ostpr. Fol., and HA EM 50a Nrs. 68 and 80 for examples of *Deputat* receipts. For *Knapkäse* descriptions, see Grimm and Grimm, *Deutsches Wörterbuch von Jacob und Wilhelm Grimm*, 11:1349–50; Goltz, *Handbuch der gesamten Landwirtschaft*, 586.

71. Elsholtz, *Diaeteticon*, 244.

72. HSTAM Bezeichnung 117 Nr. 2170.

73. Mennell, *All Manners of Food*, 51–54; Wheaton, *Savoring the Past*.

74. Freedman, *Out of the East*, 2, 103; Toussaint-Samat, *A History of Food*, 494.

75. François Pierre de La Varenne's *Le cuisinier françois* of 1651 is the most famous literary expression of this food "revolution." See also Peterson, *Acquired Taste*.

76. Johnson, *The German Discovery of the World*, 143–44.

77. Heinzelmann, *Beyond Bratwurst*, 85. There is a tremendous amount of debate about when French classical cuisine really took off in the seventeenth century, as cookbook authors who espoused its principles in their front

matter often did not reflect the rhetoric of new, more skillfully produced food in their actual menus. See Hyman and Hyman, "La Chapelle and Massialot," and Mennell, *All Manners of Food*, 75–83.

78. König, *Versuch einer Historischen Schilderung*, 2:319.

79. GStA PK, XX HA Ostpr. Fol. 13100, 3 and 5.

80. This number reflects the relative consumption of spices without sugar. For details, see the Königsberg Foodstuffs Database, https://www.taylor -poleskey.net/koenigsbergfood.html.

81. Heinzelmann, *Beyond Bratwurst*, 85.

82. Elsholtz, *Diaeteticon*, 245.

83. The practice of handling sugar with other spices went back to the medieval period. Henisch, *Fast and Feast*, 105.

84. Mintz, *Sweetness and Power*.

85. See Königsberg Food Database, https://www.taylor-poleskey.net/koenigsbergfood.html.

86. Flandrin, "L'ordre de succession des mets en France," and *Arranging the Meal*.

87. Coutts and Day, "Sugar Sculpture, Porcelain and Table Layout." See GStA PK, XX HA Ostpr. Fol. for inventories of wooden molds. One famous example of such a display of sugar sculptures was at the wedding of Johan Wilhelm, duke of Jülich-Cleves-Berg (1562–1609), and Jakobea of Baden (1558–1597) in 1685 in Düsseldorf, at which guests were expected to break the sculptures for souvenirs. Reed, *The Edible Monument*, 29.

88. To capitalize on the growing taste for sugar, Friedrich Wilhelm attempted to stimulate the economy of the Mark Brandenburg with a new beet sugar refinery.

89. See, for example, the recipes for veal, wild boar, ox, and pork. Elsholtz, *Diaeteticon*, 387.

90. Almost all the honey accounted for in the Königsberg palace went into the "New Year's dough." GStA PK, XX HA Ostpr. Fol. for 1631, 1646, 1651–52, and 1655. It is nearly impossible to pinpoint when sugar eclipsed honey in Friedrich Wilhelm's territories because of their different units of measure (sugar was weighed and honey was measured by liquid capacity of volume) and also because of their different sucrose concentrations.

91. Orlich, *Geschichte des preußischen Staates*, 1:583. This New Year's treat was baked as early as the plagues of the fourteenth century. According to local lore, during a plague year, each loaf was designated for a particular friend or neighbor. If a loaf cracked in the oven, that served as an omen that the loaf's intended recipient would die in the coming year. This story from 1575 was reprinted in David, *Preussische Chronik*, 8:92–99.

92. Rudolf Holberg, Ursula Hoberg, and Jürgen Folz, "Gemüse," in *Duden, Deutsches Universalwörterbuch* (Mannheim: Dudenverlag, 2011), 697.
93. Kirchschlager, *Ich will ein guter Koch sein,* 131.
94. Ibid.
95. Johann Heinrich Zedler, "Zugemüse, Zumus, Mußwerck, oder Zukost," in *Grosses vollständiges Universal-Lexicon aller Wissenschafften und Künste, Welche bißhero durch menschlichen Verstand und Witz erfunden und verbessert worden* (Leipzig, 1737), 63:1227–28.
96. Elsholtz, *Diaeteticon.* Marperger does use the word *Zugemüse* to define cress as, "im Frühling fast das erste kleine Salat-Kraut / und war vor Zeiten der Perser Zugemüse / as welche nach demm Zeugniß *Platonis.*" Marperger, *Vollständiges Küch- und Keller-Dictionarium,* 668 and 1337.
97. "Vegetable," *Online Etymology Dictionary,* www.etymonline.com.
98. See, for example, GStA PK, XX HA Ostpr. Fol. 13100.
99. "An allerleÿ Gartten gewächs, kömbt die Noturfft, aus den Gärtten." GStA PK, I HA Rep. 36 1066 [104]. This was part of the problem of the lack of accountability for natural wares (or products procured *in natura*) that court administrators and reformers complained of when trying to reform court finances in this period.
100. Albala, *Eating Right in the Renaissance,* 91.
101. Grieco, "The Social Politics of Pre-Linnaean Botanical Classification," 135.
102. Marperger, *Vollständiges Küch- und Keller-Dictionarium,* 689.
103. Günter Duwe, *Das Teltower Rübchen* (Teltow: Teltower Stadt-Blatt Verlags- und Presse, 2005).
104. Elsholtz, *Diaeteticon,* 23.
105. Elsholtz, *Hortus Berolinensis.* STABI Ms. Boruss. Qu. 12, 215, and *Vom Garten Baw,* 1666, 384.
106. Elsholtz, *Diaeteticon,* 24.
107. The Königsberg accounts record common white (or green), Savoy, red, and, of course, sauerkraut (sometimes referred to as *sauer kohl*) as well as other cole crops of kale, broccoli, cauliflower, brussels sprouts, and Swiss chard.
108. Davidson, "Europeans' Wary Encounter."
109. Kiple and Ornelas, *The Cambridge World History of Food.*
110. GStA PK, XX HA Ostpr. Fols. 13075–131.
111. Elsholtz, *Diaeteticon,* 352.
112. The expert source he quotes from is Peter Lauremberg (1585–1639), a professor in Rostock. Elsholtz, *Diaeteticon,* 31.

2. Someone's in the Kitchen

1. The kitchen alone was 20–30 percent of overall expenses. This range is derived from a sample of four annual budgets of direct kitchen expenses

(*Küchengelder*) in 1673, 1674, 1679, and 1680. GStA PK, I HA Rep. 36 Nr. 39, 48–49; I HA Rep. 36 Nr. 40, 56–57; I HA Rep. 36 Nr. 47, [14]; and BPH Rep. 35 B Nr. 8, [676–77]; GStA PK, BPH Rep. 35 B. Nr. 8, 1–16.

2. There are notable exceptions, such as Pennell, *Birth of the English Kitchen*, and Kühn, "Die Macht der Diener."

3. Scappi, *Opera de Bartolomeo Scappi*; and Messisbugo, *Banchetti*.

4. Rumpolt, *Ein new Kochbuch*.

5. Kühn, "Die Macht der Diener."

6. The Palaces and Gardens Foundation of Berlin-Brandenburg (SPSG) has a few silver and glass table ornaments and drinking vessels in their collections, and the Oranienburg and Köpernick palaces have a few pieces of furniture on display (but no dining table) from the time of Elector Friedrich Wilhelm.

7. Peter Bahl's extensive prosopography is a notable exception, and even though he has missed some of the servants named in the archives of Friedrich Wilhelm's reign, his work is very useful for seeing connections between people through marriage and office. Bahl, *Der Hof des Grossen Kurfürsten*.

8. Kühn, "Die Macht der Diener."

9. André Holenstein, "Introduction: Empowering Interactions: Looking at Statebuilding from Below," in Blockmans, Holenstein, and Mathieu, *Empowering Interactions*, xxxiii.

10. Stollberg-Rilinger, *The Emperor's Old Clothes*, 133.

11. Stollberg-Rilinger, "Höfische Öffentlichkeit," 148. Stollberg-Rilinger writes that the Great Elector was making a "planned ascent to the circle of sovereigns" by enacting these strategies.

12. GStA PK, BPH Rep. 35 B Nr. 8, 1–16 (*Hofordnungen* of 1652 and 1656).

13. For more on the undocumented female kitchen workers, see Michael Pölzl, "Von Obersthofmeisterinnen, Hofzuckerbäckerinnen und Leibwäscherinnen. Der Wiener Hof als Arbeitsplatz für Frauen—Möglichkeiten und Grenzen (1700–1750)," *Österreichische Zeitschrift für Geschichtswissenschaften* 33 (2022), 11–34. Thanks to Sebastian Kühn for the reference.

14. "2. Topff und ein Klein Junge, 1 Pasteten becker junge, 1 Ritter Kochs Knechts junge, 1 Aufspülerin, 2 bratenwender, 1 Einheitzer, 1 angewelbe, 1 Waßerzieher." GStA PK, BPH Rep. 35, 8 and 13. For a comparison under the previous elector, Georg Wilhelm, in 1640, see GStA PK, XX HA EM 50a Nr. 21, 50–56.

15. "1. Bradt Junge, 2. Ein Ritterkochts Knecht, 3. Ufspielern, 4. kleine Junge, 5. Bratenwender, 6. Ritterkochsjunge, 7. Pastetenbeckers Junge, 8. Hoffschlachters Knechte, 9. Ufwarter im Wiltbret gewölbe, 10. Die Ein Keufferin, 11. Hoffschlechters Junge, 12. Küchen thür knecht, 13. Hoz- und Kohlenträger." GStA PK, I HA Rep. 36 Nr. 775, 120–21v.

16. The reform account that is quoted here lists eight menial kitchen servants who between them would share six dishes. The silver- and tinware washers received even less food per person (three dishes for six people). GStA PK, I HA Rep. 36 Nr. 919, 35. Peter Bahl has also transcribed a list of servants who got a food allowance from 1656, which also lists a number of menial kitchen servants, including two silver servants, a confectioner's servant, a bread carrier (*Brotträger*), one silver and one tin washer (both female), a knights cook's servant, a butcher's boy, and two servants each in the wine and beer cellars. Bahl, *Der Hof des Grossen Kurfürsten*, 371.

17. König, *Versuch einer Historischen Schilderung*, 402–6.

18. See Müller, *Der Fürstenhof in der Frühen Neuzeit*, 20. The eighteenth-century lexicographer Krünitz defined a kitchen boy (*Kuchenjunge*) as "angenommen nurs als ein Handlanger, Holz und kohlen zu tragen, Feuer anzumachen, Wasser zu hohlen, und andere dergleichen Dienste in einer küche zu verrichten, oder auch die Koch-Kunst selbst zu erlernen, da ihm dann reinliche Arbeit angewiesen ist, als: Hasen, Hühner und andere Braten zu spicken, mit dem Backwerke umzugehen, u. d. gl." Johann Georg Krünitz, Hans-Ulrich Seifert, and Hagen Reinstein, "Oekonomische Encyklopädie oder allgemeines System der Staats- Stadt-, Haus- und Landwirthschaft in alphabetischer Ordnung" Online Edition of the Universität Trier, 1773, 54, 314, http://kruenitz1.uni-trier.de/. I could not find a definition of the *Topfjungen* in other sources. For an appointment of two *Topfjungen*, Conrad Brandt and Jacob Bleyer, in 1677, see GStA PK, I HA Rep. 36 Nr. 1017. This document, unfortunately, does not describe the duties of the job.

19. Havemann, *Geschichte der Lande Braunschweig und Lüneburg*, 191. Spiel, ed., "Herzog's Georg Wilhelm zu Celle hohe und niedere Minister und Diener und deren Besoldung, vom Jahre 1682," 308–20.

20. Furthermore, Georg Wilhelm's gardening staff included many French and Italian gardeners, while the Berlin palace gardens favored local and Dutch gardeners. See chapter 4 for more about the palace gardens.

21. See Bahl, *Der Hof des Großen Kurfürsten;* and Almer, "Zur Struktur und Organisation."

22. This was to have been funded by the 180,000 thalers anticipated combined income from manorial estates, taxes, tolls, and privileges. There seems to be an addition error, since the sum of expenses is 172,000 thalers, not 176,000 as König transcribed it and as I also read it in the original document. König, *Versuch einer Historischen Schilderung*, 2:273. GStA PK, BPH 35 B Nr. 8 [67–72]. See GStA PK, I HA Rep. 36 Nr. 1066 [51–56] for a 1627 comparison; GStA PK, I HA Rep. 36 Nr. 777, 24v–25v for 1665–66; GStA PK, I HA Rep. 36 Nr. 29, 72 for 1669; GStA PK, I HA Rep. 36 Nr. 777, 50 for 1670; GStA PK, I HA 36 Nr. 919, 5 for 1672; GStA PK. I HA Rep. 36 Nr. 29, 88 for 1679; and GStA PK, I HA Rep. 36 Nr. 775, 132–33 for 1659.

23. The other expenses were 2.8 percent each to the stable master, handwork-
    ers, general expenses and debts; 17.4 percent to the granary (likely for oats
    to feed horses); 10.5 percent to winter livery; and 12.8 percent to servants'
    salaries. König, *Versuch einer Historischen Schilderung,* 2:273, or GStA PK,
    BPH 35 B Nr. 8 [67–72]. To expand on this, we can look at the relative
    expenses in 1665–66, 1667, and 1670 in GStAa PK, I HA Rep. 36 Nr. 777,
    24v–25; GStA PK, IHA Rep. 36 Nr. 777, 38v–39; and GStA PK, I HA Rep.
    36 Nr. 777, 50.
24. Bahl, *Der Hof des Großen Kurfürsten,* 90.
25. GStA PK, BPH Rep. 35 B. Nr. 8, 13–16.
26. Müller, *Der Fürstenhof in der Frühen Neuzeit,* 21.
27. Alexander August Mützell and Leopold Krug, *Neues topographisch-
    statistisch-geographisches Wörterbuch des preussischen Staats,* vol. 1 (Halle:
    Karl August Kümmel, 1821), 9.
28. More on the court baker at the residence in Königsberg is in chapter 6.
29. GStA PK, I HA Rep. 9 F1, Fasz. 2 [22–23].
30. GStA PK, I HA Rep. 9 E7 [3–6].
31. GStA PK, XX EM 50a 80, 23–25. These were made with beef and had a rye
    crust.
32. Hörmann, "Die Königliche Hofapotheke in Berlin."
33. I say "other" spices because sugar was always cited among lists of *Gewürze*
    consumed by the court. Sugar was used in the apothecary in mixtures or
    pills to help the medicine go down. "Zucker heissen in der Apothecke
    unterschiedliche Zubrereitungen [. . . illegible]." Johann Heinrich Zedler,
    *Zedler Johann Heinrich Zedlers Grosses vollständiges Universallexicon aller
    Wissenschafften und Künste,* n.d., vol. 63, p. 0529, zedler-lexikon.de.
34. GStA PK, I HA Rep. 36 Nr. 1066 [121–22].
35. The synonym, *Zuckerbäcker,* appears in some later court correspondence
    concerning foreign and local bakers of *Pfefferkuchen* in Berlin. GStA PK,
    I HA Rep. 9, JJ Nr. 14.
36. The *Apoteke und Condit Cammer* shared the same accounting line in a
    1627–28 record. GStA PK, I HA Rep. 36 Nr. 1066, 51–56. See also Almer,
    "Zur Struktur und Organisation."
37. Krünitz also assigns the task of decorating the table to the *Konditor.*
38. GStA PK, I HA Rep. 36 Nr. 948, 52.
39. GStA PK, I HA Rep. 36 Nr. 948, 74.
40. GStA PK, I HA Rep. 36 Nr. 946, 6.
41. GStA PK, I HA Rep. 36, Nr. 948, 75–80, and 100–101, a decree of 1699,
    refers to "Regina Tiegelin, gewesene Hoff Conditorin," which might con-
    note that she was the widow of a court confectioner.
42. Bahl, *Der Hof Des Grossen Kurfürsten.* Rainer Müller claims this was be-
    cause it was beneath the nobility to deal with commerce and to keep house;

these types of tasks were completed by commoners. Müller, *Der Fürstenhof in Der Frühen Neuzeit*, 20. The steward was not listed in the 1657 order of procession during ceremonies: GStA PK, BPH Rep. 35 B. Nr. 8, 14. Immediately beneath the *Oberhofmarschall* were the *Schloßhauptmann* (this was a position particular to the Berlin palace) and the *Oberschenk*. Bahl claims these positions were not as important as the *Oberhofmarschall* as they were filled with younger members of the lower nobility. The *Oberschenk* served drinks from the *Schenktisch*, or buffet credenza, to the elector.

43. Müller, *Der Fürstenhof in der Frühen Neuzeit*, 20. For these roles under Elector Johann Sigismund (1572–1619), see Isaacsohn, *Das preußische Beamtenthum*, 1:22–23.

44. Graupius's 1664 contract reiterated the place of the steward in the hierarchy of the court administration: he would first of all obey the elector and his officers, then the *Hofmarschall* and *Schloßhauptmann*. GStA PK, I HA Rep. 36 Nr. 974, [67].

45. GStA PK, I HA Rep. 21 Nr. 13b 1, Fasc. 3 [55]. Oranienburg also sold some grains to the court this year.

46. GStA PK, I HA Rep. 36 Nr. 974 [35–38].

47. Hönn, "Koch," in *Betrugs-Lexicon*.

48. Graupius's birth and death dates from Wagner, *Das Königsberger Schloss*, 187.

49. GStA PK, I HA Rep. 36 Nr. 974 [54].

50. Ibid. [52]. Graupius's appointment as steward in 1664 (upon the death of Schmoll) did grant him more payment in kind, consisting of an ox, two sheep, twenty tons of "lordly" or *Herren* beer, four *Achtell* butter, a tun of salts, 360 pieces of cheese, and two *viertalls* of oats daily (for his horses). Ibid. [65].

51. Wagner, *Das Königsberger Schloss*, 187. See also Kühn, "Masters as Debtors of Their Servants in Early Modern Brandenburg and Saxony."

52. GStA PK, I HA Rep. 36 Nr. 3027: "Benutzung des Lusthauses im Lustgarten in Königsberg als Wohnung durch den Küchenmeister Daniel Graupius."

53. GStA PK, I HA Rep. 36 Nr. 974 [57].

54. GStA PK, I HA Rep. 36 Nr. 974 [65].

55. Bahl, *Hof des Grossen Kurfürsten*, 91.

56. Arnold Körte, *Martin Gropius: Leben und Werk eines Berliner Architekten 1824–1880*. Berlin: Lukas Verlag, 2013.

57. P. Bahl, *Hof des Grossen Kurfürsten*, 489–90. His property at Gertraudenstraße 16 was expanded in 1671 with a purchase of a small garden from the court butcher Galle Gerigke. That garden was next to one owned by the court chaplain Johann Kunschius.

58. GStA Pk, I HA Rep. 36 Nr. 974 [78].
59. Stollberg-Rilinger, "Höfische Öffentlichkeit."
60. Albala, *Banquet*, 139.
61. Müller, *Der Fürstenhof in der frühen Neuzeit*, 20–21.
62. There was also an "assistant kitchen clerk" and a separate "fish clerk" (*Fischschreiber*) on the payroll in 1652 and 1655. Erdmannsdörffer, "Zur Geschichte der Kammerstaats-Reform," 570–73.
63. GStA PK, XX HA Ostpr. Fol. 13124 [50v]: "Von höltzern Formen ist alles von den Würmen verzehret, und nichts mehr verhanden."
64. Kopytoff, "The Cultural Biography of Things," 67.
65. Ibid., 66–67.
66. Bruno Blondé and Ilja Van Damme, "Retail Growth and Consumer Changes in a Declining Urban Economy: Antwerp (1650–1750)," *Economic History Review* 63, no. 3 (2010): 644.
67. Ago, *Gusto for Things*, 9.
68. Riello. "Things Seen and Unseen," 127.
69. GStA PK, XX Ostpr. Fol. 13124, 51: "von Blech über Zint" and "Einn *Servis* von Blech über Zinnt in Einer höltzern Lahden."
70. "Tin," in Holleman and Wiberg. *Lehrbuch der Anorganischen Chemie*, 793–800. In his late eighteenth-century lexicon, Johann Krünitz defines a *Zinnblech*, which was beaten into sheets to strengthen pots, jars, pitchers, and a number of other things.
71. Roche, *History of Everyday Things*, 242.
72. Roche also notes that stationary lamps increasingly replaced candelabras and other sources of light that were mobile. Ibid., 112.
73. To see this table, visit Königsberg Foodstuffs Database, https://www.taylor-poleskey.net/koenigsbergfood.html.
74. Riello, "Things Seen and Unseen," 127.
75. Scappi and Scully, *The Opera of Bartolomeo Scappi*.
76. GStA PK, XX HA Ostpr. Fol. 13094, 4v. Most of the kitchen clerks were simultaneously responsible for the court fisheries.
77. "Das Küchen *Inventarium* fleisig bewahren, davon nichts wegkommen lassen." GStA PK XX HA Ostpr. Fol. 13043, 273.
78. Wagner, *Das Königsberger Schloss*, 187.
79. GStA PK, I HA Rep. 36 Nr. 1112.
80. Ibid.
81. Wagner, *Das Königsberger Schloss*, 187.
82. Ibid.
83. GStA PK, XX HA Ostpr. Fol. 13098.
84. Transcription of 1652 court order from Cleves, in König, *Versuch einer Historischen Schilderung*, 312. "Specification aller Churf. Bedienten in der Chur

B'burg anno 1656," transcribed in P. Bahl, *Der Hof des Grossen Kurfürsten*, 362–69. Originals in GStA PK, BPH Rep. 36, B 6 [138r–141v], and GStA PK, I HA Rep. 9, H2, Fasz. 1. "Graupius Kuchschreiber, wird Reise Kuchemeister mit der aussicht auf das Kuchemeister amt in Preußen a. 1657. Den 14. Decembris Ad. 1657," in GStA PK, I HA Rep. 36 Nr. 974, 52–53.

85. GStA PK, I HA Rep. 36 Nr. 974, Fol. [57].
86. The Mühlenhoff was the site where provisions arrived and were distributed within the Berlin residence. Ibid., and GStA PK, I HA Rep. 9, H2, Fasz. 1.
87. GStA PK, XX HA Ostpr. Fol. 13043, 273.
88. Birth and death years quoted from P. Bahl, *Der Hof des Grossen Kurfürsten*, 774.
89. Rumpolt, *Ein new Kochbuch* [10].
90. Bahl, "Die Berlin-Potsdamer Hofgesellschaft," 42.
91. See chapter 6 for the Maastricht baker Martin Hones, who came with Luise Henriette when she left the Netherlands for Brandenburg-Prussia.
92. GStA PK, I HA Rep 36 Nr. 972, 25.
93. See the book's conclusion, and BPH Rep. 35 Nr. 334: "Acta betr.: die vermeintliche Vergiftung des Markgrafen Ludwig, 1687."
94. GStA PK, I, HA Rep. 36 Nr. 919, 53; and HA Rep. 36 Nr. 780, 179.
95. Peter-Michael Hahn, "Die Hofhaltung der Hohenzollern. Der Kampf um Anerkennung," in Bahners and Roellecke, *Preussische Stile*, 73–89; Lademacher, *Oranien Nassau* and *Onder den Oranje Boom*.
96. GStA PK, I HA Rep. 36, H2 Fasz. 1, as quoted in P. Bahl, *Der Hof des Grossen Kurfürsten*, 366.
97. GStA PK, I HA Rep. 36 Nr. 972, 27–31.
98. GStA PK, I HA Rep. 92; König, Versuch einer Historischen Schilderung, 369, P. Bahl, *Der Hof des Grossen Kurfürsten*, 374.
99. P. Bahl, *Der Hof des Grossen Kurfürsten*, 374, quoting GStA PK, I HA Rep. 92 Nr. 369; and GStA PK, I HA Rep. 972, 33.
100. The road was likely between Schleusengraben and (Nieder)Wallstaße and can be seen in the 1688 plan of Berlin from Schulze, "Kreuzgasse in Mitte," in *Berlin von A Bis Z* (Berlin: Zepter und Krone, 2008); and Heiko Noack, "Berliner Stadtrundgang 1690," Stiftung Stadtmuseum Berlin, accessed April 8, 2022, https://www.stadtmuseum.de/objekte-und-geschichten/berlin-stadtrundgang-1690.
101. Schachinger, *Die Berliner Vorstadt Friedrichswerder*, 71.
102. Ibid., 70–71.
103. Ibid.
104. GStA PK, I HA Rep. 21 Nr. 191 b, 153–54, as quoted in Schachinger, *Die Berliner Vorstadt Friedrichswerder*, 68–69.
105. Ibid.

106. Schachinger, *Die Berliner Vorstadt Friedrichswerder,* 84, as quoted from Nicolai, *Beschreibung der königlichen Residenzstädte,* 1:152.
107. Schachinger, *Die Berliner Vorstadt Friedrichswerder,* 77.
108. GStA PK, I HA Rep. 36 Nr. 972, 38–39.
109. GStA PK, I HA Rep. 36 Nr. 972, 46.
110. Steege et al., "The History of Everyday Life," 376.

3. The Field and Forest and River Richly Provide

The title of this chapter is an excerpt from Bödiker, *Einzug und Feuerwerck, als* [. . .] *Friderich* [. . .] *Chur-Printz zu Brandenburg,* [. . .] *Seine allerliebste Gemahlinn, die* [. . .] *Sophia Charlotta, geborne Hertzoginn zu Braunschweig und Lüneburg* [. . .] *mit allgemeiner Freude heimführete* (Cölln an der Spree: Georg Schultze, 1684).

1. One *Last* was equivalent to 60 *Scheffel* of grain and each *Scheffel* is approximately 55 liters, making 50 *Last* about 165,000 liters, according to Heidecke, "Alte Maße Altpreußens," 54.
2. GStA PK, I HA Rep. 36 Nr. 1066, 61.
3. Ibid. [63–66]. November 18, 1630, extract from the letter of the high councilors in Königsberg.
4. Ibid. [67–68]. Letter from *Amtskammer* in Cöln an der Spree to Georg Wilhelm, November 26, 1630.
5. Palfox y Mendoz, "Juicio interior secreto de la monarquía para mí solo," appended to José Maria Jover Zamora, "Sobre los conceptos de monarquia y nación en el pensamiento político español del XVII," *Cuadernos de historia de España* 13 (1950): 145–46, as quoted by Elliott, "A Europe of Composite Monarchies," 71.
6. Elliott, "A Europe of Composite Monarchies."
7. See Theibault, "Germany, Early and Medieval Periods," 406. This binary distinction has been criticized as too narrow, but the *Gutsherrschaft* model fits this explanation of agricultural possessions of the elector Brandenburg. See Wunder, "Agriculture and Social Change."
8. For more specifics about this diverse and complex economic economic system see, for example, Eddie, *Freedom's Price.*
9. Wunder, "Agriculture and Social Change," 71; Hagen, *Ordinary Prussians,* 36.
10. Escher, *Berlin und sein Umland,* 60; McKay, *The Great Elector,* 112–13; and Michael North. "Germany, Early and Medieval Periods," in *Oxford Encyclopedia of Economic History,* 404.
11. Although these contributions were a legal obligation, the court had to maintain a balance in setting the terms of the contributions so as not to overburden struggling farms or cause the noble, landed estates to revolt.

12. During the Second Northern War, this office was streamlined to manage the elector's income from all of his territorial holdings and the wider-reaching *Hofkammer* took over. See Bahl, *Der Hof des Grossen Kurfürsten,* 115; and Clark, *Iron Kingdom,* 61.

13. Heinrich Berghaus, "Mölenammet und Mölenhof," in *Der Sprachschatz der Sassen, ein Wörterbuch der plattdeütschen Sprache in den hauptsächlichsten ihrer Mundarten* (Brandenburg: Müller, 1880), 642–43.

14. Peter Bahl claimed that although this office did not officially belong to the highest rung of court offices, its importance was unquestionable. Bahl, *Der Hof des Grossen Kurfürsten,* 48.

15. These wares were either directly used by the court household or were paid out as part of the salaries of the court servants (known as *Deputat*).

16. Hammer, *Kurfürstin Luise Henriette.*

17. Wiesner, *Early Modern Europe, 1450–1789,* 406–7.

18. Theibault, "Germany, Early and Medieval Periods," 407. Orlich, *Friedrich Wilhelm der Grosse Kurfürst,* 440.

19. Personal communication with Mary Lindemann, July 16, 2023, about her study of the aftermath of the war in Brandenburg, 1648–1721.

20. GStA PK, I HA 94 IV Hc 7 and 8. There is too little written in these two account books by Luise Henriette to be able to assess much about the details of her administration of Oranienburg.

21. GStA PK, I HA Rep. 21 13b 1, Fasc. 3, Blatt 1. In 1655, Oranienburg had also been paid (in cash) for grains delivered to the court in Berlin.

22. McKay, *The Great Elector,* 110.

23. GStA PK, XX HA Ostpr. Fol. 13236 implies that at least honey was delivered to Königsberg from those local estates.

24. GStA PK, I HA Rep. 36 Nr. 779 [119]. This is a record for the provisioning of the court household and marshal with grains and grain feed.

25. H. W. Koch, *A History of Prussia* (London; New York: Longman, 1978), 25.

26. Mundy, *The Travels of Peter Mundy,* 4:90–92.

27. See chapter 1.

28. GStA PK, I HA Rep. 36 Nr. 1066 [109]; and I HA Rep. 36 Nr. 1109.

29. GStA PK, I HA Rep. 36 Nr. 1066 [116, 118]. When these 66 tons of butter and 210 sides of bacon reached Berlin, the steward and clerk were instructed not to give out the provisions to anyone—not even to pay a *Deputat* to the court servants—because they were to be transported to Hornburg, presumably to supply the war effort.

30. GStA PK, I HA Rep. 36 Nr. 1109.

31. GStA PK, XX HA EM 50a Nrs. 71 and 96.

32. Letter from Kneyer (or Knyer) in Prussia to Friedrich Wilhelm, October 11, 1862, GStA PK, I HA Rep. 36 Nr. 1109 [4]

33. GStA PK, I HA Rep. 36 Nr. 1065 [67–68].

34. See Schulze, "Von der Mark Brandenburg zum Preußenstaat," 52; Isaacsohn, *Geschichte des preussischen Beamtenthums*, 2:254. The hypothesis that administration was centralized even under King Friedrich Wilhelm (1713–1740) has also been disputed. Rodney Gothelf, "Frederick William I and the Beginnings of Prussian Absolutism, 1713–1740," in *The Rise of Prussia: 1700–1830*, ed. Philip G. Dwyer (New York: Longman, 2000), 47–67; Neugebauer, *Zentralprovinz im Absolutismus*.

35. Johannes Bödiker, *Einzug und Feuerwerck* (Cölln an der Spree: Georg Schultze, 1684).

36. Schevill, *The Great Elector*, 374; König, *Versuch einer historischen Schilderung*, 2:228, 362, 525; Opgenoorth, *Friedrich Wilhelm*, 2:325; Vehse, *Preussische Hofgeschichten*, 143.

37. König, *Versuch einer historischen Schilderung*, 2:243. See the final chapter for more on the poison scandal.

38. Elsholtz, *Vom Garten-Baw*, 347–48.

39. See chapter 7.

40. König mistranscribed *Taffelzeug* (tableware) as *Kaffeezeug* (coffee ware) in a 1673 dining order made by Friedrich Wilhelm regarding dining protocol at his sons' table. König, *Versuch einer historischen Schilderung*, 2:362. Compare with the original, GStA PK, BPH Rep. 35 Nr. 42.

41. Leti, *Ritratti*, 1:391.

42. Elsholtz, *Diaeteticon*, 323.

43. HSTAM Bezeichnung 117 Nr. 2170.

44. Elsholtz, *Diaeteticon*, 368, 370, and 377.

45. GStA PK I HA Rep. 36 Nr. 1066 [45–48].

46. Isinglass was used as a gelling and clarifying agent in desserts and other dishes, while juniper berries frequently flavored meat roasts.

47. König, *Versuch einer Historischen Schilderung*, 2:146.

48. Even though given to flattery, Elsholtz could not claim that Brandenburg wine could compete with wine produced elsewhere: he said it was the worst of the "lesser" wines and might, with time and thanks to the elector's prodigious efforts, improve in time. Elsholtz, *Diaeteticon*, 318–19.

49. Records of wine purchases include GStA PK, I HA Rep. 36 Nr. 42; I HA Rep. 36 Nr.919, 61; I HA Rep. 36 Nr. 950, 13; I HA Rep. 36 Nr. 1065 [51–52], [54], [73]; I HA Rep. 36 Nr. 1074, 46 and 55; XX HA Ostpr. Fols. 13557 and 13566.

50. Elsholtz, *Diaeteticon*, 312.

51. Volker Henn, "Der hansische Handel mit Nahrungsmitteln," in *Nahrung und Tischkultur im Hanseraum* (Münster: Waxmann, 1996), 23–48.

52. GStA PK, I HA Rep. 36 Nr. 1080, 26; I HA Rep. 36 Nr. 1065, [73]; I HA Rep. 36 Nr. 1065, [56]; I HA Rep. 36 Nr. 950, 13.

53. Johann Georg Krünitz, "Zerbster," in *Oekonomischen Encyklopädie* (1773).

54. Kindermann, *Lob-Gesang des Zerbster Biers.*
55. GStA PK, I HA Rep. 36 Nr. 1074, 46 and 55.
56. GStA PK, I HA Rep. 36 Nr. 1065 [25–26]. In the 1673–74 order, there were also three barrels of "Breyhan" beer. König, *Versuch einer historischen Schilderung,* 2:345–46.
57. GStA PK, I HA Rep. 36 Nr. 1083, 2–5 1602 kitchen inventory; HSTAM 117 Nr. 2170 1651–52 kitchen account; Elsholtz, *Diaeteticon,* 135.
58. An engineer from the Piedmont region of Italy, Philippe de Chieze, managed the technical aspects of the earthworks, and a Dutch shipbuilder, Michael Smids, built the locks. Mittenzwei and Erika, *Brandenburg-Preußen,* 73–75.
59. See McKay, *The Great Elector,* 182; and Rachel, "Der Merkantilismus in Brandenburg-Prueßen."
60. McKay, *The Great Elector,* 183.
61. For the foundational argument about the reciprocal relationship of environment and humanity, see White, "American Environmental History: The Development of a New Historical Field."
62. Michael Rohrschneider, "Die Statthalter des Großen Kurfürsten als außenpolitische Akteure," in Kaiser and Rohrschneider, *Membra unius capitis,* 233.
63. H. G. Koenigsberger, "Dominium Regale or Dominium Politicum et Regale: Monarchies and Parliaments in Early Modern Europe," in *Politicians and Virtuosi,* 1–25. More recently, see Kaiser and Rohrschneider, *Membra unius capitis.*
64. Elliott, "A Europe of Composite Monarchies," 69–70.

4. Prince of the Living World

1. GStA PK, I HA Rep. 36 Nr. 2879, 49.
2. Ibid.
3. Seidel, "Lustgarten am Schlosse in Berlin," 3:103.
4. GStA PK, I HA Rep. 36 Nr. 2879, 33.
5. Cunningham, "The Culture of Gardens," 39.
6. The garden in Königsberg was also renovated for Friedrich Wilhelm's mother early in his reign and bears many similarities to the Berlin garden project. Wagner, *Das Königsberger Schloss,* 227–31.
7. Seidel, "Der Lustgarten am Schlosse in Berlin," 91.
8. Opgenoorth, *Friedrich Wilhelm,* 2:67.
9. Seidel, "Lustgarten am Schlosse in Berlin," 93.
10. König, *Versuch einer Historischen Schilderung,* 2:248.
11. Seidel, "Lustgarten am Schlosse in Berlin," 94.

12. Ibid.; and GStA PK, I HA, Rep. 36 Nr. 2879 [13].
13. Seidel, "Lustgarten am Schlosse in Berlin," 100; and Nadler, "Der Lustgärtner Michael Hanff und seine Familie," 151.
14. Hammer, *Kurfürstin Luise Henriette;* and Goldgar, *Tulipmania.*
15. Michael Hanff was one of the gardeners killed in the 1655 fire.
16. This occurred sometime before the end of 1645. Nadler, "Lustgärtner Michael Hanff," 145–61. Royer published a well-circulated description of the gardens of the Hessen court: *Beschreibung des ganzen fürstl.*
17. Bahl, *Der Hof des Grossen Kurfürsten,* 89; and Wiesinger, *Das Berliner Schloss,* 88.
18. For more on Elsholtz, see chapter 5.
19. Wiesinger, *Das Berliner Schloss,* 88–101.
20. Ibid., 91.
21. Elizabeth Hyde, "Introduction: Views and Perspectives of the Renaissance Garden, 1400–1700," in *A Cultural History of Gardens in the Renaissance,* 1–16; and, in the same volume, Luke Morgan, "Design," 26.
22. Johnson, *Nature Displaced, Nature Displayed,* 3.
23. Elsholtz, *Hortus Berolinensis,* trans. Fischbacher and Fink; and Elsholtz, *Hortus Berolinensis: erstes Buch,* trans. Mundt and Humar.
24. STABI, Ms. Boruss. Qu. 12.
25. *Plantae Singulares Horti Electoralis Brandenburgici Coloniensis pro Eystettensis Appendice,* STABI Ms. Boruss. Fol. 450. This fragmentary manuscript contains watercolors of forty-five plants in the elector's garden (which, according to its title page, were not printed in the earlier 1613 *Hortus Eystettensis,* describing plants in the bishop's garden in Eichstätt in Bavaria). See Krausch, "Die Pflanzen des Elsholtz-Florilegiums 1659/1660." *Plantae Singulares* has been digitized and is freely available online in the Staatsbibliothek zu Berlin's digital collection.
26. This work went through multiple editions (in 1666, 1672, 1684, 1690, and in a combined edition with his dietary manual in 1715). Elsholtz, *Vom Garten-Baw.* The dietary manual will be discussed further in chapter 7.
27. Johnson, *Nature Displaced, Nature Displayed,* 4–5.
28. Elsholtz, *Hortus Berolinensis: erstes Buch,* trans. Mundt and Humar, 69.
29. *Hortus Berolinensis,* STABI Ms. Boruss. Qu. 12, 243–46.
30. Ibid., 71. This statement corresponds with court administrative documents that indicate fruit arriving at court from the administrative districts. In preparation for the return of the court to Königsberg in late September 1655, the court ordered the *Amt* administrator in Marienwerder on the far western outskirts of Prussia to supply twenty tons of apples (half of them Borsdorfer apples) and twenty tons of "good pears." GStA PK, XX HA EM 50a Nrs. 71 and 92.

31. I counted 205 plant foods in the catalog. This number does not include the many different kinds of apple trees, for example, because Elsholtz only cataloged "garden and wild apples" (even though he listed several dozen specific varieties in *Vom Garten-Baw*). *Hortus Berolinensis*, 178–79, and *Vom Garten-Baw*, 263–65. Edibility is a culturally specific classification; therefore the "edibility" of a plant here is determined by the more detailed plant description Elsholtz provides in his later work on plants in the Mark Brandenburg.

32. Elsholtz, *Vom Garten-Baw*, 133.

33. Ibid.

34. Elsholtz, *Hortus Berolinensis*, 203 and 233; and *Vom Garten-Baw*. 1684, 131 and 133. *Doll* was an early modern spelling of the word *toll*, which means "great" in German. The eggplant is an example of an unfamiliar foreign food that took many centuries to be assimilated into European cuisine (outside of Spain), according to Alan Davidson, because there was no similar precedent. Davidson, "Europeans' Wary Encounters."

35. Heilmeyer and Humm, "Wie sich die Kartoffel in Brandenburg verbreitete," in their *König & Kartoffel*, 43–46.

36. Elsholtz, *Hortus Berolinensis*, 231: "*Solanum tuberosum esculentum*, Nachschatten mit knolligen würzeln zur speise dienlich, Grublinger Erdbirnen, Tartuffoli."

37. Elsholtz, *Vom Garten-Baw*, 131–32.

38. It is possible that potatoes were also purchased by the Königsberg palace kitchen in 1663. The annual kitchen register records that 11 thaler 19 gulden were paid that year for "Erdtäppell," another common name for potatoes in the seventeenth and eighteenth centuries. GStA PK, XX, HA Ostpr. Fol. 13100, 4.

39. Elsholtz, *Hortus Berolinensis*, 139; and *Vom Garten-Baw*, 229.

40. *Vom Garten Baw*, 131 and 133.

41. *Hortus Berolinensis*, SBB PK, MS. Boruss Qu. 12, 129.

42. Elsholtz, *Diaeteticon*, 54.

43. Elsholtz, *Hortus Berolinensis*, 201–2; s.v. "Beans," in Kiple and Ornelas, *Cambridge World History of Food*.

44. Elsholtz, *Vom Garten-Baw*, 229.

45. Ibid.

46. Ibid, 225.

47. GStA PK, I HA Rep. 36 Nr. 775, 63v–64; I HA Rep. 36 Nr. 780, 175; I HA Rep. 1066 [105–6]; XX HA EM 50a Nr. 57, 160–61; XX HA Ostpr. Fol. 13075–131.

48. GStA PK, I HA Rep. 36 Nr. 948, 52: contract with the confectioner Johann Tiegeln, July 27, 1647.

49. Ibid., 71: Friedrich Wilhelm to the *Amtskammer* in Berlin from Königsberg, September 18, 1656.
50. Ibid., 73: Friedrich Wilhelm to the *Amtskammer* in Berlin from Königsberg, August 13, 1657.
51. Ibid. These four apple varieties were listed as among "the most popular" by Elsholtz, *Vom Garten-Baw*, 263–64.
52. GStA PK, I HA Rep. 36 Nr. 2879, 36a.
53. Elsholtz, *Vom Garten-Baw*, 5.

5. Feasts and Everyday Dining

1. *Ausführlicher Bericht.*
2. Friedrich and Smart, *The Cultivation of Monarchy and the Rise of Berlin*, 44–45.
3. GStA PK, BPH Rep. 35 B Nr. 8, 20–42: *Hoffordnung*, September 21, 1665.
4. See Streich, "Fürstliche Repräsentation und Alltag am Hofe," 140.
5. Simmel, "Soziologie der Mahlzeit." See also Barlösius, *Soziologie des Essens;* and Kolmer and Rohr, *Mahl und Repräsentation.*
6. Douglas, "Deciphering a Meal."
7. Paravicini, *Alltag bei Hofe*, 9.
8. Emich, "Frühneuzeitliche Staatsbildung und politische Kultur," 195.
9. Alf Lüdtke, "Introduction: What Is the History of Everyday Life and Who Are Its Practitioners?" in *The History of Everyday Life*, 7.
10. Steege et al., "The History of Everyday Life."
11. Newton, *Hinter den Fassaden von Versailles.*
12. For example, Barbara Stollberg-Rilinger has written about a particular case in which the leaders of Protestant Ulm in 1546 were made to kneel and perform the ritual of *deditio* before the emperor in order to make their surrender to him after a defeat of the Schmalkaldic League. The ritual had to be slightly altered in order to accommodate concerns of the Protestants about idolizing a secular ruler. In this way, the *deditio* ritual was agreeable to all participants, but still carried the weight of a traditional surrender. Stollberg-Rilinger, "Kneeling before God—Kneeling before the Emperor," in *Resonances: Historical Essays on Continuity and Change (Ritus et Artes. Traditions and Transformation)*, ed. Nils Holger Petersen (Turnhout: Brepols, 2011), 149–72.
13. For more on festival literature, see Watanabe-O'Kelly and Simon, *Festivals and Ceremonies.*
14. Friedrich Wilhelm's court published relatively few festival descriptions relative to peer courts. For example, there are approximately twice as

many published festival books from the Saxon court as from the Brandenburg court. See ibid.

15. Zwantzig, *Ceremoniale Brandenburgicum,* 31.

16. Ibid., 19 and 186.

17. Ibid., 185.

18. Oelrichs, "Historische Nachricht von dem raren Buche."

19. Ibid., 539–40.

20. Ibid., 539.

21. Zwantzig, *Ceremoniale Brandenburgicum,* 13–14.

22. Scharfenort, *Die Pagen am Brandenburg-Preussischen Hofe,* 22.

23. Meiselman, *Dimensions of the Meal,* 313.

24. Elsholtz, *Diaeteticon,* 338. GStA PK, I HA Rep. 36 Nr. 40, 32. By the end of Friedrich Wilhelm's reign, there is evidence that he did not eat this meal every day. König, *Versuch einer Historischen Schilderung,* 2:282.

25. Schmidt, "'weil kuchen und keller die herrn reich und arm machen'"; and Kern, ed., *Deutsche Hofordnungen.*

26. Jacobsen, "Die Blütezeit der Residenzkultur im 17. und 18. Jahrhundert," 55.

27. Karl-Heinz Ahrens, "Hofordnungen," in *Lexikon des Mittelalters,* ed. Robert Auty (Munich: Artemis-Verlag, 1991), 74.

28. I say approximately ten because there is room for interpretation as to what qualifies as a court order. It was not a standardized document, even at just one court in a contained period. There is no fixed name for these types of orders throughout the century and a variety of terms are used to describe them, such as *Ordnung, Hofordnung, Verordnung, Hofstadts Reformation, Hofstats Reduction,* and *Hoffstaatsordnung.* These can be found at GStA PK, I HA Rep. 36 Nr. 27, 8; I HA Rep. 36 Nr. 775, 59, and 120–21; I HA Rep. 36 Nr. 919, 35; BPH 35 B Nr. 8, 13; BPH Rep. 35 B Nr. 8, 20–42; XX HA EM 50a Nr. 21, 50–56. The parts of court orders I discuss below pertain particularly to dining and food distribution, and I exclude parts of the court orders that deal with other aspects of household management such as income, horse feed, and court payrolls. I also include records that are not court orders per se but which provide similar information about dining, such as receipts, menus, and indices of diners.

29. GStA PK, I HA Rep. 36 Nr. 27, 8.

30. Scharfenort, *Pagen am Brandenburg-Preussischen Hofe,* 22.

31. Ibid., 30. In the September 1665 court order described at the start of this chapter, the steward was to send food to the hall (*Sahl*) for the nobility, the court parlors (*Hoffstuben*) for the servants, or "wherever else food was to be brought."

32. Elector Georg Wilhelm ordered that his court marshal and a particular "Herr von Brunne" have the leftover dishes (from the princely tables)

at their lodgings. GStA PK, XX HA EM 50a 21, 50–56: "in des Hl. Hoff-marschallen und Herrn von Brunne logementen die abgesezte Eßen."

33. GStA PK, I HA Rep. 36 27, 8. The Stadtholder, as the stand-in for the ruler, also ate at a *Tafel*. When the elector was traveling, for example in 1615, when he traveled between Berlin and Königsberg, his was the only *Tafel* in an entourage with ten *Tische* for the accompanying officers and servants. The electoress and electoral prince, who remained behind, dined at two *Tafeln*, with nine *Tische* for the remaining members of the court.

34. Krünitz, "Tisch" and "Tafel," in *Oekonomischen Encyklopädie*.

35. In his late eighteenth-century lexicon, Krünitz specifies many ways that bread names can be applied, one of which is by use. His examples are: *Commißbrod, Gesindebrod, Herrenbrod, Hunde-Brod, Kaffee-Brod,* and *Pferdebrod*. Krünitz, *Oekonomischen Encyklopädie*, 6:721.

36. At least early in the century, five times as much rye was used in the court bakery as wheat flour, signifying that the majority of the bread was rye or pumpernickel bread. GStA PK, I HA Rep. 36 Nr. 1074, 55; Elsholtz, *Diaeteticon*, 96. One recipe for *Semmel* called for beating down the rising dough and leaving it to leaven five times before baking. Marperger, *Vollständiges Küch- und Keller-Dictionarium*, 1083. According to Elsholtz, *Herren-Brodt* belonged to the first order of bread. Quoting from Galen, Elzholtz claimed it was the *panem primarium,* which would only be laid before the most genteel guests at banquets. *Diaeteticon,* 95. Krünitz is also not entirely explicit in describing exactly how *Herrenbrodt* differed from other breads and defined it simply as "bread that is meant for the table of the lord, in contrast to *Gesindebrod*. A fine white bread that tends to be baked for distinguished gentlemen." *Oekonomische Encyklopädie,* 6:721. For specific mentions at Friedrich Wilhelm's court, see GStA PK, I HA Rep. 36 Nr. 919, 62, and Nr. 775, 68.

37. See GStA PK, I HA Rep. 36 2, 36–37, for more on the distinctions between *Jungbier* and *Speisebier*. Also I HA Rep. 36 Nr. 1065 [25–26] 1628–29; XX HA EM 50c, 18.

38. GStA PK, I HA Rep. 36 Nr. 947, 6.

39. GStA PK, I HA Rep. 36 Nr. 919, 7.

40. König, *Versuch einer historischen Schilderung,* 2:282.

41. Ibid., 2:284.

42. Ibid., 2:282.

43. This was listed as "*Mundtkoch zu kochen.*" GStA PK, I HA Rep. 36 Nr. 919, 61.

44. HSTAM Bezeichnung 117 Nrs. 89 and 2170.

45. HSTAM Bezeichnung 117 Nr. 89.

46. Veblen and Chase, *The Theory of the Leisure Class.*

47. Laurence Fontaine, *Alternative Exchanges: Second-Hand Circulations from the Sixteenth Century to the Present* (Berghahn Books, 2008).

48. Timothy J. Tomasik, "Fishes, Fowl, and *La Fleur de Toute Cuysine:* Gaster and Gastronomy in Rabelais's Quart Livre," in *Renaissance Food from Rabelais to Shakespeare: Culinary Readings and Culinary Histories,* ed. Joan Fitzpatrick (Burlington, VT: Ashgate, 2010), 25–51.

49. See chapter 1.

50. For the instruction of the princes at the table of their parents and guardian, Otto von Schwerin, see his diary of their education, *Briefe aus England über die Zeit von 1674–1678,* transcribed in Orlich, *Geschichte des preußischen Staates,* vol. 1.

51. GStA PK, XX HA EM 50a 21, 50.

52. Ibid., 51.

53. Ibid.

54. Rabb, *The Struggle for Stability.*

55. Smart and Friedrichs. *The Cultivation of Monarchy,* 44–45.

6. The Northern War and the Prussian Bread War

A version of this chapter was published as "A Baker, the Great Elector and Prussian State-Building in the Everyday," *German History* 37, no. 1 (2019): 17–31, reprinted by permission of the German History Society and Oxford University Press.

1. GStA PK, XX HA EM 50b 3, 104: Martin Hones to Elector Friedrich Wilhelm, July 1, 1669.

2. Ibid.

3. Rulers generally responded favorably to supplications. Würgler, "Bitten und Begehren," 38.

4. GStA PK, XX HAEM 50b 3, 86: Elector Friedrich Wilhelm to Bogislaw Radziwill, April 15, 1667.

5. Examples of this classic centrist approach with regard to Prussia's territorial integration include Droysen, *Geschichte der preußischen Politik,* vol. 3; and Hajo Holbonn, *History of Modern Germany, 1840–1945* (New York: Knopf, 1969).

6. See, for example, Carsten, *Origins of Prussia;* Rosenberg, *Bureaucracy, Aristocracy, and Autocracy;* and Baumgart, *Ständetum und Staatsbildung in Brandenburg-Preußen.* Not all recent Prussian historians agree with this theory; see for example Hagen, *Ordinary Prussians.*

7. Beik, "The Absolutism of Louis XIV"; Kettering, *Patrons, Brokers, and Clients in Seventeenth-Century France;* and for the German perspective, Asch and Freisch, *Staatsbildung als kultureller Prozess.*

8. Kümin, "Political Culture in the Holy Roman Empire," 134.
9. Blockmans, Holenstein, and Mathieu, *Empowering Interactions.*
10. See Emich, "Frühneuzeitliche Staatsbildung und politische Kultur."
11. Emich, "Frühneuzeitliche Staatsbildung," 196.
12. Hones later called himself the electress's *Mundbecker* in 1657. GStA PK, XX HA EM 50b 3, 100, 2. The *Mundbecker* was responsible only for the needs of the ruler or ruling family, as opposed to a *Hofbäcker* or *Backmeister,* who was responsible for the bread for an entire court.
13. Gause, *Die Geschichte der Stadt Königsberg,* 441.
14. In early modern Europe, it was common practice for nobility and royalty to move frequently for family reasons, for education, for reasons of state, and for health. These mobile nobles brought retinues of servants, including chefs and bakers, who were instrumental in cultural exchange throughout Europe through their language, practices, and tastes.
15. The *Bürgerrecht* was granted on September 27, 1657, and Radziwill was appointed on October 1. See GStA PK, XX HA EM 50b 3, 111, Beilage sub NB and 1105, 5, Beilage 1.
16. GStA PK, XX HA EM 50b 3, 111. Hones called the citizenship "very expensive" in a later appeal—indeed, his yearly salary as Luise Henriette's *Mundbecker* was fifty thalers. Ibid., 100.
17. GStA PK, XX HA EM 50b3, 117 and 121; and I, HA Rep. 36 1105, 5.
18. Contract record: GStA PK, XX HA Ostpr. Fol. 13569; XX HA EM 501 80, 85 (*Deputat* receipt from October 4, 1651); XX HA EM 50b 3, 65; and Wagner, *Das Königsberger Schloss,* 18–90.
19. GStA PK; XX HA EM 50 80, 85; XX HA EM 50b 3, 65; and XX HA Ostpr. Fol. 13227, 105. For Grabe's history, see Wagner, *Das Königsberger Schloss,* 190.
20. GStA PK, I HA Rep. 36 Nr. 974 [78].
21. Carsten, *Origins of Prussia,* 209.
22. Gause, *Die Geschichte der Stadt Königsberg,* 480.
23. Ibid., 481.
24. Ibid. Building Fort Friedrichsburg enabled Friedrich Wilhelm to get around the terms of the Peace of Oliva, which said he could not keep an armed guard in Königsberg. Construction on Fort Friedrichsburg also began in 1657.
25. Ibid. Gause quotes from an unnamed source that the trades "were imprisoned as if with a chain" and excluded from the fort. Presumably, this is from the *Bedenken* or other official complaint that the estates lodged in 1661.
26. Ibid., 482–83.
27. See GStA PK, XX HA Ostpr. Fol.; and Stein, *Das alte Königsberg,* 88.
28. Stein, *Das alte Königsberg,* 82.

29. GStA PK, XX HA Ostpr. Fol. 13569, 363.
30. Story related by von Rekoski, "Ein mittelalterliches Volksfes." See also Rachel, "Handel und Handelsrecht von Königsberg."
31. For more on the communal rites of Carnival, see Muir, *Ritual in Early Modern Europe;* Burke, *Popular Culture in Early Modern Europe;* and Davis, *Society and Culture in Early Modern France.*
32. *Kringel* were circular pretzels that were a specialty of Königsberg and often found on the shop signs or signets of a baker. See Frischbier, "Kringel," in *Preussisches Wörterbuch,* 1:430.
33. The *Stritzel* was 4¾ Ellen (approximately 5½ meters), according to H. Frischbier, "Stritzel," in ibid., 2:382.
34. "Die Städte Königsberg klagen absonderlich, dass auf Kurfürstlicher Freiheit Handwerker, Schenken und Händler, welche mit Gewerksgerechtigkeit, Rollen und Freiheiten versehen worden, zu Hunderten ihr Wesen treiben, so dass sie neben ihnen nicht aufkommen können." See "Bedenken der Stände über die übrigen Punkte der kurfürstlichen Proposition. Praes. Königsberg 12 Juli 1661," in *Urkunde und Aktenstücke,* 15:521–31.
35. GStA PK, I HA Rep. 36 Nr. 1105, 4. The decree was given by Radzilwill, who presumably acted on instructions from Friedrich Wilhelm.
36. Herms Bahl records many hundreds of Ansbacher with particular privileges from the margrave and very few instances of complaint by the city craftspeople. Bahl, *Ansbach.*
37. Scott, *Weapons of the Weak.*
38. GStA PK, XX HA EM 50b 3, 102.
39. Ibid.
40. Rubel, *Bread,* 20.
41. Hönn, *Fortgesetztes Betrugs-Lexicon,* 49.
42. Carsten, *Origins of Prussia,* 219; and Orlich, *Geschichte des Preußischen Staates,* 3:360.
43. Von Krünitz, "Backen," in *Oekonomischen Encyklopädie oder allgemeines System der Staats- Stadt- Haus- und Landwirthschaft.*
44. Middleton, "How It Came," 354.
45. C. Müllerum, "Brodt- und Semmel Rechnung, wie die Becker bey der Churfürstl. Brandenb. Resdez-Städte Berlin und Cölln an der Spree, das Brod und die Semmel nach dem Gewicht backen . . . vom 20ten Juni 1626," in *Corpus Constitutionum Marchicarum* (Berlin, 1740), 625–32.
46. GStA PK, XX, EM 50b 3, 107.
47. The guilds did not always adhere to quality controls either, it should be noted. See Ogilvie, "Rehabilitating the Guilds."
48. GStA PK, XX HA EM 50b 3, 105.

49. "Bedenken aller Stände. Preas. 11. Oktober 1657," in *Urkunden und Akten-stücke*, 15:403.

50. In the terms of the resolution, the elector agreed to call parliament every three years and obtain its approval to raise taxes for war unless he deemed the taxes absolutely necessary (which, in essence, gave him ultimate control). The estates agreed to pay seventy thousand thalers annually until 1666 and, most important, to swear an oath of fealty to Friedrich Wilhelm as their sovereign ruler. This compromise conceded enough for parliament to agree to a very public acknowledgment of Friedrich Wilhelm's sovereignty, but was vague enough to invite a second flare-up between the elector and parliament a decade later.

51. "Kurfürstliche Resolution. Dat. Königsberg 1. Mai 1663," *Urkunden und Aktenstücke*, vol. 16, no. 2:417.

52. McKay, *The Great Elector*, 21.

53. GStA PK, XX HA Ostpr. Fol. 13043.

54. Ibid., and GStA PK, I HA Rep. 36 Nr. 1105, 12.

55. The kitchen account shows that twenty-one marks went to the *Backmeis-ter* "Merten" Hones for milk and yeast for these baked goods on December 24. GStA PK, XX HA Ostpr. Fol. 13576.

56. GStA PK, I HA Rep. 36 Nr. 1105, 3.

57. GStA PK, I HA Rep. 36 Nr. 1106, 13.

58. Ibid., 3.

59. GStA PK, I HA Rep. 36 Nr. 1105, 2.

60. Ibid., 3.

61. Ibid., 4.

62. Ibid., 6.

63. GStA PK, I HA Rep. 36 Nr. 1106, 3.

64. GStA PK, I HA Rep. 36 Nr. 1022.

65. GStA PK, I HA Rep. 36 Nr. 1023. Letter of Hones's widow to Friedrich Wilhelm, March 22, 1685. (Her own name is never given. Even after she remarried, she referred to herself as "Hones's remaining widow.")

66. Ibid. Friedrich Wilhelm to the Prussian governors, January 29, 1685.

67. Ibid. Letter of Ernst von Croy to Friedrich Wilhelm with Hones's widow's supplication, March 3, 1685.

68. Ibid.

69. Ibid. Handwritten letter of Friedrich Wilhelm to Prussian governors, October 28, 1685.

70. Ibid. Letter of the four high councilors in Königsberg, November 26, 1685.

71. He eventually ended up in Berlin. There was a question about what to do with Hones's daughter and with the children of Hones's widow and Zoll. GStA PK, I HA Rep. 36 Nr. 1023.

72. Ibid. Letter of the four high councilors (*Oberräte*) in Königsberg, November 26, 1685. Berovsky is also variously spelled Bersowski, Brühofsky, Brohsofsky, Brahofsky, Bersoffski, Brusofski, Brosofski.

73. These two patents were signed by a judge in Berlin, April 12, 1688. Ibid.

74. GStA PK, XX HA EM 50b 3, 125. Letter of the *Oberräte* to Friedrich III, July 6, 1690.

75. Ibid.

76. GStA PK, XX HA EM 50b 3, 127. Letter of the *Oberräte* to Friedrich III, October 8, 1691.

77. Robisheaux, *The Last Witch of Langenburg.*

78. Other historians have noted the extraordinary quantity of administrative correspondence that Friedrich Wilhelm wrote himself. Rohrschneider, *Der Große Kurfürst,* 227. The ambassador of the Holy Roman emperor wrote of him in 1663, "I am amazed at this elector, who delights in long accounts of minute detail and expressly demands such from his servants. He reads, considers, and takes care of everything; he combines one thing with another and neglects nothing." As quoted in Gloger, *Friedrich Wilhelm,* 158.

7. The Great Elector's Legacy

1. Pufendorf arrived from Sweden (where he had also been the historiographer royal) only a few months before Friedrich Wilhelm's death. As privy councilor to Friedrich III, Pufendorf completed and published his biography of Friedrich Wilhelm, *De rebus gestis Frederici Wilhelmi Magni* (Berlin: Joannis Schrey, 1695). See too Fischer, "Die offizielle brandenburgische Geschichtsschreibung."

2. Fehling, *Urkunden und Actenstücke,* vol. 20, pt. 2:1065–70. Reports of François de Pas de Feuquières, comte de Rebenac, envoy extraordinary of Louis XIV from December 1685.

3. November 29, 1681, Poley to Conway, British Library, Add. Ms. 37986, as quoted by McKay, *The Great Elector,* 236n9.

4. Elsholtz, *Diacteticon,* 1682 [iv].

5. Artelt, *Medizinische Wissenschaft,* 1:22.

6. Privy Councilor Meinders to Count von Waldeck, January 19, 1684, as quoted in Arthur Strecker, *Franz von Meinders, ein brandenburgisch-preussischer Staatsmann im siebzehnten Jahrhundert* (Duncker und Humblot, 1892), 97n3.

7. Marion Mücke, "Johann Sigismund Elsholz. Kurfürstlich brandenburgischer Hofmedikus zu Cölln an der Spree in der zweiten Hälfte des 17. Jahrhunderts," in Hilber and Taddei, *In fürstlicher Nähe—Ärzte bei Hof (1450–1800),* 171–88.

8. Axel Klausmeier, "Johann Sigismund Elscholtz-'Botanicus,'" in Hingst und Heilmeyer, *Schön und nützlich,* 88.

9. See Mücke, "Johann Sigismund Elsholtz."

10. See Siraisi, *Medieval and Early Renaissance Medicine,* 62. In Wittenberg, Elsholtz contributed to the 1642 dissertation of Martin Heins, *De Quatuor Monstris* (Frankfurt an der Oder: Eichhorn, 1642).

11. Elsholtz, *Anthropometria accessit doctrina naevorum* (Patavii: Typis M. Cadorini, 1654); Elsholtz, *Anthropometria, sive, de mutua membrorum corporis humani proportione, & naevorum harmonia libellus.* (Frankfurt an der Oder: Prælo Andreæ Becmani, 1663); Elsholtz, *Anthropometria sive de mutua membrorum corporis humani proportione, & naevorum harmonia libellus* (Stadae: apud Ernestum Gohlium, 1672); Jean Antoine Rampalle, Nicola Spadoni, and Elsholtz, *Höchstfürtreflichstes chiromantisch- und . . . . Anthropometrie oder Meßkunst des menschlichen Körpers* (Nürnberg: Zieger, 1695).

12. Elsholtz, Werner Rolfinck, and Georg Wolffgang Wedel, *Destillatoria curiosa* (Berlin: Typis Rungianis, impensis Ruperti Volcheri, 1674); Elsholtz and Thomas Sherley, *The Curious Distillatory* (London: Printed by J.D. for Robert Boulter, 1677); Elsholtz, *De Phosphoris Observationes* (Berlin: Schultz, 1681).

13. Mücke, "Johann Sigismund Elsholtz," 173.

14. Ibid., 175.

15. Ibid., 187.

16. SBB PK, Ms. Boruss. Fol. 233, 20–21 (list of rarities owned by Elsholtz, perhaps at the time of his death). For more on collecting in this period, see Findlen, *Possessing Nature* and "The Economy and Scientific Exchange in Early Modern Italy," in *Patronage and Institutions,* 5–24.

17. Winau, "Leibärzte des Großen Kurfürsten" and *Medizin in Berlin.*

18. Winau, *Medizin in Berlin,* 25.

19. Winau cites three letters he believes indicate Mentzel's disdain for Elsholtz in "Medizin und Botanik am Hof des Großen Kurfürsten," 105–6.

20. Winau, "Medizin und Botanik am Hof des Großen Kurfürsten," 104.

21. Winau, *Medizin in Berlin,* 31.

22. Elsholtz, *Clysmatica Nova,* 1667, 5.

23. Gladstone, "The Lure of Medical History," 433. See also Dorrington and Poole, "The First Intravenous Anesthetic"; and French and Wear, *The Medical Revolution of the Seventeenth Century,* 2.

24. Cook, "Living in Revolutionary Times," 111–35.

25. Gladstone, "The Lure of Medical History," 47.

26. Cook, "Living in Revolutionary Times."

27. Many contemporaries also pursued such seemingly contradictory lines of inquiry. Siraisi, "Medicine and the History of Science," 501.

28. Marschke, "The Crown Prince's Brothers and Sisters," 115.
29. Elsholtz, *Diaeteticon,* [v].
30. Ibid.
31. Albala, *Eating Right in the Renaissance,* 25. Albala classified three periods in the genre. During the first period (1470–1530), works contained dining advice tailored to the likely patrons of the authors: banqueting courtiers. Albala's second period (1530–70) saw a "Galenic revival" when writers tried, with mixed results, to apply the ancient humoral food classifications to Renaissance foods and practices throughout the continent. In this period, Albala claims, "dietary literature became increasingly removed from everyday practice." The final period lasted from 1570 to 1650 and was characterized by a wide discrepancy in interpretations and a more practical tone, which condemned gluttony without recommending a poor man's diet. In other words, these later vernacular manuals were directed toward an upper-middle instead of a courtly class.
32. Von Güldenklee devoted more attention than Elsholtz to the nonfood aspects of one's daily regimen (air quality, sleep, exercise, etc.), but both Elsholtz and von Güldenklee wrote about the specific dietary needs of different ages. Güldenklee, *Baldassaris Timaei von Guldenklee .*
33. The vast majority of authors come from the Italian peninsula, both ancient (19 percent) and Renaissance (22 percent).
34. Manfred Lemmer, "Nachwort," in Elsholtz, *Diaeteticon* (1984 ed.), 3.
35. Johann Hübner and Georg Heinrich Zincke, *Curiöses und reales Natur-Kunst- Berg- Gewerck- und Handlungs-Lexicon* ([Leipzig]: Verlegt von Johann Friedrich Gleditsch, 1746).
36. Ibid.
37. One copy formerly owned by the Fürstbischöfliche Hofbibliothek Eichstätt is now at the Anna Amalia Library in Weimar. Others came from the collections of naturalists, such as the Bamberg copy formerly owned by Johann Theophil Hoeffel (1704–1781), who published on minerals, and the copy belonging to the Swiss anatomist and physiologist Albrecht von Haller (1708–1777), now at the Braidense National Library in Milan. Another copy was owned by Balthasar Friedrich von Logau (1645–1702), son of the most famous German Baroque epigrammatist. Catalog searches on WorldCat (http://worldcat.org).
38. The work was Claude St. Etienne, *Nouvelle instruction pour connaître les bon fruits* (1670).
39. Ibid.
40. Elsholtz, *Diaeteticon,* 87.
41. MacLean, "The Medical Republic of Letters before the Thirty Years War."
42. Elsholtz, *Diaeteticon,* 340.
43. Ibid.

44. König, *Versuch einer historische Schilderung,* 2:281.

45. Ibid., 340–41.

46. Ibid.

47. GStA PK, I HA Rep. 36 Nr. 40, 26; and Nr. 42, 245–52.

48. Elsholtz, *Diaeteticon,* 117. This practice of artificially stocking the elector's hunting grounds with deer began in the 1650s. The park did not provide the deer with enough grain for feed, so the diet of this "wild" game was supplemented with oats. König, *Versuch einer historische Schilderung,* 2:87.

49. Elsholtz, *Diaeteticon,* 116–17.

50. Ibid., 172.

51. GStA PK, I HA Rep. 36 Nr. 1066, 57–60; XX HA Ostpr. Fols. 13096 and 13098.

52. Ibid., 133–34.

53. Ibid., 135.

54. After Parmesan and Edam, Elsholtz listed some other well-regarded cheeses, such as Swiss, Swedish, Limburger, and something known as *Terter* cheese. Ibid. Parmesan cheese is listed in only two accounts from the court of Brandenburg-Prussia: once in 1602 in Königsberg and once in 1652 in Cleves. GStA PK, I HA Rep. 36 Nr. 1083; and HSTAM Bezeichnung 117 Nr. 2170, respectively.

55. See chapter 1 for more about these *Küchenzetteln* of 1652.

56. Elsholtz, *Diaeteticon,* 105.

57. Ibid., 113.

58. Ibid. "Heut zu Tage richtet man nicht mehr nach des *Apicii* seltsame Koch-kunst / sondern hält das Braten vor das beste Mittel / die schleumige Feuchtigkeit den Span-Ferckeln zu benehmen."

59. See Susan Broomhall, "The Body In/as Text: Medical Knowledge and Technologies in the Renaissance," in Kalof and Bynum, *A Cultural History of the Human Body in the Renaissance,* 3:73–98; Siraisi, *Medieval and Early Renaissance Medicine,* x.

60. Cook, "Living in Revolutionary Times"; Moran, "Patronage and Institutions: Courts, Universities, and Academies in Germany: An Overview 1550–1750," in Moran, *Patronage and Institutions,* 169–84; Wear, "Medical Practice in Late Seventeenth- and Early Eighteenth-Century England: Continuity and Union," in French and Wear, *The Medical Revolution of the Seventeenth Century,* 294–320; Smith, "Curing the Body Politic: Chemistry and Commerce at Court, 1664–70," in Moran, *Patronage and Institutions,* 195–211.

61. Elsholtz, *Diaeteticon,* 348. My translation of Elsholtz's German translation from the Latin of Galen, *De alimentorum facultatibus,* bk. 2, c. 27.

62. Elsholtz, *Diaeteticon,* 16. Bonnefons, *Les délices de la campagne.*

63. Freedman, *Out of the East,* 216.

64. Ibid.

65. Wheaton, *Savoring the Past,* 136.

66. Brunt, *The Influence of the French Language,* 232.

67. Along with François Pierre La Varenne (1615–1678), Bonnefons's work marked the end of the long period without any printed French cookbooks during the wars of religion. Pinkard, *A Revolution in Taste,* 238.

68. Shumacher-Voelker, "German Cookery Books," 41. A new, related genre that appeared in Germany in the 1670s was *Hausväterliteratur,* which promoted the efficient and economic running of the household, or *oikos.*

69. Bonnefons, *Les délices de la campagne,* 19.

70. Ibid., 35.

71. Elsholtz, *Diaeteticon,* 11.

72. Ibid., 464; and Bonnefons, *Der Frantzösische Beckerr,* 14.

73. Wheaton, *Savoring the Past,* 121; Pinkard, *A Revolution in Taste,* 64; Willan, Cherniavsky, and Claflin, *The Cookbook Library,* 149, 162–63.

74. See also Lademacher, *Onder den Oranje Boom.*

75. Bonnefons, *Le Jardinier François.*

76. Elsholtz, *Vom Garten-Baw,* 1666. Following this first edition were editions in 1672, 1684, 1690 (see below), 1715, and 1728. A reprint of the 1684 edition was made in 1987.

77. Elsholtz, *Artzney- Garten- und- Tisch-Buch oder Fortsetzung des Gartenbaws / Wie man die von Gott erzeigte Erd-Gewächse / Kräuter/Blumen und Wurzeln / zur Erhaltung guter Gesundheit / wol gebrauchen und anwenden/ auch durch eine ordentlich Diaet, insonderheit durch rechmäßigen Gebrauch der Speisen und des Geträncks sein Leben erhalten und fristen könne: So wol hohen als Niedrigen/ absonderlich aber Den Gärtnern/Wegen der darin enthaltenen fremden Gewächse/Blumen und Kräuter / sehr dienlich; Wie sie selbige auff den Teuschen Climate zu rechter Zeit zeigen/ warten und anrichten müssen. In VI. Bücher verfasset / und mit nöhtigen Figuren als auch einen vollkommenen Register versehen / Wobey der Französche Koch / Becker und Cofitirer / Mit Rom. Kaiserl. Majest. als auch Churfürstl. Churfürstl. Sachs. und Brandenb. Priviligiis* (Frankfurt and Leipzig: Rupert Völkers, Buchhändlers in Berlin und Cölln, 1690).

78. Elsholtz had cited Bonnefons, *Le Jardinier François,* in his 1684 edition of *Vom Garten Baw,* 5.

CONCLUSION

1. Droysen, *Geschichte der preussischen Politik,* 3:557.

2. Marschke, "The Crown Prince's Brothers and Sisters."

3. The *sekt* referred to in the witness's account was likely the sweet Canarian wine called Malmsey. Krünitz, "Sect," in *Oekonomischen Encyklopädie,* 151.

4. *Urkunden und Aktenstücke,* vol. 20, pt. 2, 1213–15. Rébénacq [*sic*] to Louis XIV. Berlin, April 12, 1687. The midday time of death is given in the announcement letters written by Ludwig's wife and other members of the court. GStA PK, I HA Rep. 35 Nr. 336.

5. Rébénacq, in *Urkunden und Aktenstücke,* vol. 20, pt. 2, 1213–15.

6. Ibid.

7. Ibid, 1214.

8. Opgenoorth, *Der Grosse Kurfürst von Brandenburg,* 2:2:322; Prutz, *Aus des Grossen Kurfürsten letzten Jahren,* 178; and Wintzingerode, *Schwierige Prinzen,* 48.

9. The *Affaire de poisons* is the most famous of several such episodes in the widespread premodern European culture of poison. Historians have drawn a number of conclusions about the affair related to ancien régime political culture, legal history, the Catholic Reformation, and the history of medicine. Somerset, *The Affair of the Poisons;* Mollenauer, *Strange Revelations,* and "Poisons and Secrets: The Court, the King, and the Problem of Drug Knowledge in Late Seventeenth-Century France," lecture presented by Emma Spary at the Intoxicating Spaces Lectures Series, February 17, 2021. https://www.crowdcast.io/e/poisons-and-secrets-the.

10. Somerset, *The Affair of the Poisons,* 181–87.

11. Ibid., 186.

12. Ibid., 225.

13. Ibid., 224–25.

14. GStA PK, I HA Rep. 35 Nr. 334.

15. Thanks to Dr. Claire West of the University of North Carolina for the *pro bono* medical consultation. The diagnosis of scarlet fever was mentioned by Clark, *Iron Kingdom,* 103. *Fleckfieber,* which I translated as "tyhus," was mentioned in the German literature; see for example Großmann, "Jugendgeschichte Friedrichs I," 39.

16. Rébénacq, in *Urkunden und Aktenstücke,* vol. 20, pt. 2, 1214–15.

17. Wintzergerode, *Schwierige Prinzen,* 23–24.

18. Vehse, *Geschichte der deutschen Höfe,* 164.

19. GStA PK, I HA Rep. 35 Nr. 334.

20. Ibid. This testimony was appended to the *Protocol* without the question-and-answer format of the previous testimonies as "Lit. A des Pagen Fürstenbergs schriftliche *Deposition.*"

21. Ibid.

22. The detail about the sable is interesting because one of the commission's questions seemed to wonder whether Ludwig's illness stemmed from his being underdressed in cold weather. In any case, those closest to him related that they did not believe that because Ludwig dressed better (i.e., warmer) than he had in previous years.

23. Opgenoorth, *Der Grosse Kurfürst von Brandenburg*, 2:322.
24. Pufendorf, *Friedrich Wilhelms des Grossen*, 934–35.
25. Ibid., 433 and 934.
26. Prutz, *Aus des Grossen Kurfürsten letzten Jahren*, 218.
27. Karl Ludwig von Pöllnitz, *Memoiren zur Lebens- und Regierungsgeschichte der vier letzten Regenten des Preußischen Staat* (Berlin: Voss, 1791), 4.
28. Elsholtz, *Diaeteticon*, 85–86.
29. See chapter 4.
30. Laszlo, *Citrus*, 137.
31. Orlich, *Friedrich Wilhelm der Grosse Kurfürst*, 579.
32. Kluge, *Currywurst & Co.*
33. See chapter 1.
34. Elsholtz, *Diaeteticon*, 323.
35. König, *Versuch einer Historischen Schilderung*, 2:228.
36. Orlich, *Geschichte des preußischen Staates im siebzehnten Jahrhundert*, 3: 362. This is a reprinting of a court order issued by Friedrich Wilhelm on November 15, 1673.
37. Vehse, *Preussiche Hofgeschichten*, 144.
38. Buch, *Tagebuch Dietrich Sigismund's von Buch*, 1:147. See also Pöllnitz, *Memoiren zur Lebens- und Regierungsgeschichte*, 156. Vehse claimed Danckelmann used an emetic. Vehse. *Preussische Hofgeschichten*, 1:144.
39. Heinrich, *Geschichte Preussens*, 125.
40. Vehse, *Geschichte der deutschen Höfe*, 282. This is the only mention I have found of this action.
41. Eventually, Friedrich and his wife went to visit her family in Hanover, which greatly angered Elector Friedrich Wilhelm, who was in a dispute with the elector of Braunschweig-Lüneburg. Emperor Leopold I also offered Friedrich Wilhelm asylum and the Viennese ambassador in Berlin reported that the French party sought to take advantage of the disputes. *Urkunden und Actenstücke*, vol. 14, pt. 2, 1367.
42. Charlotte-Elisabeth d'Orléans, *Aus den Briefen der Herzogin Elisabeth Charlotte von Orléans*, 84–85.
43. See Prutz, *Aus des Grossen Kurfürsten letzten Jahren.*
44. Sophie von Hannover, *Briefe der Kurfürstin Sophie von Hannover*, 57. As quoted in the original French from her letter of June 26, 1687, to the Countess Charlotte of Schönburg.
45. Opgenoorth, *Der Grosse Kurfürst von Brandenburg*, 2:319.
46. Marschke, "The Crown Prince's Brothers and Sisters," 130.
47. Friedrich Wilhelm and Dorothea had seven children together.
48. Marschke, "The Crown Prince's Brothers and Sisters."
49. Ernst Kantorowicz coined the term in his 1957 book, translated as *The King's Two Bodies: A Study in Medieval Political Theology.* His objective

was to use semiotics to trace the origins of an abstract notion of "the State" or the continuity of rule beyond the death of a single person. Jussen, "The King's Two Bodies Today." Here, the term refers to early modern means of legitimizing rule.

50. Stollberg-Rilinger, *The Emperor's Old Clothes.*

51. Behringer, *A Cultural History of Climate.*

52. In 2018, 3.7 million people in the United States injected drugs, spreading HIV and hepatitis C, and leading to a record high numbers of overdoses and deaths. H. Bradley et al., "Estimated Number of People Who Inject Drugs in the United States," *Clin. Infect. Dis.* 76, no. 1 (January 6, 2023): 96–102, https://pubmed.ncbi.nlm.nih.gov/35791261/.

BIBLIOGRAPHY

Manuscript Sources

Geheimes Staatsarchiv Preußischer Kulturbesitz (GstA PK)

BPH Rep. 35—Kurfürst Friedrich Wilhelm (Der Große Kurfürst; 1620–, reg. 1640–1688)

I. HA Rep. 9: Allgemeine Verwaltung

I. HA Rep. 21: Brandenburgische Städte, Ämter und Kreise nebst einigen Materien betr. Die innere Verwaltung der Mark.

I. HA Rep. 36: Hofverwaltung

I. HA Rep. 94 IV HC 6, 7, 8

X. HA Rep. 32 Nr. 83

XX. HA EM 50a, b, c

XX. HA Ostpreussische Folianten

Hessische Staatsarchiv Marburg (HSTAM)

Bezeichnung 117: Politische Archiv Georg Friedrichs

Landeshauptarchiv Brandenburg (BLHA)

Rep. 2: Kurmärkische Kammer B, D

Rep. 7: Berlin-Mühlenhof

Rep. 7: Oranienburg Nr. 687

"Report from Cologne to King Charles II of England. State Papers Online." Gale, Cengage Learning, December 25, 1674. SP 81/74, Sequence Number 0301, 0302, 0303. The National Archives. Staatsbibliothek zu Berlin—Preußischer Kulturbesitz (STABI)

MS Boruss. Folio 63

MS Boruss. Folio 233

MS Boruss. Folio 869

Primary Printed Sources

Adamson, Melitta. *Daz Buch von Guter Spise (The Book of Good Food). A Study, Edition, and English Translation of the Oldest German Cookbook.* Medium Aevum Quotidianum, Sonderband IX. Krems, Austria: Medium Aevum Quotidianum, 2000.

Agricola, Johann Jacob. *Worinnen zu Ersehen/ wie die Feld- ynd Blumen-Garten sollen abgetheilet / [. . .] insonderheit vor den Maulwürffen/ sollen praeservirt werden.* Nördlingen: Schultes, 1677.

Appetit-Lexikon. oder alphabetisch geordnetes Auskunftbuch über alle Speisen und Getränke sowohl gewöhnlicher Art als des Luxus. Vienna: Carl Gerold, 1830.

Ausführlicher Bericht Belangend die Erb-Huldigung und Souverainität So Sr. Churfürstl. Durchl. zu Brandenburg etc. etc. Von denen Preußnischen Ständen und Städten in Gegenwart der Königl. Polnischen Herren Commissarien geleistet worden : Geschehen in Königsberg am 18. Octobr. Anno MDCLXIII. [S.I.], 1663.

Beger, Lorenz. *Thesaurus Brandenburgicus Selectus: Sive Gemmarum, et Numismatum Graecorum: in Cimeliarchio Electorali Brandenburgico, Elegantiorum Series, Commentario Illustratae.* Berlin: Liebpert, 1696.

Böckler, Georg Andream. *Nüzliche Hauß- und Feld-Schule / Das ist: Wie man ein Land-Feld-Guth und Meyeren mit aller zugehöre; als da seynd die nothwendige Gebäu / vollkommene Haußhaltung/ allerley Viehzucht / Ackerbau / Wiesen / Gärten / Fischereyen / Waldungen und dergleichen mit Nuzen anordnen solle: [. . .].* Nuremberg: Paul Fürstens, 1678.

Bonnefons, Nicolas. *Der Frantzösische Confitirer, welcher handelt von der Manier, die Früchte in ihrer natürlichen Art zu Erhalten.* Translated by Georg Greflinger. Hamburg, 1665.

———. *Der Frantzösische Küchen-Gärtner, welcher unterweiset: Wie die Küchen-Kräuter und andere rare Gewächse auffzubringen und zu bewahren seyn.* Translated by Georg Greflinger. 1665.

———. *Le Jardinier François, qui enseigne à cultiver les arbres, & herbes potagères; avec la manière de conserver les Fruicts, & faire toutes sortes de Confitures, Conserves, & Massepans.* Paris: Pierre Des-Hayes, 1651.

———. *Les délices de la campagne: suitte du Iardinier françois, ou est enseigné a preparer pour l'usage de la vie tout ce qui croist sur la terre, & dans les eaux : dedieé aux dames mesnageres.* Paris: Pierre Des-Hayes, 1654.

Buch, Dietrich Sigismund von. *Tagebuch Dietrich Sigismund's von Buch aus den Jahren 1674 bis 1683: Beitrag zur Geschichte des großen Kurfürsten von Brandenburg ; nach dem Urtexte im Königlichen Geheimen Staats-Archive zu Berlin.* Jena and Leipzig: Costenoble, 1865.

Colerus, Johannes. *Calendarium perpetuum (mit) Oeconomia ruralis et domestica, darin das gantz Ampt aller trewer Hauss-Vaetter, Hauss-Muetter, bestaendiges und allgemeines Hauss-Buch vom Hausshalten, Wein, Acker, Gaerten, Blumen und Feldbaubegriffen, auch Wild- und Voegelfang, Weidwerck, Fischereyen, Viehezucht [. . . .].* Frankfurt am Main: Johann Arnold Cholinu, 1672.

David, Lucas. *Preussische Chronik.* Vol. 8. Königsberg: Haberland, 1817.

D'Orléans, Charlotte-Elisabeth. *Aus den Briefen der Herzogin Elisabeth Charlotte von Orléans an die Kurfürstin Sophie von Hannover: Ein Beitrag zur Kulturgeschichte des 17. und 18. Jahrhunderts.* Hahn, 1891.

Eger, Susanna. *Leipziger Koch-Buch* [. . .] *Dem beygefüget XXX. curieuse Tisch-Fragen* [. . .] *wie auch Tisch- und Speise-Lexicon* [. . .] *Anitzo aufs neue übersehen, etc.* Leipzig, 1732.

Elsholtz, Johann Sigismund. *Clysmatica nova; oder, Newe Clystier-Kunst, wie eine Arzney durch eröffnete Ader bey zu bringen, dasz sie ihre Wirckung eben also verrichte, als wan sie durch den Mund genommen worden wäre (Jo. Sig. Elsholtii, D. & Sereniss. Electoris Brandenburg. Medici Ordinarii, Clysmatica Nova: Sive Ratio, qua in Venam Sectam Medicamenta Immitti Possint, Ut Eodem Modo, Ac Si per Os Assumta Fuissent, Operentur* [. . .] *Editio secunda* [. . .]). Berlin: Bey Daniel Reicheln, 1665; second Latin edition published as Berlin: Reichelius, 1667.

———. *Diaeteticon, das ist Newes Tischbuch oder Unterricht von Erhaltung guter Gesundheit durch eine ordentliche Diät.* Berlin, 1682; new ed. Leipzig: Edition Leipzig, 1984.

———. *Flora marchica, sive Catalogus plantarum, quae partim in hortis electoralibus Marchiae Brandenburgicae primariis, Berolinensi, Aurangiburgico, & Potstamensi excoluntur: partim sua sponte passim proveniunt.* Berlin: Reichel, 1663.

———. *Hortus Berolinensis: Der Berliner Lustgarten: Liber Primus: Erstes Buch.* Translated by Thomas Fischbacher and Thomas Fink. Weimar: Verlag und Datenbank für Geisteswissenschaften, 2010.

———. *Hortus Berolinensis: erstes Buch.* Translated by Felix Mundt and Marcel Humar. Worms: Wernersche Verlagsgesellschaft, 2010.

———. *Joan. Sigism Elszholtz Vom Garten-Baw, oder, Unterricht von der Gärtnerey auff das Clima der Chur-Marck Brandenburg: wie auch der benachbarten Länder gerichtet.* Cölln an der Spree: Druckts Georg Schultze, 1666.

Feist, Wilhelm Adolph von. *Handbuch der Fürsten und Fürstlichen Beampten: worinnen der rechte Kern der Politischen Klugheit aus den vornembsten verscheidenen newen, sowol Lateinischen als Frantzösischen Politischen Schreiberen, kurtz zusammen gezogen, und verfasset in dieses Tractätlein.* Bremen: Köhler, 1660.

France, Ministère des affaires étrangères (1588–2007). *Recueil des Instructions Données aux Ambassadeurs et Ministres de France: Depuis les Traités de Westphalie Jusqu'à la Révolution Française. XXVIII. Tome Premier, États Allemands. L'électorat de Mayence /[Ministère des Affaires Étrangères] ; Avec une Introd. et des Notes par Georges Livet.* Paris: Éd. du Centre national de la recherche scientifique, 1962. https://gallica.bnf.fr/ark:/12148/bpt6k33368779.

Frederick II, king of Prussia. *Memoirs of the House of Brandenburg* [. . .]. London : Printed for J. Nourse, 1751–58.

Frischbier, Hermann. *Preussisches Wörterbuch: Ost- und westpreussische Provinzialismen in alphabetischer Folge.* Berlin: Enslin, 1883.

Gantz Neu-vermehrter Sorgfältiger Hauß-Halter, begreiffend einen Nutz und Lust-bringenden Baum-, Küchen-, und Blumen-Garten [. . .]. Münster: Deyerlein, 1696.

Greflinger, Georg. *Ethica Complementoria, das ist: Complementir-Büchlein, In welchem enthalten, eine richtige Art, wie man so wol mit hohen als nidrigen Standes-Personen: bey Gesellschafften und Frauen-Zimmer Hofzierlich reden, und umgehen solle; Neulich wider übersehen, an vielen Orten gebessert, und vermehret; Mit angefügtem Trenchir-Büchlein, auch züchtigen Tisch- und Leber-Reimen.* Amsterdam, 1665.

———. *Der Nordischer Mercurius,* Hamburg, 1664.

Güldenklee, Balthazar Timaeus von. *Baldassaris Timaei von Guldenklee /* [. . .] *Opera Medico-Practica.* [. . .]. Leipzig: Kirchnerus, 1677.

Günther, Simon. *Hortulus Sanitatis, h.e. Tuenda et Conservanda Bona Valetudine Omnibus Literatis et Peregrinantibus Libellus Accomodatissimus et Maxime Necessarius, in Lucem Editus.* Spira, 1608.

Hannover, Sophie von. *Briefe der Kurfürstin Sophie von Hannover an die Raugräfinnen and Raugrafen zu Pfalz.* Edited by Eduard Bodemann. Leipzig: S. Hirzel, 1888.

Hesse, Heinrich, and Theodorus Phytologus. *Heinrich Hessens, Churfürstl. Mayntzischen Garten-Vorstehers, Neue Garten-Lust* [. . .]. Leipzig: Weidmann, 1690.

Hiebner, Johann Christoph. *Horticultura, das ist, Kurtz- und verständliche Anleitung, Wie ein Lust- Obst- und Küchen-Garten anzulegen* [. . .]. Leipzig: Kirchner, 1671.

Hönn, Georg Paul. *Fortgesetztes Betrugs-Lexicon.* Leipzig: Christan Samuel Krug, 1743.

Jüngken, Johann Helfrich. [. . .] *Medicus oder Leib-Arzt* [. . .]. Frankfurt and Leipzig: Thomas Fristchen, 1702.

Khumperger, Maria Euphrosina, Franziska Kolmer, and Lothar Kolmer, eds. *Kochbuch der Maria Euphrosina Khumperger: aus dem Jahr 1735 mit 285 Rezepten.* Vienna: Mandelbaum Verlag, 2015.

Kindermann, Balthasar. *Lob-Gesang des Zerbster Biers* [. . .] Wittenberg: Borckard, 1658.

Klett, Andreas. *Neu-erfundenes Trenchir-Buch* [. . .] Leipzig, 1665.

———. *Neues Trenchir-Büchlein / Wie man nach rechter Art, und ietzigen Gebrauch nach, allerhand Speisen ordentlich auff die Taffel setzen, zierlich zerschneiden und vorlegen, auch artlich wiederumb abheben soll.* Jena: Freyschmied, 1657.

König, Anton Balthasar. *Versuch einer Historischen Schilderung der Haupt-veränderungen, der Religion, Sitten, Gewohnheiten, Künste, Wissenschaften [et]c. der Residenzstadt Berlin seit den ältesten Zeiten, bis zum Jahre 1786.* 3 vols. Berlin: Wilhelm Dehmigke dem Jüngern, 1793.

La Varenne, Pierre François. *Le cuisinier françois: enseignant la manière de bien apprester et assaisonner toutes sortes de viandes . . . légumes . . . par le sieur de La Varenne.* Paris: P. David, 1651.

———. *La Varenne's Cookery: The French Cook; the French Pastry Chef; the French Confectioner.* Translated by Terence Scully. Blackawton, UK: Prospect Books, 2006.

Lemmer, Manfred, and Franz de Rontzier. *Kunstbuch von Mancherley Essen, Gesotten, Gebraten, Posteten, von Hirschen, Vogelen, Wildtprat, und andern Schawessen, so auff Fürstlichen [. . .].* Reprint. Munich: Heimeran Verlag, 1979.

Leti, Gregorio. *Ritratti Historici-Politici-Chronologici e Genealogici della Casa Serenissima [Ed] Elettorale Di Brandenburgo / Gregorio Leti 1.: Parte Prima Scritta Con Metodo Heroestorico, Divisa in Sette Libri.* Amsterdam: Roger, 1687.

Marperger, Paul Jacob. *Paul Jacob Marpergers [. . .] Vollständiges Küch- und Keller-Dictionarium [. . .]* Hamburg: Verlag Benjamin Schillers seel. Wittwe, 1716.

Messisbugo, Cristoforo di. *Banchetti. Compositioni di vivande et apparecchio generale: di Christoforo di Messisburgo [. . .].* Ferrara: G. de Buglhat et A. Hucher, 1549.

Müller, Christian. *Brod- und Semmel-Rechnung: Wie die Becker beyder Churfl. Brandenb. Residentz-Städte Berlin und Cöln an der Spree das Brod und die Semmel nach dem Gewicht backen.* Berlin: Völcker, 1686.

Nicolai, Friedrich. *Beschreibung der königlichen Residenzstädte Berlin und Potsdam, aller daselbst befindlicher Merkwürdigkeiten, und der umliegenden Gegend.* Vol. 3. Berlin: Bey Friedrich Nicolai, 1786.

Orléans, Charlotte-Elisabeth de. *Aus den Briefen der Herzogin Elisabeth Charlotte von Orléans an die Kurfürstin Sophie von Hannover: Ein Beitrag zur Kulturgeschichte des 17. und 18. Jahrhunderts.* Hanover: Hahn, 1891.

Panckow, Thomas. *Thomae Pancovii, D. Sereniss: Elect: Brandeb: Aulae Medici, Herbarium Portatile, oder Behendes Kräuter- und Gewächs-Buch.* Leipzig: C. Kirchner, 1656.

Pascha, Johann Georg. *Neu vermehrtes vollständiges Trincier-Buch [. . .].* Naumburg: Müller, 1665.

Platina, and Mary Ella Milham. *Platina, on Right Pleasure and Good Health: A Critical Edition and Translation of "De Honesta Voluptate et Valetudine."* Tempe, AZ: Medieval & Renaissance Texts & Studies, 1998.

Pöllnitz, Karl Ludwig von. *Nouveaux Memoires du Baron de Pöllnitz: Contenant l'histoire de Sa Vie, et La Relation de Ses Premiers Voyages.* Amsterdam:

Changuion, 1737. German ed., *Memoiren zur Lebens- und Regierungsge-schichte der vier letzten Regenten des Preußischen Staat* (Berlin: Voss, 1791).

Prasmofskey, Stanislaum. *Neu-verfertigtes vollständiges Koch-Buch* [. . .]. Nuremberg: Johan Philip Miltenberger, 1671.

Procacci, Giacomo. *Trincier- Oder Vorleg-Buch: Darinnen Berichtet* [. . .]. Leipzig: Grosse, 1620.

Pufendorf, Samuel von. *De rebus gestis Friderici Wilhelmi Magni, Electoris Brandenburgici commentariorum libri novendecim.* Berlin: Impensis Jeremiæ Schrey, & Hered. Henrici Johanni Meyeri, 1695.

———. *Friederich Wilhelms des Grossen, Chur-Fürstens zu Brandenburg Leben und Thaten.* Berlin: Schrey- und Mayersche Buchladen, 1710.

Rosalia, Eleonora Maria. *Ein gantz neues und nutzbahres Koch-Buch* [. . .]. Vienna: Voigt, 1699.

Roselli, Giovanni de. *Epulario Quale Tratta Del Modo de Cucinare Ogni Carne Vcelli Pesci de Ognj Sorte Fare Sapore: Torte, Pastellj al Modo de Tutte Le Proujncje.* Venice: Giovanni Andrea Valvassore, 1549.

Royer, Johann. *Beschreibung des ganzen fürstl: Braunschw: Gartens zu Hessen* [. . .] *auch* [. . .] *Specification aller derer Simplicium und Gewechse, so von Aō 1607 bis in dass 1651. Jahr.* Braunschweig: G. Müller, 1651.

Rumpolt, Marx. *Ein new Kochbuch, das ist ein gründtliche Beschreibung, wie man recht und wol, nicht allein von vierfüssigen, heymischen und wilden Thieren* [. . .] *allerley Speiß als gesotten, gebraten* [. . .] *zubereiten solle.* Frankfurt am Main: Feyerabendt, 1587; Frankfurt: Johann Saurn, 1604.

Scappi, Bartolomeo. *Opera de Bartolomeo Scappi, Cvoco Secreto Di Papa Pio V.* Venice, 1570.

———. *The Opera of Bartolomeo Scappi (1570).* Translated by Terence Scully. Toronto: University of Toronto Press, 2011.

Schellhammer, Maria Sophia. *Das brandenburgische Koch-Buch* [. . .]. Berlin: Bey Johann Andreas Rüdiger, 1723.

Schindler, Wolfgang Erich. *Speiß- und Keller wie auch Frölich- und trauriger Geschichten Calenders Grosse Practica* [. . .]. Nuremberg: Hoffmann, 1684.

Schnurr, Balthasar. *Kunst und Wunderbüchlein* [. . .]. Frankfurt am Main: Johann Press, 1643.

Schwänder, Johann Georg. *Der Sorgfältige Hausshalter, Oder Gründliche Anleitung zum GARTEN-BAW, Nach den zwölf Monaten des Jahrs eingerichtet Sambt Einem Anhang von kochen / Condiren und Destilliren, Nebenst Dazu gehörigen Figuren* [. . .]. Osnabrück: Johann Georg Schwänders, 1674.

Seckendorf, Veit Ludwig von. *Teutscher Fürsten-Staat mit einer gantz neuen Zugabe sonderbahrer und wichtiger Materien üm ein grosses Theil vermehret.* Frankfurt and Leipzig: Verlegts Johann Meyer, Buchhändler, 1703.

Seyler, Georg Daniel. *Leben und Thaten Friedrich Wilhelms des Großen: Churfürstens zu Brandenburg.* Frankfurt and Leipzig: Zu finden bey George Marcus Knochen, 1730.

Spiel, Georg Heinrich Gerhard, ed. "Herzog's Georg Wilhelm zu Celle hohe und niedere Minister und Diener und deren Besoldung, vom Jahre 1682 (Aus einem offiziellen Besoldungsregister)." *Neues vaterländisches Archiv oder Beiträge zur allseitigen Kenntniß des Königreichs Hannover und des Herzogthums Braunschweig* 1, nr. 13 (1828): 308–20.

Thiemen, Johann Christoph. *Haus- Feld- Arzney- Koch- Kunst- und Wunder-Buch* [. . .]. Nuremberg: Johann Hofmann, 1682.

"Über die Zubereitung des Zuckers, und den Handel, der damit geführt wird." *Allgemeines europäisches Journal* 2, no. 2 (1794): 262–72.

Volkamer, Johann Christoph, and Paul Decker. *Nürnbergische Hesperides, Oder Gründliche Beschreibung Der Edlen Citronat, Citronen, und Pomerantzen-Früchte* [. . .]. Nuremberg: Endter, 1708.

Wecker, Anna. *Neu / köstlich und nutzliches Koch-Buch* [. . .] Basel: König, 1667.

Weise, Christian. *Der Kluge Hoff-Meister / Das ist / Kurtze und eigentliche Nachricht* [. . .] Weissenfels: Brühl, 1676.

Winterfeld, Friedrich Wilhelm von. *Teutsche Ceremonial-Politica.* Frankfurt and Leipzig: Carl Christian Neuenhahn, 1700.

Wolley, Hannah. *Frauen-Zimmers Zeit-Vertreib / oder Reiches Gemach von außerlesenen Experimenten und Curiositäten bestehend in einen neuen Vollkommenen Koch-Buch* [. . .]. Hamburg: Schultz, 1688.

Zwantzig, Zacharias. *Ceremoniale Brandenburgicum.* Freiburg, 1700.

Secondary Sources

Abel, Wilhelm. *Agricultural Fluctuations in Europe from the Thirteenth to the Twentieth Centuries.* New York: St. Martin's Press, 1980.

———. *Stufen der Ernährung: eine historische Skizze.* Göttingen: Vandenhoeck & Ruprecht, 1981.

Achilles, Walter. "Getreidepreise und Getreidehandelsbeziehungen europäischer Räume im 16. und 17. Jahrhunderts." *Zeitschrift für Agrargeschichte und Agrarsoziologie* 7, no. 1 (April 1959): 32–47.

———. *Landwirtschaft in der frühen Neuzeit.* Munich: R. Oldenbourg, 1991.

Adamson, Melitta Weiss. *Food in Medieval Times.* Westport, CT: Greenwood Press, 2004.

———. *Regional Cuisines of Medieval Europe.* New York and London: Routledge, 2002.

Ago, Renata. *Gusto for Things: A History of Objects in Seventeenth-Century Rome.* Translated by Bradford Bouley and Corey Tazzara. Chicago: University of Chicago Press, 2013.

Ahrens, Theodore G. "Breeding Back the Extinct Auerochs." *Journal of Mammalogy* 17, no. 3 (August 1936): 266–68.

Albala, Ken, ed. *The Banquet: Dining in the Great Courts of Late Renaissance Europe.* Urbana: University of Illinois Press, 2007.

———. *A Cultural History of Food in the Renaissance.* London: Bloomsbury, 2014.

———. *Eating Right in the Renaissance.* Berkeley: University of California Press, 2002.

———. *Food in Early Modern Europe.* Westport, CT: Greenwood Press, 2003.

———. "Ludovicus Nonnius and the Elegance of Fish." In *The Dining Nobility. From the Burgundian Dukes to the Belgian Royalty,* 38–43. Brussels: Brussels University Press, 2008.

Albarella, Umberto, et al., eds. *Pigs and Humans: 10,000 Years of Interaction.* Oxford: Oxford University Press, 2007.

Albinus, Robert. *Königsberg Lexikon. Stadt und Umgebung.* Würzburg: Flechsig, 2002.

Alewyn, Richard. *Das grosse Welttheater die Epoche der höfischen Feste.* Munich: Beck, 1985.

Allen, Robert C. "Economic Structure and Agricultural Productivity in Europe, 1300–1800." *European Review of Economic History* 4, no. 1 (2000): 1–26.

Almer, Gabriel. "Zur Struktur und Organisation des Berlin-Cöllner Hofes um 1700." Master's thesis, Freie Universität Berlin, 2009.

Andressen, B. Michael. *Barocke Tafelfreuden: Tischkultur an Europas Höfen.* Niedernhausen: Orbis, 2001.

Appadurai, Arjun. "The Social Life of Things: Commodities in Cultural Perspective." Cambridge: Cambridge University Press, 1986.

Appelbaum, Robert. "Newe Bokes of Cookerie." *Journal for Early Modern Cultural Studies* 1, no. 1 (April 1, 2001): 128–43.

Artelt, Walter. *Medizinische Wissenschaft und ärztliche Praxis im alten Berlin in Selbstzeugnissen: ein Lesebuch.* Vol. 1. Berlin: Urban & Schwarzenberg, 1948.

Asch, Ronald. *Europäischer Adel in der Frühen Neuzeit: eine Einführung.* Cologne: Böhlau, 2008.

Asch, Ronald, and Adolf M. Birke, eds. *Princes, Patronage, and the Nobility: The Court at the Beginning of the Modern Age, c. 1450–1650.* London: German Historical Institute London, 1991.

Asch, Ronald, and Heinz Duchhardt, eds. *Der Absolutismus—Ein Mythos?: Strukturwandel monarchischer Herrschaft in West- und Mitteleuropa (ca. 1550–1700).* Cologne: Böhlau, 1996.

Asch, Ronald, and Dagmar Freist, eds. *Staatsbildung als kultureller Prozess: Strukturwandel und Legitimation von Herrschaft in der Frühen Neuzeit.* Cologne: Böhlau, 2005.

Asche, Matthias. *Neusiedler im verheerten Land. Kriegsfolgenbewältigung, Migrationssteuerung und Konfessionspolitik im Zeichen des Landeswiederaufbaus. Die Mark Brandenburg nach den Kriegen des 17. Jahrhunderts.* Münster: Aschendorff, 2006.

Aston, T. H., and C. H. E. Philpin, eds. *The Brenner Debate. Agrarian Class Structure and Economic Development in Pre-Industrial Europe.* Cambridge: Cambridge University Press, 1985.

Atorf, Lars. *Der König und das Korn: die Getreidehandelspolitik als Fundament des brandenburg-preussischen Aufstiegs zur europäischen Grossmacht.* Berlin: Duncker & Humblot, 1999.

Bahl, Herms. *Ansbach: Strukturanalyse einer Residenz vom Ende des dreissigjährigen Krieges bis zur Mitte des 18. Jahrhunderts : Verfassung, Verwaltung, Bevölkerung und Wirtschaft.* Ansbach: Historischer Verein für Mittelfranken, 1974.

Bahl, Peter. *Der Hof des Grossen Kurfürsten: Studien zur höheren Amtsträgerschaft Brandenburg-Preussens.* Cologne: Böhlau, 2001.

———. "Die Berlin-Potsdamer Hofgesellschaft unter dem Großen Kurfürsten und König Friedrich I. Mit einem prosopographischen Anhang für die Jahre 1680–1713." In *Im Schatten der Krone: die Mark Brandenburg um 1700*, edited by Frank Göse, 31–98. Potsdam: Verlag für Berlin-Brandenburg, 2003.

Bahners, Patrick, and Gerd Roellecke, eds. *Preussische Stile: Ein Staat als Kunststück.* Stuttgart: Klett-Cotta, 2021.

Bairoch, Paul. *La population des villes européennes de 800 a 1850.* Geneva: Droz, 1988.

Barcia, Franco. *Gregorio Leti, informatore politico di principi italiani.* Milan: F. Angeli, 1987.

Barlösius, Eva. *Soziologie des Essens: Eine sozial- und kulturwissenschaftliche Einführung in die Ernährungsforschung.* Weinheim: Juventa, 2011.

Barockes Tafelsilber. Ausstellung vom 12. Dezember 1981 bis 29. Februar 1982. Frankfurt am Main: Museum für Kunsthandwerk Frankfurt am Main, 1981.

Barta-Fliedl, Ilsebill, Andreas Gugler, and Peter Parenzan. *Tafeln bei Hofe: zur Geschichte der fürstlichen Tafelkultur.* Hamburg: Dölling und Galitz, 1998.

Bartoschek, Gerd. *Preußisch Grün: Hofgärtner in Brandenburg-Preußen.* Berlin: Henschel, 2004.

———. *Sophie Charlotte und ihr Schloss: ein Musenhof des Barock in Brandenburg-Preussens.* Munich: Prestel, 1999.

Bauer, Volker. *Hofökonomie: der Diskurs über den Fürstenhof in Zeremonialwissenschaft, Hausväterliterature und Kameralismus.* Vienna: Böhlau, 1997.

Bauernfeind, Walter, and Ulrich Woitek. *Business Cycles in Germany, 1339—1670: A Spectral Analysis of Grain Prices and Production in Nuremberg.* Munich: Volkswirtschaftliche Fakultät der Ludwig Maximilian Universität, 1994.

Baumgart, Peter, ed. *Ständetum und Staatsbildung in Brandenburg-Preussen.* Berlin: De Gruyter, 1983.

Bavel, Bas J. P. van, and Erik Theon. *Land Productivity and Agro-Systems in the North Sea Area : Middle Ages–20th Century, Elements for Comparison.* Turnhout: Brepols, 1999.

Becker, Annelies. *Berlin-Brandenburgische Küchengeschichten.* Berlin: Maritim Hotels, 2008.

Behre, Karl-Ernst. "The Role of Man in European Vegetation History." In *Vegetation History,* edited by B. Huntley and T. Webb III, 632–72. Dordrecht: Kluwer, 1988.

Behringer, Wolfgang. *A Cultural History of Climate.* English ed. Cambridge: Polity Press, 2010.

Beik, William. "The Absolutism of Louis XIV as Social Collaboration." *Past & Present* 188, no. 1 (August 1, 2005): 195–224.

Bencard, Mogens. *Rosenborg studier: de Danske kongers kronologiske samling.* Copenhagen: De Samling, 2000.

Bepler, Jill. "Welfen und Hohenzollern vom 16. bis zum 18. Jahrhundert." In *Frauensache: wie Brandenburg Preussen wurde,* edited by Julia Klein, Eric Hartmann, and Jürgen Luh, 122–31. Dresden: Sandstein Verlag, 2015.

Berger, Günter, and Franziska Sick. *Französisch-deutscher Kulturtransfer im Ancien Régime.* Tübingen: Stauffenburg, 2002.

Berns, Andrew. "Food, Social Politics and the Order of Nature in Renaissance Italy." *Food, Culture & Society* 24, no. 1 (January 1, 2021): 169–70.

Berns, Jörn Jochen. *Zeremoniell als höfische Ästhetik in Spätmittelalter und Früher Neuzeit.* Berlin: De Gruyter, 1995.

Bertelli, Sergio. *The King's Body: The Sacred Rituals of Power in Medieval and Early Modern Europe.* University Park: Pennsylvania State University Press, 2001.

Beuys, Barbara. *Der Große Kurfürst: Friedrich Wilhelm von Brandenburg, der Mann, der Preußen schuf.* Munich: Deutscher Taschenbuch Verlag, 2012.

Beyer, Achim. *Die kurbrandenburgische Residenzenlandschaft im "langen 16. Jahrhundert."* Berlin: Berliner Wiss.-Verl., 2014.

Biagioli, Mario. *Galileo, Courtier: The Practice of Science in the Culture of Absolutism.* Science and Its Conceptual Foundations. Chicago: University of Chicago Press, 1993.

Biewer, Ludwig. *Preußen und Berlin: Beziehungen zwischen Provinz und Hauptstadt.* Edited by Udo Arnold. Lüneburg: Verlag Nordostdeutsches Kulturwerk, 1982.

Bloch, Marc. *Feudal Society.* Chicago: University of Chicago Press, 1961.

Bloch, Marc, and Léopold Benjamin. *The Royal Touch; Sacred Monarchy and Scrofula in England and France.* London: Routledge & Kegan Paul, 1973.

Blockmans, Wim, André Holenstein, and Jon Mathieu, eds. *Empowering Interactions: Political Cultures and the Emergence of the State in Europe, 1300–1900.* Farnham, UK: Ashgate, 2009.

Bohstedt, John. *The Politics of Provisions: Food Riots, Moral Economy, and Market Transition in England, c. 1550–1850.* Farnham, UK: Ashgate, 2010.

Bornhak, Friederike. *Luise Henriette von Nassau-Oranien: Kurfürstin von Brandenburg, erste Gemahlin des grossen kurfürsten Friedrich Wilhelnm von Brandenburg, geboren 1627, gestorben 1667.* Altenburg: S. Geibel, 1889.

Bourdieu, Pierre. *Outline of a Theory of Practice.* Cambridge: Cambridge University Press, 1977.

Brady, Thomas, Heiko Oberman, and James D Tracy. *Handbook of European History, 1400–1600: Late Middle Ages, Renaissance, and Reformation.* Leiden: E. J. Brill, 1994.

Braudel, Fernand. *Civilization and Capitalism, 15th–18th Century.* Vol. 1. London: Collins, 1981.

Brears, Peter C. D. *All the King's Cooks: The Tudor Kitchens of King Henry VIII at Hampton Court Palace.* London: Souvenir, 1999.

Brett, Gerard. *Dinner Is Served: A Study in Manners.* Hamden, CT: Archon Books, 1969.

Breunlich, Maria, and Helga Haas. *Karpfen, Krebs und Kälbernes: ein bürgerliches Kochbuch aus der Barockzeit.* Vienna: Mandelbaum, 2004.

Breysig, Kurt, and Friedrich Wolters. *Geschichte der brandenburgischen Finanzen in der Zeit von 1640 bis 1697: Darstellung und Akten.* Leipzig: Duncker & Humblot, 1895.

Brunt, Richard J. *The Influence of the French Language on the German Vocabulary (1649–1735).* Berlin: De Gruyter, 1983.

Bürger, Thomas, et al. *Das Kräuterbuch des Johannes Kentmann von 1563.* Munich: Prestel, 2004.

Burke, Peter. *Popular Culture in Early Modern Europe.* Aldershot, UK: Ashgate, 1996.

Büsch, Otto, and Wolfgang Neugebauer. *Moderne preussische Geschichte, 1648–1947: eine Anthologie.* Berlin: De Gruyter, 1981.

Bynum, Caroline Walker. *Holy Feast and Holy Fast: The Religious Significance of Food to Medieval Women.* Berkeley: University of California Press, 1987.

Cachée, Josef. *Die Hofküche des Kaisers: die k.u.k. Hofküche, d. Hofzuckerbäckerei u.d. Hofkeller in d. Wiener Hofburg.* Vienna: Amalthea, 1985.

Calabi, Donatella, and Stephen Christensen, eds. *Cities and Cultural Exchange in Europe, 1400–1700.* Cambridge: University of Cambridge Press, 2013.

Calaresu, Melissa. "Introduction: The Material Worlds of Food in Early Modern Europe." *Journal of Early Modern History* 24, no. 1 (February 2020): 1–16.

Campbell, Jodi. *At the First Table: Food and Social Identity in Early Modern Spain.* Early Modern Cultural Studies. Lincoln: University of Nebraska Press, 2017.

Camporesi, Piero. *Bread of Dreams: Food and Fantasy in Early Modern Europe.* Chicago: University of Chicago Press, 1989.

———. *Exotic Brew: The Art of Living in the Age of Enlightenment.* Oxford: Polity Press, 1994.

Carbone, Valentina, and Elisabeth Gouvernal. "Supply Chain and Supply Chain Management: Appropriate Concepts for Maritime Studies." In *Ports, Cities, and Global Supply Chains,* edited by James Wang et al., 11–26. Aldershot, UK: Ashgate, 2007.

Carlin, Martha. *Food and Eating in Medieval Europe.* London: Hambledon Press, 1998.

Carsten, F. L. "The Great Elector and the Foundation of the Hohenzollern Despotism." *English Historical Review* 65, no. 255 (April 1, 1950): 175–202.

———. *The Origins of Prussia.* Oxford: Clarendon Press, 1954.

Cassidy-Geiger, Maureen, ed. *Fragile Diplomacy: Meissen Porcelain for European Courts ca. 1710–63.* New Haven: Published for The Bard Graduate Center for Studies in the Decorative Arts, Design, and Culture, New York, by Yale University Press, 2007.

———. "The Hof-Conditorey in Dresden: Traditions and Innovations in Sugar and Porcelain." In *Triumph of the Blue Swords. Meissen Porcelain for Aristocracy and Bourgeoisie, 1710–1815,* edited by Ulrich Pietsch and Claudia Banz, 121–31. Dresden: E. A. Seemann, 2010.

Chester, Robert N., III, and Nicolaas Mink. "Having Our Cake and Eating It Too: Food's Place in Environmental History, a Forum [Introduction]." *Environmental History* 14, no. 2 (April, 2009): 309–11.

Cinqueterre, Berengario delle. *The Renaissance Cookbook: Historical Perspectives through Cookery.* Crown Point, IN: Dunes Press, 1975.

Claflin, Kyri W. "Food among the Historians: Early Modern Europe." In *Writing Food History: A Global Perspective,* edited by Peter Scholliers and Kyri Claflin, 38–58. London and New York: Berg, 2012.

Claflin, Kyri W., and Peter Scholliers. *Writing Food History: A Global Perspective.* London: Berg, 2012.

Clark, Christopher. *Iron Kingdom: The Rise and Downfall of Prussia, 1600–1947.* London: Allen Lane, 2006.

———. *Time and Power: Visions of History in German Politics, from the Thirty Years' War to the Third Reich.* Lawrence Stone Lectures. Princeton, NJ: Princeton University Press, 2019.

Clark, Peter, and Bernard Lepetit, eds. *Capital Cities and Their Hinterlands in Early Modern Europe.* Aldershot, England: Scolar Press, Ashgate, 1996.

Collet, Dominik. "Storage and Starvation: Public Granaries as Agents of Food Security in Early Modern Europe." *Historical Social Research* 35, no. 4 (January 2010): 234–52.

Conan, Michel, and Dumbarton Oaks, eds. *Baroque Garden Cultures: Emulation, Sublimation, Subversion.* Washington, DC: Dumbarton Oaks Research Library and Collection, 2005.

Cook, Daniel Thomas. "The Sociology of Taste by Jukka Gronow." *American Journal of Sociology* 104, no. 4 (January 1, 1999): 1198–200.

Cook, Harold. "Living in Revolutionary Times: Medical Change under William and Mary." In *Patronage and Institutions: Science, Technology, and Medicine at the European Court, 1500–1750,* edited by Bruce T Moran, 111–35. Rochester, NY: Boydell Press, 1991.

———. *Matters of Exchange: Commerce, Medicine, and Science in the Dutch Golden Age.* New Haven, CT: Yale University Press, 2007.

———. "Victories for Empiricism, Failure for Theory: Medicine and Science in the Seventeenth Century." In *Body as Object and Instrument of Knowledge,* edited by Charles T. Wolfe and Ofer Gal, 9–32. Dordrecht: Springer, 2010.

Cooper, Alix. *Inventing the Indigenous. Local Knowledge and Natural History in Early Modern Europe.* Cambridge: Cambridge University Press, 2007.

Counihan, Carole, Penny van Esterik, and Alice Julier, eds. *Food and Culture: A Reader.* New York: Routledge, 2008.

Cruyningen, Piet van, and E. Thoen. *Food Supply, Demand and Trade: Aspects of the Economic Relationship between Town and Countryside (Middle Ages–19th Century).* Turnhout: Brepols, 2012.

Cunningham, Andrew. "The Culture of Gardens." In *Cultures of Natural History,* edited by Nicholas Jardine, James A. Secord, and E. C. Spary, 38–57. Cambridge: Cambridge University Press, 1996.

Czarra, Fred R. *Spices: A Global History.* London: Reaktion, 2009.

Czok, Karl. *Am Hofe Augusts des Starken.* Stuttgart: Deutsche Verlags-Anhalt, 1990.

Daston, Lorraine, and Katharine Park. *The Cambridge History of Science.* Cambridge: Cambridge University Press, 2006.

Davidson, Alan. "Europeans' Wary Encounter with Tomatoes, Potatoes, and Other New World Foods." In *Chilies to Chocolate: Food the Americas Gave the World,* edited by Nelson Foster and Linda S. Cordell, 1–14. Tucson: University of Arizona Press, 1992.

———. *The Oxford Companion to Food.* Oxford: Oxford University Press, 1999.

Davis, Jennifer J. *Defining Culinary Authority the Transformation of Cooking in France, 1650–1832.* Baton Rouge: Louisiana State University Press, 2013.

Davis, Natalie Zemon. "History's Two Bodies." *American Historical Review* 93, no. 1 (1988): 1–30.

———. *Society and Culture in Early Modern France: Eight Essays*. Stanford, CA: Stanford University Press, 1975.

De Vries, Jan. *The Dutch Rural Economy in the Golden Age, 1500–1700*. Yale Series in Economic History. New Haven: Yale University Press, 1974.

———. "The Industrial Revolution and the Industrious Revolution." *Journal of Economic History* 54, no. 2 (June 1994): 249–70.

Dickhaut, Kirsten, Jörn Steigerwald, and Birgit Wagner, eds. *Soziale und ästhetische Praxis der höfischen Fest-Kultur im 16. und 17. Jahrhundert*. Wiesbaden: Harrassowitz, 2009.

Dietrich, Richard. *Preussen, Epochen und Probleme seiner Geschichte*. Berlin: De Gruyter, 1964.

Dietz, Johann. *Master Johann Dietz, Surgeon in the Army of the Great Elector and Barber to the Royal Court; from the Old Manuscript in the Royal Library of Berlin*. London: G. Allen & Unwin; New York: E. P. Dutton, 1923.

Dorrington, K. L., and W. Poole. "The First Intravenous Anesthetic: How Well Was It Managed and Its Potential Realized?" *British Journal of Anesthesia* 110, no. 1 (January 2013): 7–12.

Douglas, Mary. "Deciphering a Meal." *Daedalus* 101, no. 1 (January 1, 1972): 61–81.

Droysen, Johann Gustav. *Abhandlungen [. . .] zur neueren Geschichte*. Leipzig: Veit, 1876.

———. *Das Testament des Grossen Kurfürsten*. Leipzig: Hirzel, 1866.

———. *Der Staat des großen Kurfürsten: 31*. Leipzig: Veit, 1861.

———. *Geschichte der preußischen Politik*. Leipzig: Veit, 1855–68.

Duchhardt, Heinz. "Anspruch und Architektur: das Beispiel Berlin." *Forschungen zur Brandenburgischen und Preussischen Geschichte*, Neue Folge, 1, no. 1 (1991): 31–52.

Duelmen, Richard van. *Kultur und Alltag in der Fruehen Neuzeit: das Haus und seine Menschen*. Vol. 1. 3 vols. Munich: C. H. Beck, 1999.

Dugo, Giovanni, and Angelo di Giacamo. *Citrus: The Genus Citrus*. London: Taylor & Francis, 2002.

Dümpelmann, Sonja, Carsten Neumann, and Clemens Alexander Wimmer. *Preussisch Grün: Hofgärtner in Brandenburg-Preussen*. Berlin: Henschel, 2004.

Duval, Marguerite. *The King's Garden*. Charlottesville: University Press of Virginia, 1982.

Dwyer, Philip G., ed. *The Rise of Prussia: 1700–1830*. New York: Longman, 2000.

Eddie, S. A. *Freedom's Price: Serfdom, Subjection, and Reform in Prussia, 1648–1848*. Oxford: Oxford University Press, 2013.

Egmond, Florike. *The World of Carolus Clusius Natural History in the Making, 1550–1610*. London: Pickering & Chatto, 2010.

Ehlert, Trude. *Haushalt und Familie in Mittelalter und Früher Neuzeit.* Wiesbaden: Vertrieb Modernes Antiquariat Verlag, 1997.

Elias, Norbert. *The Civilizing Process: Sociogenetic and Psychogenetic Investigations.* 1st American ed. Mole Editions. New York: Urizen Books, 1978.

———. *The Court Society.* New York: Pantheon Books, 1983.

Ellerbrock, Karl-Peter. *Geschichte der deutschen Nahrungs- und Genußmittelindustrie: 1750–1914.* Stuttgart: Steiner, 1993.

Elliott, J. H. "A Europe of Composite Monarchies." *Past & Present* 137, no. 1 (November 1, 1992): 48–71.

Elsas, Moritz John. *Umriss einer geschichte der preise und löhne in Deutschland.* Leiden: A. W. Sijthoff, 1936.

Elton, G. *The Reformation, 1520–1559.* 2nd ed. Cambridge: Cambridge University Press, 1990.

Emich, Birgit. "Frühneuzeitliche Staatsbildung und politische Kultur: für die Veralltäglichung eines Konzepts." In *Was heisst Kulturgeschichte des Politischen?,* 191–205. Berlin: Duncker & Humblot, 2005.

Endres, Rudolf. *Adel in der frühen Neuzeit.* Munich: R. Oldenbourg, 1993.

Engel, Evamaria. *Die deutsche Stadt des Mittelalters.* Munich: C. H. Beck, 1993.

Epstein, Stephan R., and Maarten Roy Prak. *Guilds, Innovation, and the European Economy, 1400–1800.* Cambridge: Cambridge University Press, 2008.

Erdmannsdörfer, Bernhard. *Graf Georg Friedrich von Waldeck: E. Preuß. Staatsmann im 17. Jh.* Berlin: Reimer, 1869.

———. "Zur Geschichte der Kammerstaats-Reform von 1652. Aktenstücke." *Zeitschrift für preussische Geschichte und Landeskunde,* no. 13 (1876): 560–90.

Ertman, Thomas. *Birth of the Leviathan: Building States and Regimes in Medieval and Early Modern Europe.* Cambridge : Cambridge University Press, 1997.

Escher, Felix. *Berlin und sein Umland: zur Genese der Berliner Stadtlandschaft bis zum Beginn des 20. Jahrhunderts.* Berlin: Colloquium, 1985.

Etcheverry, Michel. "Un seigneur béarnais ambassadeur de France en Espagne." *Bulletin hispanique* 50, no. 3 (1948): 483–94.

Etzlstorfer, Hannes. *Küchenkunst und Tafelkultur: Culinaria von der Antike bis zur Gegenwart.* Vienna: Brandstätter, 2006.

Evan-Thomas, Owen. *Domestic Utensils of Wood.* London: Evan-Thomas, 1932.

Eveleigh, David J. *Old Cooking Utensils.* Princes Risborough, UK: Shire, 1986.

Ferguson, Priscilla. *Accounting for Taste. The Triumph of French Cuisine.* Chicago: University of Chicago Press, 2004.

———. "Eating Orders: Markets, Menus, and Meals." *Journal of Modern History* 77, no. 3 (2005): 679–700.

Fidicin, Ernst. "Die Wendland'sche Chronik von 1648 bis 1701." *Schriften des Vereins für die Geschichte der Stadt Berlin,* no. 1 (1865): 45–104.

Field, Rachael. *Irons in the Fire: A History of Cooking Equipment.* Ramsbury, UK: Crowood Press, 1984.

Findlen, Paula. "The Economy and Scientific Exchange in Early Modern Italy," in *Patronage and Institutions,* edited by Bruce Moran, 5–24. Rochester, NY: Boydell Press, 1991.

———. *Possessing Nature: Museums, Collecting, and Scientific Culture in Early Modern Italy.* Berkeley: University of California Press, 1996.

Fischer, Ernst. "Die offizielle brandenburgische Geschichtsschreibung zur Zeit Friedrich Wilhelms, des Großen Kurfürsten (1640–1688)." *Zeitschrift für preussische Geschichte und Landeskunde* 15 (1878): 377–430.

Fitzpatrick, Joan, ed. *Renaissance Food from Rabelais to Shakespeare Culinary Readings and Culinary Histories.* Farnham, UK; Burlington, VT: Ashgate, 2010.

Flandrin, Jean-Louis. *Arranging the Meal: A History of Table Service in France.* Translated by Julie E. Johnson. Berkeley: University of California Press, 2007.

———. "Le goût et la nécessité: sur l'usage des graisses dans les cuisines d'Europe occidentale (XIVe–XVIIIe siècle)." *Annales: Paris* 38, no. 2 (1983): 369–401.

———. *Le sucre dans les livres de cuisine francais, du XIVe siecle au XVIIIe.* Paris: Museum d'histoire naturelle, 1988.

———. "L'ordre de succession des mets en France aux XVIIe et XVIIIe siècles." In *Mahl und Repräsentation: der Kult ums Essen,* edited by Lothar Kolmer and Christian Rohr, 167–79. Paderborn: Ferdinand Schöningh, 2000.

———. *Pour une histoire du gout.* Liege: Sect. d'Histoire, 1982.

Flandrin, Jean-Louis, Philip Hyman, and Mary Hyman, eds. "La cuisine dans la littérature de Colportage." In *Le cuisinier françois* by François Pierre de La Varenne, 11–99. Paris: Montalba, 1983.

Flandrin, Jean-Louis, Massimo Montanari, and Albert Sonnenfeld, eds. *Food: A Culinary History from Antiquity to the Present.* New York: Columbia University Press, 1999.

Földes, László, and Akadémiai Kiadó (Budapest). *Viehwirtschaft und Hirtenkultur: Ethnographische Studien.* Budapest: Akadémiai Kiadó, 1969.

Forster, Elborg. *European Diet from Pre-Industrial to Modern Times.* New York: Harper and Row, 1975.

Foster, Nelson, and Linda S. Cordell. *Chilies to Chocolate: Food the Americas Gave the World.* Tucson: University of Arizona Press, 1992.

Fouquet, Gerhard, Jan Hirschbiegel, and Werner Paravicini, eds. *Hofwirtschaft: ein ökonomischer Blick auf Hof und Residenz in Spätmittelalter und Früher Neuzeit.* Ostfildern: Thorbecke, 2008.

Foxcroft, Louise. *Calories & Corsets: A History of Dieting over 2000 Years.* London: Profile, 2012.

Francke, August Hermann. *Speise-Ordnung im Waysenhauße zu Halle 1702.* Halle (Saale): Franckeschen Stiftungen, 2011.

Frantzen, Allen J. *Food, Eating and Identity in Early Medieval England.* Woodbridge: Boydell Press, 2014.

Franz, Günther. *Der Dreißigjährige Krieg und das Deutsche Volk: Untersuchungen zur Bevölkerungs- und Agrargeschichte.* Jena: Gustav Fischer, 1943.

Fraser, Evan D. G., and Andrew Rimas. *Empires of Food: Feast, Famine, and the Rise and Fall of Civilizations.* New York: Free Press, 2010.

Freedman, Paul, Joyce E. Chaplin, and Ken Albala. *Food in Time and Place: The American Historical Association Companion to Food History.* Berkeley: University of California Press, 2014.

——. *Food: The History of Taste.* Berkeley: University of California Press, 2007.

——. *Out of the East: Spices and the Medieval Imagination.* New Haven: Yale University Press, 2008.

French, R. K., and A. Wear. *The Medical Revolution of the Seventeenth Century.* Cambridge: Cambridge University Press, 1989.

Frey, Linda. *Friedrich I.* Graz: Styria, 1984.

Friedland, Klaus, ed. *Maritime Food Transport.* Cologne: Böhlau, 1994.

Friedrich, Karin. *Brandenburg-Prussia, 1466–1806: The Rise of a Composite State.* Houndmills, UK: Palgrave Macmillan, 2012.

Friedrich, Karin, and Sara Smart, eds. *The Cultivation of Monarchy and the Rise of Berlin: Brandenburg-Prussia, 1700.* Farnham, UK: Ashgate, 2010.

Fuhrich-Grubert, Ursula. *Handbuch der preußischen Geschichte.* Vol. 1. Berlin: De Gruyter, 2009.

Gagliardo, John G. *Germany under the Old Regime, 1600–1790.* London: Longman, 1991.

Garber, Klaus, Manfred Komorowski, and Axel E. Walter. *Kulturgeschichte Ostpreussens in der Frühen Neuzeit.* Tübingen: M. Niemeyer, 2001.

Gause, Fritz. *Acta Prussica; Abhandlungen zur Geschichte Ost- und Westpreussens.* Würzburg: Holzner-Verlag, 1968.

——. *Die Geschichte der Stadt Königsberg in Preussen.* Cologne: Böhlau, 1965.

Gautier, Alban, and Allen J. Grieco. "Food and Drink in Medieval and Renaissance Europe: An Overview of the Past Decade (2001–2012)." *Food and History* 10, no. 2 (July 1, 2012): 73–88.

Gentilcore, David. *Food and Health in Early Modern Europe Diet, Medicine and Society, 1450–1800.* London: Bloomsbury, 2016.

Georg, Carl. *Verzeichnis der Litteratur über Speise und Trank bis zum Jahre 1887.* Hanover: Klindworth's, 1888.

George, Richard. "Die ersten Regierungsjahre des Großen Kurfürsten." In *Hie gut Brandenburg alleweg!: Geschichts- und Kulturbilder aus der Vergangenheit der Mark und aus Alt-Berlin bis zum Tode des Grossen Kurfürsten,* 374–80. Berlin: Pauli, 1900.

Geyer, Albert. "Der Festsaal des Großen Kurfürsten." *Hohenzollern Jahrbuch* 1 (1897): 146–73.

———. *The Historical Private Apartments in Berlin Castle.* Berlin: Deutsche Kunst Verlag, 1929.

Geyer, Albert, and Jürgen Julier, *Geschichte des Schlosses zu Berlin: erster band: die kurfürstliche zeit bis zum jahre 1698.* Berlin: Nicolaische, 2010.

Giersberg, Hans-Joachim. *Der Grosse Kurfürst: 1620–1688: Sammler, Bauherr, Mäzen.* Potsdam-Sanssouci: Generaldirektion der Staatlichen Schlösser und Gärten, 1988.

Gilman, Sander L. *Diets and Dieting: A Cultural Encyclopedia.* New York: Routledge, 2008.

Gladstone, Ethel. "The Lure of Medical History: Johann Sigismund Elsholtz†: Clysmatica Nova (1665): Elsholtz' Neglected Work on Intravenous Injection: Parts I–IV." *California and Western Medicine* nos. 38–39 (1933–39).

Glanville, Philippa. "Protocole et usages des tables à la cour d'Angelterre." In *Versailles et les tables royales en Europe, XVIIème–XIXème siècles,* edited by Guorarer Zeev and Jean-Pierre Babelon, 156–59. Paris: Editions de la Réunion des musées nationaux, 1993.

Glanville, Philippa, and Hilary Young, eds. *Elegant Eating. Four Hundred Years of Dining in Style.* London: V&A Publications, 2002.

Glinski, Gerhard von. *Die Königsberger Kaufmannschaft des 17. und 18. Jahrhunderts.* Marburg/Lahn: J. G. Harder, 1964.

Glinski, Gerhard von, and Peter Wörster. *Königsberg: die ostpreussische Hauptstadt in Geschichte und Gegenwart.* Berlin: Westkreuz, 1990.

Gloger, Bruno. *Friedrich Wilhelm: Kurfürst von Brandenburg.* Berlin: Verl. Neues Leben, 1986.

Gloning, Thomas. "Monumenta Culinaria et Diaetetica Historica, Corpus of Culinary & Dietetic Texts of Europe from the Middle Ages to 1800, Corpus älterer deutscher Kochbücher und Ernährungslehren." Justus-Liebig-Universität Gießen. Accessed April 5, 2023. https://www.uni-giessen.de/de/fbz/fb05/germanistik/absprache/sprachverwendung/gloning/kobu.htm.

Goldgar, Anne. *Tulipmania: Money, Honor, and Knowledge in the Dutch Golden Age.* Chicago: University of Chicago Press, 2007.

Gollub, Hermann. *Der Grosse Kurfürst und Polen von 1660 bis 1668.* Dissertation at the Friedrich-Wilhelms Universität zu Berlin. Berlin: Universitäts-Buchdruckerei von Gustav Schade, 1914.

Goltz, Theodor Alexander Ludwig Georg. *Handbuch der gesamten landwirtschaft: Die landwirtschaftliche tierhaltung und die landwirtschaftlichen nebengewerbe.* Tübingen: Verlag der H. Laupp'schen buchhandlung, 1890.

Göschen, G. T., ed. *Jahresberichte für neuere deutsche Literaturgeschichte.* Berlin: B. Behrs Verlag, 1907.

Göse, Frank. *Friedrich I. (1657–1713): ein König in Preußen.* Regensburg: Pustet, 2012.

———. *Rittergut—Garnison—Residenz: Studien zur Sozialstruktur und Politischen Wirksamkeit des Brandenburgischen Adels, 1648–1763*. Berlin: Berliner Wissenschafts-Verlag, 2005.

Grafton, Anthony, April Shelford, and Nancy G. Siraisi. *New Worlds, Ancient Texts: The Power of Tradition and the Shock of Discovery*. Cambridge, MA: Harvard University Press, 1995.

Grafton, Anthony, and Nancy G. Siraisi. *Natural Particulars Nature and the Disciplines in Renaissance Europe*. Cambridge, MA: MIT Press, 1999.

Grebe, Anja, and Heinrich Häffner. "Truhe und Wandschrank—Mobile und Feste Ausstattungen im Burgen- und Frühen Schlossbau." In *Raumkunst in Burg und Schloss. Zeugnis und Gesamtkunstwerk.*, 25–47. Jahrbuch der Stiftung Thüringer Schlösser und Gärten 8. Regensburg: Schnell & Steiner, 2004.

Greenblatt, Stephen. "Introduction: Fifty Years of The King's Two Bodies." *Representations* 106, no. 1 (May 1, 2009): 63–66.

Grew, Marion Ethel Tuckwell. *The House of Orange*. London: Methuen, 1947.

Grieco, Allen J. *Food, Social Politics and the Order of Nature in Renaissance Italy*, Florence: I Tatti, 2019.

———. "Medieval and Renaissance Wines: Taste, Dietary Theory, and How to Choose the 'Right' Wine (14th–16th Centuries)." *Mediaevalia* 30 (2009): 15.

———. "The Social Politics of Pre-Linnaean Botanical Classification." *I Tatti Studies in the Italian Renaissance* 4 (January 1, 1991): 131–49.

Grieco, Allen J., and Peter Scholliers. "Corresponding Members." *Reports, Food Historiography: Periods, Places and Themes* 18, nos. 1–2 (January 2020): 187–89.

Großmann, Julius. "Jugendgeschichte Friedrichs I. Ersten Königs in Preußen." *Hohenzollern Jahrbuch* 4 (1900): 10–59.

Günther, Harri, ed. *Vom Garten-Baw. 1684*. Reprint, Hildesheim; New York: G. Olms, 1987.

Gutmann, Anita. *Hofkultur in Bayreuth zur Markgrafenzeit: 1603–1726*. Bayreuth: Rabenstein, 2008.

Haag, Sabine. *Fürstlich Tafeln: eine Ausstellung des Kunsthistorischen Museums Wien Schloss Ambras Innsbruck 25. März bis 31. Mai 2015*. Vienna: KHM-Museumsverband, 2015.

Habermas, Jürgen. *The Structural Transformation of the Public Sphere: An Inquiry into a Category of Bourgeois Society*. Studies in Contemporary German Social Thought. Cambridge, MA: MIT Press, 1989.

Häcker, Andreas. "Mangeurs et cuisiniers dans la littérature moderne de langue allemande." *Food and History* 10, no. 2 (July 1, 2012): 169–79.

Haffner, Sebastian. *Preußen ohne Legende*. Berlin: Siedler, 2001.

Hagen, William W. "Capitalism and the Countryside in Early Modern Europe: Interpretations, Models, Debates." *Agricultural History* 62, no. 1 (January 1988): 13–47.

———. *Ordinary Prussians: Brandenburg Junkers and Villagers, 1500–1840.* Cambridge: Cambridge University Press, 2002.

———. "Seventeenth-Century Crisis in Brandenburg: The Thirty Years' War, The Destabilization of Serfdom, and the Rise of Absolutism." *American Historical Review* 94, no. 2 (April 1989): 302–35.

———. "Working for the Junker: The Standard of Living of Manorial Laborers in Brandenburg, 1584–1810." *Journal of Modern History* 58, no. 1 (March 1986): 143–58.

Hahn, Peter-Michael. *Pracht und Herrlichkeit: adlig-fuerstliche Lebensstile im 17. und 18. Jahrhundert.* Potsdam: Verlag für Berlin-Brandenburg, 1998.

Hahn, Peter-Michael, et al., eds. *Zeichen und Raum: Ausstattung und höfisches Zeremoniell in den deutschen Schlössern der Frühen Neuzeit.* Munich: Deutscher Kunstverlag, 2006.

Halén, Widar. *Royal Silver Services.* Translated by Elinor Ruth Waaler. Oslo: Kunstindustrimuseet I Oslo, 2000.

Hamling, Tara, and Catherine Richardson. *Everyday Objects: Medieval and Early Modern Material Culture and Its Meanings.* Farnham, UK: Ashgate, 2010.

Hammer, Ulrike. *Kurfürstin Luise Henriette: eine Oranierin als Mittlerin zwischen den Niederlanden und Brandenburg-Preussen.* Münster: Waxmann, 2001.

Harvey, Karen, ed. *History and Material Culture: A Student's Guide to Approaching Alternative Sources.* London: Routledge, 2009.

Havemann, Wilhelm. *Geschichte der Lande Braunschweig und Lüneburg für Schule und Haus.* Brunswick: Herold & Wahlstab, 1838.

Hays, J. N. *The Burdens of Disease: Epidemics and Human Response in Western History.* New Brunswick, NJ: Rutgers University Press, 2009.

Heegewaldt, Werner. *(Adlige) Herrschafts-, Guts- und Familienarchive (Rep. 37).* Vol. 60. Veroeffentlichungen des Brandenburgischen Landeshauptarchivs. Berlin: Berliner Wissenschafts-Verlag, 2010.

Heeres, W. G, and J. A Faber. *From Dunkirk to Danzig: Shipping and Trade in the North Sea and the Baltic, 1350–1850.* Hilversum: Verloren Publishers, 1988.

Heidecke, Wolfgang. "Alte Maße Altpreußens." *Altpreußische Geschlechterkunde* 13 (1939): 22–23, 53–54, 92.

Heidegger, Maria, et al. "'Gutachterei': Beiträge der Medical Humanities zu Ambivalenzen der Begutachtung." *Österreichische Zeitschrift für Geschichtswissenschaften* 31, no. 3 (2020): 7–17.

Heilmeyer, Marina. *Kirschen für den König.* Potsdamer pomologische Geschichten. Potsdam: Vacat, 2001.

Heilmeyer, Marina, and Antonia Humm. *König & Kartoffel: Friedrich der Grosse und die preussischen "Tartuffoli."* Potsdam: Verlag für Berlin-Brandenburg, 2012.

Heilmeyer, Marina, and Michael Seiler. *Maulbeeren—zwischen Glaube und Hoffnung.* Potsdam: Vacat, 2006.

Hein, Max. *Otto von Schwerin: der Oberpräsident des Grossen Kurfürsten.* Königsberg: Gräfe und Unzer, 1929.

Heinrich, Gerd, ed. *Ein Sonderbares Licht in Teutschland: Beiträge zur Geschichte des Grossen Kürfursten von Brandenburg (1640–1688).* Berlin: Duncker & Humblot, 1990.

———. *Geschichte Preussens: Staat und Dynastie.* Frankfurt am Main: Propyläen, 2016.

Heinzelmann, Ursula. *Beyond Bratwurst: A History of Food in Germany,* 2014.

———. *Food Culture in Germany.* Westport, CT: Greenwood Press, 2008.

———. "Rumohr's Falscher Rehschlegel: The Significance of Venison in German Cuisine." *Gastronomica* 6, no. 4 (2006): 53–58.

Helstosky, Carol, ed. *The Routledge History of Food.* London: Routledge, 2015.

Henisch, Bridget Ann. *Fast and Feast: Food in Medieval Society.* University Park: Pennsylvania State University Press, 1976.

Hennert, Forstrat. "Anekdoten von den Reisen der Kurfürstin Dorothea von Brandenburg, besonders als sie ihren Gemahl Kfft Friedrich Wilhelm den Gr. in seinen letzten Feldzügen begleitete." *Neue Berlinische Monatsschrift* 3 (1800): 3–31.

Henning, Friedrich-Wilhelm. *Landwirtschaft und Ländliche Gesellschaft in Deutschland.* Paderborn: Schöningh, 1978.

Henry, John. *The Scientific Revolution and the Origins of Modern Science.* Basingstoke, UK: Palgrave Macmillan, 2008.

Herman, Eleanor. *The Royal Art of Poison: Fatal Cosmetics, Deadly Medicines, and Murder Most Foul.* New York: St. Martin's Press, 2019.

Hess, Volker. "Die Anfänge ärztlicher Standesvertretung zwischen korporativer Autonomie und staatlicher Behörde. Das Medizinaledikt von 1685. " *Berliner Ärzte* 47, no. 8 (2010): 16–19.

Heyde, Johann Friedrich. *Der Roggenpreis und die Kriege des grossen Königs: Chronik und Rezeptsammlung des Berliner Bäckermeisters Johann Friedrich Heyde, 1740 bis 1786.* Berlin: Siedler Verlag, 1988.

Hilber, Marina, and Elena Taddei, eds. *In fürstlicher Nähe—Ärzte bei Hof (1450–1800).* Innsbruck: Innsbruck University Press, 2021.

Hingst, Monika, and Marina Heilmeyer, eds. *Schön und nützlich: aus Brandenburgs Kloster-, Schloss- und Küchengärten* Leipzig: Henschel, 2004.

Hintze, Otto. *Die Hohenzollern und ihr Werk: Fünfhundert Jahre vaterländischer Geschichte.* Berlin: Paul Parey, 1915.

Hirsch, Ferdinand. "Die Erziehung des älteren Söhne des Großen Kurfürsten." *Forschungen zur brandenburgischen und preussischen Geschichte* 7 (1906): 141–71.

Hirschfelder, Gunther. *Europäische Esskultur: eine Geschichte der Ernährung von der Steinzeit bis heute.* Frankfurt am Main: Campus, 2001.

Hoffman, Julius. *Die Hausväterliteratur und die Predigten üben den christlichen Hausstand.* Goettinger Studien zur Paedagogik 37. Berlin: Weinheim, 1959.

Hoffmann, Andreas. *Der Umbau des Berliner Stadtschlosses zur barocken Residenz unter Friedrich III./I. und seinem Baumeister Andreas Schlüter.* Munich: GRIN Verlag, 2007.

Holleman, A. F., and Egon Wiberg. *Lehrbuch der Anorganischen Chemie.* Berlin: De Gruyter, 1985.

Holm, LeRoy, et al. *World Weeds: Natural Histories and Distribution.* New York: John Wiley & Sons, 1997.

Holtze, Friedrich. "Das Amt Mühlenhof bis 1600." In *Schriften des Vereins für die Geschichte Berlins* 30.2:19–32. Berlin: Zentral- und Landesbibliothek Berlin Zentrum für Berlin-Studien, 1893.

Hörmann, Johannes. "Die Königliche Hofapotheke in Berlin 1598–1898." *Hohenzollern Jahrbuch* 2 (1898): 208–26.

Hornsey, Ian S. *A History of Beer and Brewing.* Cambridge: Royal Society of Chemistry, 2003.

Humm, Antonia Maria, Marina Heilmeyer, Kurt Winkler, and Haus der Brandenburgisch-Preussischen Geschichte. *König & Kartoffel: Friedrich der Grosse und die preussischen "Tartuffoli."* Potsdam: Haus der Brandenburgisch-Preussischen Geschichte, VBB, Verlag für Berlin-Brandenburg, 2012.

Hüttl, Ludwig. *Friedrich Wilhelm von Brandenburg: Der Große Kurfürst, 1620–1688. Eine Politische Biographie.* Munich: Süddeutscher Verlag, 1981.

Hyde, Elizabeth, ed. *A Cultural History of Gardens in the Renaissance.* London: Bloomsbury Academic, 2013.

Hyman, Philip, and Mary Hyman. "La Chapelle and Massialot: An Eighteenth-Century Feud." *Petits propos culinaires* 2 (1979): 44–54.

Isaacsohn, Siegfried. "Das Erbpachtsystem in der preußischen Domänenpolitik." *Zeitschrift für preussische Geschichte und Landeskunde* 11 (1874): 698–737.

———. *Das preußische Beamtenthum des siebenzehnten Jahrhunderts.* 3 vols. Berlin: Puttkammer & Mühlbrecht, 1874–78.

———. "Die Reform des kurfürstlich brandenburgischen Kammerstaats 1651/52." *Zeitschrift für preussische Geschichte und Landeskunde,* no. 13 (1876): 161–208.

Jacobsen, Roswitha. "Die Blütezeit der Residenzkultur im 17. und 18. Jahrhundert." In *Neu entdeckt: Thüringen—Land der Residenzen; 1485–1918; 2. Thüringer Landesausstellung Schloss Sondershausen 15. Mai–3. Oktober 2004,* edited by Martin Salesch, 52–64. Sondershausen: Philipp von Zabern, 2004.

Jacoby, Jörg. *Boguslaus Radziwill, der Statthalter des Grossen Kurfürsten in Ostpreussen.* Marburg: J. G. Herder Institut, 1959.

Jacomet, Stefanie, and Angela Kreuz. *Archäobotanik: Aufgaben, Methoden und Ergebnisse Vegetations- und Agrargeschichtlicher Forschung.* Stuttgart: Ulmer, 1999.

Jahn, Hans. *Berlin im Todesjahr des Grossen Kurfürsten.* Schriften des Vereins für die Geschichte Berlins. Berlin: Verlag des Vereins für die Geschichte Berlins, 1935.

Jähnig, Bernhart, Udo Arnold, Mario Glauert, and Jürgen Sarnowsky. *Preussische Landesgeschichte: Festschrift für Bernhart Jähnig zum 60. Geburtstag.* Marburg: Elwert, 2001.

Jaine, Tom, ed. *The Cooking Pot: Proceedings, Oxford Symposium on Food & Cookery, 1988.* London: Prospect Books, 1989.

Jancke, Gabriele, and Daniel Schläppi. "Ökonomie sozialer Beziehungen. Wie Gruppen in frühneuzeitlichen Gesellschaften Ressourcen bewirtschafteten." In *Mitgift,* edited by Margareth Lanzinger and Karin Gottschalk, 85–97. Cologne: Böhlau, 2011.

Jochums, Gabriele. *Bibliographie Friedrich III./I. Schrifttum von 1657 bis 2008.* Berlin: Geheimes Staatsarchiv PK, 2009.

———. *Bibliographie Friedrich Wilhelm, Kurfürst von Brandenburg: Schrifttum von 1640 bis 2013.* Berlin: Geheimes Staatsarchiv PK, 2005.

Johnson, Christine R. *The German Discovery of the World: Renaissance Encounters with the Strange and Marvelous.* Charlottesville: University of Virginia Press, 2008.

Johnson, Nuala Christina. *Nature Displaced, Nature Displayed: Order and Beauty in Botanical Gardens.* London: I. B. Tauris, 2011.

Jussen, Bernhard. "The King's Two Bodies Today." *Representations* 106, no. 1 (2009): 102–17.

Kaak, Heinrich. *Die Gutsherrschaft: theoriegeschichtliche Untersuchungen zum Agrarwesen im ostelbischen Raum.* Berlin: De Gruyter, 1991.

Kaiser, Hermann, and Helmut Ottenjann. *Das alltägliche Brot über Schwarzbrot, Pumpernickel, Backhäuser und Grobbäcker: ein geschichtlicher Abriß.* Cloppenburg: Museumsdorf Cloppenburg, 1989.

Kaiser, Michael, and Michael Rohrschneider, eds. *Membra unius capitis: Studien zu Herrschaftsauffassungen und Regierungspraxis in Kurbrandenburg (1640–1688).* Berlin: Duncker & Humblot, 2005.

Kalinke, Heinke M. *Esskultur und Kulturelle Identität: ethnologische Nahrungsforschung im Östlichen Europa.* Munich: Oldenbourg, 2010.

Kalof, Linda, and William F. Bynum, eds. *A Cultural History of the Human Body in the Renaissance.* Vol. 3. Oxford: Berg, 2010.

Kamke, Hans-Ulbrich. *Barnim und Lebus. Studien zur Entstehung und Entwicklung Agrarischer Strukturen Zwischen Havel und Oder.* Vol. 1106. Deutsche Hochschulschriften. Frankfurt am Main: Egelsbach, 1996.

Kampmann, Christoph, et al., eds. *Bourbon, Habsburg, Oranien: konkurrierende Modelle im dynastischen Europa um 1700*. Cologne: Böhlau 2008.

Kantorowicz, Ernst Hartwig. *The King's Two Bodies: A Study in Mediaeval Political Theology*. Princeton: Princeton University Press, 1957.

Kaphahn, Fritz. *Die wirtschaftlichen Folgen des 30jährigen Krieges für die Altmark ein Beitrag zur Geschichte des Zusammenbruchs der deutschen Volkswirtschaft in der ersten Hälfte des 17. Jahrhunderts*. Gotha: F. A. Perthes, 1911.

Kaplan, Steven Laurence. *The Bakers of Paris and the Bread Question, 1700–1775*. Durham, NC: Duke University Press, 1996.

———. *Bread, Politics and Political Economy in the Reign of Louis XV*. The Hague: Nijhoff, 1976.

———. *Provisioning Paris: Merchants and Millers in the Grain and Flour Trade during the Eighteenth Century*. Ithaca, NY: Cornell University Press, 2018.

Katz, Solomon, and William Weaver. *Encyclopedia of Food and Culture*. New York: C. Scribner, 2003.

Keblusek, Marika, and Jori Zijlmans, eds. *Princely Display: The Court of Frederik Hendrik of Orange and Amalia van Solms*. The Hague: Historical Museum, Waanders, 1997.

Keisch, Christine. *Das grosse Silberbuffet aus dem Rittersaal des Berliner Schlosses*. Berlin: Staatliche Museen Preussische Kulturbesitz Kunstgewerbemuseum, 1997.

Kellenbenz, Hermann. "Der Kammerdiener, ein Typus der höfischen Gesellschaft: Seine Rolle als Unternehmer." *Vierteljahrschrift für Sozial- und Wirtschaftsgeschichte* 72 (1985): 476–507.

Kern, Arthur, ed. *Deutsche Hofordnungen des 16. und 17. Jahrhunderts*. 2 vols. Vol. 1: *Brandenburg, Preußen, Pommern, Mecklenburg*. Berlin: Weidmannsche Buchhandlung, 1905.

Kettering, Sharon. *Patrons, Brokers, and Clients in Seventeenth-Century France*. New York: Oxford University Press, 1986.

Kinder, Sebastian, and Haik Thomas Porada. *Brandenburg an der Havel und Umgebung: eine landeskundliche Bestandsaufnahme im Raum Brandenburg an der Havel, Pritzerbe, Reckahn und Wusterwitz*. Cologne: Böhlau, 2006.

Kiple, Kenneth F. *A Movable Feast: Ten Millennia of Food Globalization*. Cambridge: Cambridge University Press, 2007.

Kiple, Kenneth F., and Kriemhild Coneè Ornelas. *The Cambridge World History of Food*. Cambridge: Cambridge University Press, 2000.

Kirchschlager, Michael. *Ich will ein guter Koch sein: Küchengeheimnisse des Mittelalters und der Renaissance*. Arnstadt: Kirchschlager, 2004.

Kissane, Christopher. *Food, Religion and Communities in Early Modern Europe*. London: Bloomsbury Academic, 2020.

Klein, Julia, Eric Hartmann, and Jürgen Luh, eds. *Frauensache: Wie Brandenburg Preussen Wurde*. Dresden: Sandstein Verlag, 2015.

Klein, Ulrich. *Küche—Kochen—Ernährung: Archäologie, Bauforschung, Natur-wissenschaften: Tagung Schwäbisch Hall, 6. bis 8. April 2006.* Paderborn: Deutsche Gesellschaft für Archäologie des Mittelalters und der Neuzeit, 2007.

Kleinschmidt, Wolfgang. *Essen und Trinken in der frühneuzeitlichen Reichsstadt Speyer: die Rechnungen des Spitals St. Georg (1514-1600).* Münster: Wax-mann, 2012.

Kloosterhuis, Elisabeth M. *Soldatenkönigs Tafelfreuden: die Tafelkultur am Hofe Friedrich Wilhelms I.* Berlin: Berlin-Story-Verlag, 2009.

Kloosterhuis, Jürgen, ed. *Schloss: Macht und Kultur: Entwicklung und Funktion Brandenburg-Preußischer Residenzen.* Berlin: Berliner Wiss.-Verl., 2012.

Kluge, Arnd. *Currywurst & Co.: Die Geschichte des Fast Food in Deutschland.* Stuttgart: Franz Steiner, 2021.

Koch, H. W. *A History of Prussia.* London: Longman, 1978.

Koenigsberger, H. G. *Politicians and Virtuosi: Essays in Early Modern History.* London: Hambledon Press, 1986.

Kolmer, Lothar, and Christian Rohr, eds. *Mahl und Repräsentation: der Kult ums Essen.* Paderborn: Ferdinand Schöningh, 2000.

Koopmann, Torben. "Höfische Repräsentation bei Graf Anton Günther am Beispiel des Besuches des Kurprinzen Friedrich Wilhelm von Brandenburg." *Oldenburger Jahrbuch* 112 (2012): 53–76.

Kopytoff, Igor. "The Cultural Biography of Things: Commoditization as Pro-cess." In *The Social Life of Things,* edited by Arjun Appadurai, 64–91. Cam-bridge: Cambridge University Press, 1986.

Koslofsky, Craig. "Court Culture and Street Lighting in Seventeenth-Century Europe." *Journal of Urban History* 28, no. 6 (September 1, 2002): 743–68.

Kotzsch, Lothar. *Königsberg in Preussen seit Peter dem Grossen: die Beziehungen zwischen Deutschen und Russen in den letzten drei Jahrhunderten.* Berlin: Edition Ost, 2001.

Krausch, Hans-Dieter. "Die Pflanzen Des Elsholtz-Florilegiums 1659/1660." *Feddes Repertorium* 112, nos. 7–8 (December 1, 2001): 597–612.

Krohn, Deborah L. "Carving and Folding by the Book in Early Modern Eu-rope." *Journal of Early Modern History* 24, no. 1 (February 20, 2020): 17–40.

———. *Food and Knowledge in Renaissance Italy: Bartolomeo Scappi's Paper Kitchens.* London: Routledge Taylor & Francis, 2018.

———. "Picturing the Kitchen: Renaissance Treatise and Period Room." *Studies in the Decorative Arts* 16, no. 1 (2008): 20–34.

———. *Staging the Table in Europe, 1500–1800.* New York: Bard Graduate Cen-ter, 2023.

Kudriaffsky, Eufemia von. *Die Historische Küche: ein Kulturbild.* Vienna: A. Hartleben's Verlag, 1880.

Kühn, Sebastian. "Die Macht der Diener: Hausdienerschaft in hofadligen Haushalten (Preußen und Sachsen, 16.–18. Jahrhundert)." *Mitteilungen der*

Residenzen-Kommission der Akademie der Wissenschaften zu Göttingen, Neue Folge: Stadt und Hof 6 (2017): 159–69.

——. "Küchenpolitik. Annäherungen an subalterne Handlungsweisen in hofadligen Haushalten des 17. und 18. Jahrhunderts." *L'Homme. Europäische Zeitschrift für Feministische Geschichtwissenschaft* 28, no. 2 (2017): 69–84.

——. "Masters as Debtors of Their Servants in Early Modern Brandenburg and Saxony." In *Early Modern Debts,* edited by Laura Kolb and George Oppitz-Trotman, 53–82. Cham: Springer, 2020.

——. "Teil-Habe am Haushalt. Dienerschaften in Adelshaushalten der Frühen Neuzeit." In *Von der Allmende zur Share-Economy,* 113–36. Beiträge zur Rechts-, Gesellschafts- und Kulturkritik 15. Berlin: Berliner Wissenschafts Verlag, 2018.

Kümin, Beat, ed. *A Cultural History of Food in the Early Modern Age.* London: Bloomsbury, 2014.

——. *Drinking Matters: Public Houses and Social Exchange in Early Modern Central Europe.* Basingstoke, UK: Palgrave Macmillan, 2007.

——. "Political Culture in the Holy Roman Empire." *German History* 27, no. 1 (January 2009): 131–44.

——. "Rural Autonomy and Popular Politics in Imperial Villages." *German History* 33, no. 2 (June 2015): 194–213.

Kunisch, Johannes. "Der Grosse Kurfürst als Feldherr." *Zeitschrift für Historische Forschung* 33, no. 1 (2006): 67–87.

Küntzel, Georg, and Martin Hass. *Die politischen testamente der Hohenzollern nebst ergänzenden aktenstücken.* Leipzig: B. G. Teubner, 1911.

Kunz, Ludvik. "Die Traditionfelle Milch- und Käsewirtschaft in Mittel- und Westmähren." In *Viehwirtschaft und Hirtenkultur: ethnographische Studien,* 706–34. Budapest: Akadémiai Kiadó, 1969.

Kürbis, Holger. *Johann Moritz von Nassau-Siegen.* Erfurt: Sutton, 2005.

Kurzel-Runtscheiner, Monica. *Glanzvolles Elend: die Inventare der Herzogin Jacobe von Jülich-Kleve-Berg (1558–1597) und die Bedeutung von Luxusgütern für die höfische Frau des 16. Jahrhunderts.* Vienna: Böhlau, 1993.

Küster, Hansjörg. *Wo der Pfeffer wächst: ein Lexikon zur Kulturgeschichte der Gewürze.* Munich: C. H. Beck, 1987.

Lademacher, Horst. *Onder den Oranje Boom : Niederländische Kunst und Kultur im 17. und 18. Jahrhundert an Deutschen Fürstenhöfen.* Munich: Hirmer, 1999.

——. *Oranien-Nassau, die Niederlande und das Reich: Beiträge zur Geschichte einer Dynastie.* Münster: Lit, 1995.

Ladendorf, H. "Die Geschichte des Schlosses zu Berlin." *Sonderdruck aus der Zeitschrift des Vereins für die Geschichte Berlins,* no. 4 (1836): 136–38.

Laszlo, Pierre. *Citrus.* Chicago: University of Chicago Press, 2007.

Laszlovszky, József, and Péter Szabó. *People and Nature in Historical Perspective.* Budapest: Central European University, Dept. of Medieval Studies, 2003.

Leach, Helen M., and Raelene Inglis. "The Archaeology of Christmas Cakes." *Food and Foodways* 11, nos. 2–3 (January 1, 2003): 141–66.

Ledebur, Leopold von. *Schauplatz der Thaten oder Aufenthalts-Nachweis des Kurfürsten Friedrich Wilhelm des Großen.* Berlin: W. Hayn, 1840.

Lévi-Strauss, Claude. *The Raw and the Cooked.* Chicago: University of Chicago Press, 1996.

Lindemann, Mary. *Health & Healing in Eighteenth-Century Germany.* Baltimore: Johns Hopkins University Press, 1996.

———. *Medicine and Society in Early Modern Europe.* Cambridge: Cambridge University Press, 1999.

Linklater, Andrew, and Stephen Mennell. "Norbert Elias, The Civilizing Process: Sociogenetic and Psychogenetic Investigations—An Overview and Assessment." *History and Theory* 49, no. 3 (2010): 384–411.

Linnemeier, Bernd-Wilhelm. *Ein Gut und sein Alltag: Neuhof an der Weser.* Münster: F. Coppenrath, 1992.

Lüdtke, Alf, ed. *The History of Everyday Life : Reconstructing Historical Experiences and Ways of Life.* Princeton, NJ: Princeton University Press, 1995.

Luh, Jürgen. *Der Grosse Kurfürst: Sein Leben Neu Betrachtet.* Munich: Siedler, 2020.

Lupin, Matthew. "Poisoning as a Means of State Assassination in Early Modern Venice." In *Medieval and Early Modern Murder: Legal, Literary, and Historical Contexts,* edited by Larissa Tracy, 227–53. Woodbridge, UK: Boydell Press, 2018.

Lupton, Julia Reinhard. "Thinking with Things: Hannah Woolley to Hannah Arendt." *Postmedieval: A Journal of Medieval Cultural Studies* 3, no. 1 (March 2012): 63–79.

Macartney, C. A. *The Habsburg and Hohenzollern Dynasties in the Seventeenth and Eighteenth Centuries.* New York: Walker, 1970.

MacLean, Ian. "The Medical Republic of Letters before the Thirty Years War." *Intellectual History Review* 18 (2008): 15–30.

Mączak, Antoni, Henryk Samsonowicz, and Peter Burke. *East-Central Europe in Transition: From the Fourteenth to the Seventeenth Century.* Editions de la Maison des sciences de l'Homme. Cambridge: Cambridge University Press, 1985.

Mager, Friedrich. *Der Wald in Altpreussen als Wirtschaftsraum.* Vol. 1 of 2 vols. Cologne: Böhlau, 1960.

Malacarne, Giancarlo. "Il convivio tra specttacolarita e mode imperati." *Appunti di gastronomia* 53 (2007): 83–102.

———. *Sulla mensa del principe: alimentazione e banchetti alla Corte dei Gonzaga.* Modena: Il Bulino, 2000.

Manthey, Jürgen. *Königsberg: Geschichte einer Weltbürgerrepublik*. Munich: Hanser, 2005.

Marriott, John Arthur Ransome, and Charles Grant Robertson. *The Evolution of Prussia, the Making of an Empire*. Revised edition. Oxford: Clarendon Press, 1946.

Marschke, Benjamin. "The Crown Prince's Brothers and Sisters: Succession and Inheritance Problems and Solutions among the Hohenzollerns, from the Great Elector to Frederick the Great." In *Sibling Relations and the Transformations of European Kinship, 1300–1900*, edited by Christopher Johnson and David Sabean, 111–44. Oxford: Berghahn Books, 2011, 111–44.

———. "Vater und Sohn: Friedrich der Große und die Dynastie der Hohenzollern." Paper presented at the Fifth Conference in the series Friedrich300, September 30–October 1, 2011. In *Friedrich der Große und die Dynastie der Hohenzollern*, edited by Michael Kaiser and Jurgen Luh, 2011. https://www.perspectivia.net/publikationen/friedrich300-colloquien/friedrich-dynastie/marschke_vater.

Materna, Ingo, Wolfgang Ribbe, and Kurt Adamy, eds. *Brandenburgische Geschichte*. Berlin: Akademie Verlag, 1995.

Mauer, August, and C. Roland. *Die Kurfürstin Henriette Louise Gemahlin Friedrich Wilhelms des Grossen, als Landesmutter, und ihre besondere Wirksamkeit zu Oranienburg*. Neustadt-Eberswalde, 1858.

McCabe, Ina Baghdiantz. *A History of Global Consumption, 1500–1800*. London: Routledge, 2015.

McCollum, Elmer Verner. *A History of Nutrition: The Sequence of Ideas in Nutrition Investigations*. Boston: Houghton Mifflin, 1957.

McKay, Derek. *The Great Elector*. Harlow, UK: Longman, 2001.

———. *The Rise of the Great Powers, 1648–1815*. London: Longman, 1983.

Meiselman, Herbert L. *Dimensions of the Meal: The Science, Culture, Business, and Art of Eating*. Gaithersburg, MD: Aspen, 2000.

Mellinger, Nan. *Fleisch: Ursprung und Wandel einer Lust—eine kulturanthropologische Studie*. Frankfurt am Main: Campus, 2000.

Mennell, Stephen. *All Manners of Food: Eating and Taste in England and France from the Middle Ages to the Present*. Oxford: Blackwell, 1985.

Menninger, Annerose. *Genuss im kulturellen Wandel: Tabak, Kaffee, Tee und Schokolade in Europa (16.–19. Jahrhundert)*. Stuttgart: F. Steiner, 2004.

Metz, Peter. "Ein Automatisches Tafelspielzeug der Renaissance." *Jahrbuch der Berliner Museen* 12 (1970): 5–33.

Meyer, Moritz. *Geschichte der Preussischen Handwerkerpolitik*. Reprint. Glashütten im Taunus: Detlex Auvermann, 1972.

Middleton, Simon. "'How It Came That the Bakers Bake No Bread': A Struggle for Trade Privileges in Seventeenth-Century New Amsterdam." *William and Mary Quarterly*, 3rd series, 58, no. 2 (April 1, 2001): 347–72.

Miller, Jeff, and Jonathan Deutsch. *Food Studies: An Introduction to Research Methods.* Oxford: Berg, 2010.

Mintz, Sidney Wilfred. *Sweetness and Power: The Place of Sugar in Modern History.* New York: Viking, 1985.

Mittenzwei, Ingrid, and Erika Herzfeld. *Brandenburg-Preußen 1648–1789: das Zeitalter des Absolutismus in Text und Bild.* Berlin: Verlag Nation, 1987.

Mollenauer, Lynn Wood. *Strange Revelations: Magic, Poison, and Sacrilege in Louis XIV's France.* University Park: Pennsylvania State University Press, 2007.

Montanari, Massimo. *The Culture of Food.* Oxford: Blackwell Publishers, 1994.

———. *Food Is Culture.* New York: Columbia University Press, 2006.

———. *Il formaggio con le pere: la storia in un proverbio.* 1st ed. Rome: Laterza, 2008.

Moran, Bruce T. "German Prince-Practitioners: Aspects in the Development of Courtly Science, Technology, and Procedures in the Renaissance." *Technology and Culture* 22, no. 2 (1981): 253–74.

———, ed. *Patronage and Institutions: Science, Technology, and Medicine at the European Court, 1500–1750.* Rochester, NY: Boydell Press, 1991.

———. "A Survey of Chemical Medicine in the 17th Century: Spanning Court, Classroom, and Culture." *Pharmacy in History* 38, no. 3 (1996): 121–33.

Morel, Andreas. *Der gedeckte Tisch: zur Gechichte der Tafelkultur.* Zürich: Punktum AG, 2001.

Morton, A. G. *History of Botanical Science: An Account of the Development of Botany from Ancient Times to the Present Day.* London: Academic Press, 1988.

Muchembled, Robert, et al., eds. *Cultural Exchange in Early Modern Europe.* Vol. 2 of 4. Cambridge: Cambridge University Press, 2007.

Muir, Edward. *Ritual in Early Modern Europe.* Cambridge: Cambridge University Press, 1997.

Muldrew, Craig. *Food, Energy and the Creation of Industriousness: Work and Material Culture in Agrarian England, 1550–1780.* Cambridge: Cambridge University Press, 2011.

Müllenmeister, Kurt J. "Ein Bild der Schwanenburg zu Kleve um 1660." *Weltkunst,* 1971.

Müller, Rainer A. *Der Fürstenhof in der frühen Neuzeit.* Munich: Oldenbourg, 1995.

———. "Die Deutschen Fürstenspiegel des 17. Jahrhunderts: Regierungslehren und Politische Pädagogik." *Historische Zeitschrift* 240, no. 3 (1985): 571–97.

Mulryne, J. R., et al. *Europa triumphans: Court and Civic Festivals in Early Modern Europe.* Aldershot, UK: Ashgate, 2004.

Mundy, Peter. *The Travels of Peter Mundy in Europe and Asia, 1608–1667.* Edited by Richard Carnac Temple and Lavinia Mary Anstey. Vol. 4 of 5. London: Hakluyt Society, 1924.

Murcott, Anne. "The Sociology of Food." In *The Cambridge Handbook of Sociology: Specialty and Interdisciplinary Studies*, 2 vols., edited by Kathleen Odell Korgen, 2:199–206. Cambridge: Cambridge University Press, 2017.

Nadler, Ekhard. "Der Lustgärtner Michael Hanff und seine Familie." *Willdenowia* 5, no. 1 (November 1, 1968): 145–61.

Neugebauer, Wolfgang. *Das Thema "Preussen" in Wissenschaft und Wissenschaftspolitik des 19. und 20. Jahrhunderts.* Berlin: Duncker & Humblot, 2006.

———. *Die Hohenzollern: Anfänge, Landesstaat und Monarchische Autokratie bis 1740.* Vol. 1 of 2. Stuttgart: W. Kohlhammer, 1996.

———. *Handbuch der preußischen Geschichte.* Vol. 1 of 3. Berlin: De Gruyter, 2009.

———. *Preußische Geschichte als gesellschaftliche Veranstaltung.* Paderborn: Ferdinand Schöningh, 2018.

———. *Residenz, Verwaltung, Repräsentation: das Berliner Schloss und seine historischen Funktionen vom 15. bis 20. Jahrhundert.* Potsdam: Verlag für Berlin-Brandenburg, 1999.

———. *Zentralprovinz im Absolutismus: Brandenburg im 17. und 18. Jahrhundert.* Berlin: Berlin Verlag, Arno Spitz, 2001.

Newton, William Ritchey. *Hinter den Fassaden von Versailles: Mätressen, Flöhe und Intrigen am Hof des Sonnenkönigs.* Translated by Lis Künzli. 3rd ed. Berlin: Propyläen Verlag, 2010.

Nöldeke, Ingeborg. *Einmal Emden—Berlin und zurück im Frühjahr 1683: die Reise des Reichsfreiherrn Dodo II. zu Innhausen und Knyphausen auf Lütetsburg in Ostfriesland als Präsident der Ostfriesischen Landstände im Frühjahr 1683 nach Berlin an den Hof des Kurfürsten Friedrich Wilhelm von Brandenburg, berichtet von einem ungenannten Begleiter.* Berlin: Westkreuz-Verlag, 1989.

North, Michael. *Die Amtswirtschaften von Osterode und Soldau: vergleichende Untersuchungen zur Wirtschaft im frühmodernen Staat am Beispiel des Herzogtums Preussen in der zweiten Hälfte des 16. und in der ersten Hälfte des 17. Jahrhunderts.* Berlin: Duncker & Humblot, 1982.

———. "The Export Trade of Royal Prussia and Ducal Prussia, 1550–1650." In *From the North Sea to the Baltic: Essays in Commercial, Monetary and Agrarian History, 1500–1800*, 383–90. Aldershot, UK: Variorum, 1996.

———. *From the North Sea to the Baltic; Essays in Commercial, Monetary and Agrarian History, 1500—1800.* Aldershot, UK: Variorum, 1996.

———. "Getreideanbau und Getreidehandel im Königlichen Preußen und im Herzogtum Preußen: Überlegungen zu den Beziehungen zwischen Produktion, Binnenmarkt und Weltmarkt im 16. und 17. Jahrhundert." *Zeitschrift für Ostforschung* 34, no. 1 (January 1985): 39–47.

———. *Kommunikation, Handel, Geld und Banken in der Frühen Neuzeit.* Berlin: De Gruyter, 2014.

Norton, Marcy. *Sacred Gifts, Profane Pleasures: A History of Tobacco and Chocolate in the Atlantic World.* Ithaca, NY: Cornell University Press, 2008.

Nubola, Cecilia, and Andreas Würgler, eds. *Bittschriften und Gravamina: Politik, Verwaltung und Justiz in Europa, 14.–18. Jahrhundert.* Berlin: Duncker & Humblot, 2005.

Nuki, George, and Peter A Simkin. "A Concise History of Gout and Hyperuricemia and Their Treatment." *Arthritis Research & Therapy* 8, suppl. 1 (2006): 1–5.

Nummendal, Tara E. "Practical Alchemy and Commercial Exchange in the Holy Roman Empire." In *Merchants & Marvels: Commerce, Science and Art in Early Modern Europe,* edited by Pamela H Smith and Paula Findlen, 201–22. New York: Routledge, 2002.

Nussdorfer, Laurie. "New Cultural History Review." *History and Theory* 32, no. 1 (February 1, 1993): 74–83.

Nutton, Vivian, ed. *Medicine at the Courts of Europe, 1500–1837.* London: Routledge, 1990.

Odebrecht, Theodor. "Die Amtshauptmänner des Amtes Mühlenhof in Berlin." *Beiträge zur Geschichte Berlins* 3 (1840): 88–89.

Oelrichs, Johann Carl Conrad. "Historische Nachricht von dem raren Buche: Ceremoniale Brandenburgicum dessen Verfasser, Ausgaben, und Schicksalen." *Beyträge zur Brandenburgischen Geschichte* (1761): 529–42.

Oestreich, Gerhard. *Der Brandenburg-Preußische Geheime Rat vom Regierungsantritt des Großen Kurfürsten bis zu der Neuordnung im Jahre 1651: eine behördengeschichtliche Studie.* Würzburg-Aumühle: Triltsch, 1937.

———. *Friedrich Wilhelm. Der Grosse Kurfürst von Brandenburg: eine politische Biographie.* Frankfurt am Main: Musterschmidt, 1971.

———. *Neostoicism and the Early Modern State.* Edited by Helmut Georg Koenigsberger and Brigitta Oestreich, translated by David McClintock. Cambridge: Cambridge University Press, 1982.

Ogilvie, Brian W. *The Science of Describing Natural History in Renaissance Europe.* Chicago: University of Chicago Press, 2006.

Ogilvie, Sheilagh, *A Bitter Living: Women, Markets, and Social Capital in Early Modern Germany.* Oxford: Oxford University Press, 2003.

———. *European Proto-Industrialization.* Cambridge: Cambridge University Press, 1996.

———, ed. *Germany: A New Social and Economic History.* Vol. 2: *1630–1800.* London: Arnold, 1996.

———. "Rehabilitating the Guilds: A Reply." *Economic History Review* 61, no. 1 (2008): 175–82.

Opgenoorth, Ernst. "Ausländer." In *Brandenburg-Preußen als leitende Beamte und Offiziere.* Würzburg: Holzner, 1967.

———. *Der Grosse Kurfürst von Brandenburg: eine politische Biographie.* 2 vols. Frankfurt: Musterschmidt Göttingen, 1971.

———. *Handbuch der Geschichte Ost- und Westpreussens.* Lüneburg: Institut Nordostdeutsches Kulturwerk, 1994.

———. "Zur Ständegeschichte des Herzogtums Preußen: Ergebnisse und Probleme der Forschung." In *Preussische Landesgeschichte: Festschrift für Bernhart Jähnig zum 60. Geburtstag,* edited by Udo Arnold et al., 227–36. Marburg: Elwert, 2001.

Ordi, Jaume, et al. "The Severe Gout of Holy Roman Emperor Charles V." *New England Journal of Medicine* 355, no. 5 (August 3, 2006): 516–20.

Orlich, Leopold von. *Friedrich Wilhelm der Grosse Kurfürst: nach bisher noch ungekannten Original-Handschriften—mit einem Portrait und Zwei Facsimile.* Berlin: Mittler, 1836

———. *Geschichte des Preussichen Staates im siebzehnten Jahrhundert: mit besonderer Beziehung auf das Leben Friedrich Wilhelm's des grossen Kurfuersten; aus archivalischen Quellen und aus vielen noch ungekannten Original-Handscriften.* 3 vols. Berlin: Ferdinand Duemmler, 1838–89.

Orlowska, Anna Paulina, Werner Paravicini, and Jörg Wettlaufer. *Atelier Vorbild, Austausch, Konkurrenz: Höfe und Residenzen in der gegenseitigen Wahrnehmung.* Kiel: Christian-Albrechts-Universität, 2009.

Ottomeyer, Hans, and Deutsches Historisches Museum. *Die Öffentliche Tafel: Tafelzeremoniell in Europa, 1300—1900.* Wolfratshausen: Minerva, 2002.

Pandorf, Tina. *100 Glanzstücke: europäisches Silber aus 4 Jahrhunderten.* Hanover: Museum August Kestner, 2009.

Paravicini, Werner, ed. *Alltag bei Hofe: 3. Symposium der Residenzen-Kommission der Akademie der Wissenschaften in Göttingen.* Sigmaringen: J. Thorbecke, 1995.

———. *Die ritterlich-höfische Kultur des Mittelalters.* Munich: Oldenbourg, 1994.

Paravicini, Werner, Jan Hirschbiegel, Anna Paulina Orlowska, and Jörg Wettlaufer, eds. *Höfe und Residenzen im Spätmittelalterlichen Reich.* Ostfildern: Thorbecke, 2005–12.

Park, Katharine and Lorraine Daston, eds. *The Cambridge History of Science.* Vol. 3, *Early Modern Science.* Cambridge: Cambridge University Press, 2003.

Parker, Geoffrey. *Europe in Crisis, 1598–1648.* Blackwell Classic Histories of Europe. Oxford: Blackwell, 2001.

———. *Global Crisis: War, Climate Change and Catastrophe in the Seventeenth Century.* New Haven, CT: Yale University Press, 2013.

Pavord, Anna. *The Naming of Names: The Search for Order in the World of Plants.* New York: Bloomsbury, 2005.

Pennell, Sara. *The Birth of the English Kitchen, 1600–1850.* Cultures of Early Modern Europe. London: Bloomsbury, 2016.

———. "'Pots and Pans History': The Material Culture of the Kitchen in Early Modern England." *Journal of Design History* 11, no. 3 (January 1, 1998): 201–16.

Peralta, Iris, David Spooner, and Sandra Knapp. *Taxonomy of Wild Tomatoes and Their Relatives.* Ann Arbor, MI: American Society of Plant Taxonomists, 2008.

Persson, Karl Gunnar. *Grain Markets in Europe, 1500—1900: Integration and Deregulation.* Cambridge: Cambridge University Press, 1999.

Peter, Peter. *Kulturgeschichte der deutschen Küche.* Munich: C. H. Beck, 2008.

Peters, Jan. *Märkische Lebenswelten: Gesellschaftsgeschichte der Herrschaft Plattenburg-Wilsnack, Prignitz, 1550-1800.* Berlin: Berliner Wissenschafts-Verlag, 2007.

Peterson, T. Sarah. *Acquired Taste: The French Origins of Modern Cooking.* Ithaca, NY: Cornell University Press, 1994.

Pfeifer, Helen. "The Gulper and the Slurper: A Lexicon of Mistakes to Avoid While Eating with Ottoman Gentlemen." *Journal of Early Modern History* 24, no. 1 (February 20, 2020): 41–62.

Philippson, Martin. *Der grosse Kurfürst Friedrich Wilhelm von Brandenburg.* Berlin: S. Cronbach, 1897.

Pilcher, Jeffrey M. *Food in World History.* New York: Routledge, 2006.

Pinkard, Susan. *A Revolution in Taste: The Rise of French Cuisine, 1650–1800.* Cambridge: Cambridge University Press, 2009.

Plodeck, Karin. *Hofstruktur und Hofzeremoniell in Brandenburg-Ansbach vom 16. bis zum 18. Jahrhundert: zur Rolle des Herrschaftskultes im absolutist. Gesellschafts- und Herrschaftssystem.* Ansbach: Histor. Verein für Mittelfranken, 1972.

Porter, Roy, and George Sebastian Rousseau. *Gout: The Patrician Malady.* New Haven, CT: Yale University Press, 2000.

Pounds, Norman John Greville. *Hearth & Home: A History of Material Culture.* Bloomington: Indiana University Press, 1989.

Prak, Maarten Roy. *Craft Guilds in the Early Modern Low Countries: Work, Power and Representation.* Aldershot, UK: Ashgate, 2006.

Prak, Maarten Roy, and Diane Webb. *The Dutch Republic in the Seventeenth Century: The Golden Age.* Cambridge: Cambridge University Press, 2005.

Price, J. L. *The Dutch Republic in the Seventeenth Century.* New York: St. Martin's Press, 1998.

Prutz, Hans. *Aus des Grossen Kurfürsten letzten Jahren: zur Geschichte seines Hauses und Hofes, seiner Regierung und Politik.* Berlin: G. Reimer, 1897.

———. "Zur Geschichte des Konflikts zwischen den Großen Kurfürsten und dem Kurprinzen Friedrich, 1687." *Forschungen zur brandenburgischen und, preussischen Geschichte* 11, no. 2 (1898): 230–40.

Rabb, Theodore K. *The Struggle for Stability in Early Modern Europe.* New York: Oxford University Press, 1975.

Rachel, Hugo. "Handel und Handelsrecht von Königsberg in Preußen im 16. bis 18. Jahrhundert." *Forschungen zur brandenburgischen und preussischen Geschichte* 22 (1909): 95–132.

———. "Der Merkantilismus in Brandenburg-Prueßen." In *Modern Preussische Geschichte: 1648–1947: eine Anthologie,* edited by Otto Büsche, 951–93. Berlin: De Gruyter, 1981.

Radkau, Joachim. "Wood and Forestry in German History: In Quest of an Environmental Approach." *Environment and History* 2, no. 1 (February 1996): 63–76.

———. *Nature and Power: A Global History of the Environment.* Translated by Thomas Dunlap. Cambridge: Cambridge University Press, 2008.

Rahlf, Thomas. *Getreide in der Sozial-und Wirtschaftsgeschichte vom 16. bis 18. Jahrhundert : das Beispiel Köln im regionalen Vergleich.* Trier: Auenthal, 1996.

Rahn, Thomas. *Festbeschreibung: Funktion und Topik einer Textsorte am Beispiel der Beschreibung höfischer Hochzeiten, 1568–1794.* Tübingen: M. Niemeyer, 2006.

Ranke, Leopold von. *Leopold von Ranke's sämmtliche Werke.* Duncker & Humblot, 1878.

———. *Memoirs of the House of Brandenburg, and History of Prussia, during the Seventeenth and Eighteenth Centuries.* Vol. 1 of 3. London: J. Murray, 1849.

———. *Preussische Geschichte.* Hamburg: Hoffmann & Campe, 1934.

———. *Zwölf Bücher preussischer Geschichte.* Vols. 1–2 of 12. Hamburg: Hoffmann, 1928.

Ranke, Winfried, and Gottfried Korff. *Preußen: Versuch einer Bilanz.* Vol. 1. Berlin: Rowohlt, 1981.

Rankin, Alisha. *Panaceia's Daughters: Noblewomen as Healers in Early Modern Germany.* Chicago: Chicago University Press, 2013.

———. *The Poison Trials: Wonder Drugs, Experiment, and the Battle for Authority in Renaissance Science.* Chicago: University of Chicago Press, 2021.

Raumer, Georg Wilhelm von. "Geschichte des Geheimen Staats- und Cabinets-Archivs zu Berlin bis zum Jahre 1820." *Archivalische Zeitschrift* 72 (1976): 30–75.

Raumer, Georg Wilhelm von, and Eckart Henning. *Friedrich Wilhelm des Grossen, Kurfürsten von Brandenburg Kinderjahre.* Berlin: Decker, 1850–54.

Ray, Larry, and Andrew Sayer, eds. *Culture and Economy after the Cultural Turn.* London: Sage, 1999.

Rebora, Giovanni. *Culture of the Fork. A Brief History of Food in Europe.* Translated by Albert Sonnenfeld. New York: Columbia University Press, 1998.

Reed, Marcia, ed. *The Edible Monument: The Art of Food for Festivals.* Los Angeles: J. Paul Getty Trust, 2015.

Reeds, Karen. *Botany in Medieval and Renaissance Universities.* New York: Garland, 1991.

———. "Renaissance Humanism and Botany." *Annals of Science* 33 (June 1976): 519–42.

Rehse, Birgit. *Die Supplikations- und Gnadenpraxis in Brandenburg-Preußen.* Berlin: Duncker & Humblot, 2017.

Reich, Eduard. *Die Nahrungs- und Genussmittelkunde: historisch, naturwissenschaftlich und hygieinisch.* Göttingen: Vandenhoeck & Ruprecht, 1860.

Reinhard, Wolfgang, ed. *Power Elites and State Building.* Oxford: Oxford University Press, 1996.

———. "Was ist europäische politische Kultur? Versuch zur Begründung einer politischen Historischen Anthropologie." *Geschichte und Gesellschaft* 27, no. 4 (2001): 593–616.

Reith, Reinhold. *Umweltgeschichte der frühen Neuzeit.* Munich: Oldenbourg, 2011.

Rekoski, F. W. J. von. "Ein mittelalterliches Volksfest." *Zeitung für den deutschen Adel,* no. 26 (1844): 89–102.

Revel, Jena-François. *Culture and Cuisine: A Journey through the History of Food.* Translated by Helen Lane. New York: Doubleday, 1982.

Rich, E. E., and Charles Wilson. *The Cambridge Economic History of Europe.* Vol. 5 of 8. Cambridge: Cambridge University Press, 1977.

Rich, Rachel. "The King's Dinner, Bodies in the Royal Household, and Kew Palace." Presented at the Institute of Historical Research, University College London, London, February 27, 2020. https://www.youtube.com/watch?v=MvexqtWToWE, at minute 27.

Richard, Michel. *Das Haus Oranien-Nassau.* Lausanne: Rencontre, 1969.

Richardt, Aimé, and Jean-Gérard Théobald. *Les médecins du Grand siècle.* Paris: F.-X. de Guibert, 2005.

Richie, Alexandra. *Faust's Metropolis : A History of Berlin.* New York : Carroll & Graf, 1998.

Riedel, Adolph Friedrich. *Codex diplomaticus Brandenburgensis: Sammlung der Urkunden, Chroniken und sonstigen Quellenschriften für die Geschichte der Mark Brandenburg und ihrer Regenten.* Berlin: F. H. Morin, 1847

———. *Der brandenburgisch-preussische Staatshaushalt in den beiden letzten Jahrhunderten.* Berlin: Ernst & Korn, 1866.

———. *Die Domainen und Forsten, Gruben, Hütten und Salinen des Preußischen Staates.* Berlin: Schröder, 1849.

Riello, Giorgio. "'Things Seen and Unseen': The Material Culture of Early Modern Inventories and Their Representation of Domestic Interiors." In *Early Modern Things* edited by Paula Finden, 125–50. London: Routledge, 2013.

Rittersma, Rengenier, ed. *Luxury in the Low Countries: Miscellaneous Reflections on Netherlandish Material Culture, 1500 to the Present.* Brussels: Pharo, 2010.

Robisheaux, Thomas W. *The Last Witch of Langenburg: Murder in a German Village*. New York: W. W. Norton, 2009.

Roche, Daniel. *A History of Everyday Things: The Birth of Consumption in France, 1600–1800*. Cambridge: Cambridge University Press, 2000.

Roedder, H. *Zur Geschichte des Vermessungswesens Preussens insbesondere Altpreussens aus der ältesten Zeit bis in das 19. Jahrhundert*. Stuttgart: Konrad Wittwer, n.d.

Rohrschneider, Michael. *Der Große Kurfürst Friedrich Wilhelm von Brandenburg (1620–1688). Studien zu einem frühneuzeitlichen Mehrfachherrscher*. Berlin: Duncker & Humblot, 2019.

———. "Zacharias Zwanzig: Theatrum Praecedentiae." Theatrum-Literatur der Frühen Neuzeit: Repertorium. Wolfenbüttel: Herzog August Bibliothek Digilib, 2012. http://diglib.hab.de/edoc/ed000068/tei-introduction.xml.

———. "Zusammengesetzte Staatlichkeit in der Frühen Neuzeit. Aspekte und Perspektiven der neueren Forschung am Beispiel Brandenburg-Preußens." *Archiv für Kulturgeschichte* 90 (2008): 321–49.

Rokosz, Mieczyslow. "History of the Aurochs (Bos Taurus Primigenius) in Poland." *Animal Genetics Resources Information. Food and Argriculture Organization* 16, no. 4 (1995): 5–12.

Rose, Peter G. *The Sensible Cook: Dutch Foodways in the Old and the New World*. Syracuse, NY: Syracuse University Press, 1989.

Rosenberg, Hans. *Bureaucracy, Aristocracy, and Autocracy : The Prussian Experience, 1660–1815*. 1958; Cambridge, MA: Harvard University Press, 1966.

Rousselle, M. *Zwei deutsche Fürstinnen: Luise Henriette, Kurfürstin von Brandenburg. Elisabeth Christine, Königin von Preussen; dem deutschen Volke erzählt*. Berlin: Schriftenvertriebsanstalt, 1900.

Rowen, Herbert Harvey. *The Princes of Orange: The Stadholders in the Dutch Republic*. Cambridge: Cambridge University Press, 1988.

Rubel, William. *Bread: A Global History*. London: Reaktion Books, 2011.

Runge, Christoph. *Andachtsbuch Luise Henriettens von Brandenburg, Gemahlin des Großen Kurfürsten*. Berlin: Schleiermacher, 1880.

Sachs, Julius von. *Geschichte der Botanik vom 16. Jh. bis 1860*. Munich: Oldenbourg, 1875.

Sander, Oliver. "Die Leibärzte des Großen Kurfürsten und die Entstehung des brandenburgischen Medizinaledikts von 1685." *Jahrbuch für brandenburgische Landesgeschichte* 48 (1997): 100–112.

Sarti, Raffaella. *Europe at Home: Family and Material Culture, 1500–1800*. New Haven, CT: Yale University Press, 2002.

Schachinger, Erika. *Die Berliner Vorstadt Friedrichswerder, 1658–1708*. Cologne: Böhlau, 1993.

Schama, Simon. *The Embarrassment of Riches: An Interpretation of Dutch Culture in the Golden Age*. 1st ed. New York: Knopf, 1987.

Schärer, Martin R., and Alexander Fenton, eds. *Food and Material Culture: Proceedings of the Fourth Symposium of the International Commission for Research into European Food History.* East Linton, UK: Tuckwell Press, 1998.

Scharfenort, Louis von. *Die Pagen am Brandenburg-Preussischen Hofe, 1415–1895: Beiträge zur Kulturgeschichte des Hofes, auf Grund archivalischer Quellen.* Berlin: E. S. Mittler, 1895.

Schatzker, Mark. *The Dorito Effect: The Surprising New Truth about Food and Flavor.* New York: Simon & Schuster, 2015.

Schevill, Ferdinand. *The Great Elector.* Hamden, CT: Archon Books, 1965.

Schieber, Martin, and Bernd Windsheimer. *Rotes Bier und blaue Zipfel: zur Geschichte der Ernährung in Nürnberg.* Nuremberg: Sandberg, 2004.

Schiebinger, Londa L., and Claudia Swan, eds. *Colonial Botany: Science, Commerce, and Politics in the Early Modern World.* Philadelphia: University of Pennsylvania Press, 2007.

Schilling, Heinz. "Stadt und frühmoderner Territorialstaat: Stadtrepublikanismus versus Fürstensouveränität : die politische Kultur des deutschen Stadtbürgertums in der Konfrontation mit dem frühmodernen Staatsprinzip." In *Recht, Verfassung und Verwaltung in der frühneuzeitlichen Stadt,* edited by Michael Stolleis, 19–39. Vienna: Böhlau, 1991.

Schirmer, Uwe. "Hofhaltung und Hofwirtschaft der Kurfürsten von Sachsen, 1486–1547." In *Hofwirtschaft: ein ökonomischer Blick auf Hof und Residenz in Spätmittelalter und Früher Neuzeit,* edited by Gerhard Fouquet et al., 257–76. Ostfildern: Akademie der Wissenschaften zu Göttingen, 2008.

Schmeling, Manfred. "Der gastronomische Diskurs. Essen und Trinken als Gegenstand der Kulturwissenschaft." *KulturPoetik* 3, no. 1 (January 1, 2003): 119–30.

Schmidt, Ferdinand. *Preussens Geschichte in Wort und Bild: illustrierte Geschichte von Brandenburg und Preussen.* Vol. 3 of 3. Braunschweig: Archiv Verlag, 2002.

Schmidt, Franz. *"weil kuchen und keller die herrn reich und arm machen.* Nahrungsmittelversorgung und Nahrungsmittelkonsum am Heidelberger Hof Kurfürst Karl Ludwigs." *Zeitschrift für die Geschichte des Oberrheins* 159 (2011): 389–424.

Schmidt, Georg. *Der Dreissigjährige Krieg.* Munich: Beck, 2010.

Schmidtke, Martin. *Königsberg in Preußen: Personen und Ereignisse 1255–1945 im Bild.* Husum: Husum, 1997.

Schnyder-Von Waldkirch, Antoinette, and Katerina Vatsella. *Wie Europa den Kaffee entdeckte: Reiseberichte der Barockzeit als Quellen zur Geschichte des Kaffees.* Zürich: Jacobs Suchard Museum, 1988.

Schönberger, Gesa. *Mahlzeiten: Alte Last oder neue Lust?* Wiesbaden: Verlag für Sozialwissenschaften, 2011.

Schubert, Ernst. *Essen und Trinken im Mittelalter.* Darmstadt: Primus, 2006.

Schuller, Alexander, and Jutta Anna Kleber. *Verschlemmte Welt: Essen und Trinken historisch-anthropologisch*. Göttingen: Vandenhoeck & Ruprecht, 1994.

Schultz, Helga. *Berlin, 1650–1800: Sozialgeschichte einer Residenz*. Berlin: Akademie-Verlag, 1987.

Schultz, Uwe, ed. *Das Fest: eine Kulturgeschichte von der Antike bis zur Gegenwart*. Munich: C. H. Beck, 1988.

Schulze, Johannes "Von der Mark Brandenburg zum Preußenstaat," in *Preussen, Epochen und Probleme seiner Geschichte*, edited by Richard Dietrich, 31–56. Berlin: De Gruyter, 1964.

Schweikardt, Christoph. "More than Just a Propagandist for Tea: Religious Argument and Advice on a Healthy Life in the Work of the Dutch Physician Cornelis Bontekoe (1647–1685)." *Medical History* 47, no. 3 (July 2003): 357–68.

Schwerin, Otto von. *Briefe aus England über die Zeit von 1674—1678*. Edited by Leopold von Orlich and Friedrich von Raumer. Berlin: Reimer, 1837.

Scott, James. *Weapons of the Weak: Everyday Forms of Peasant Resistance*. New Haven: Yale University Press, 1985.

Scribner, Robert. *Germany: A New Social and Economic History*. Vol. 1 of 3 vols. London: Arnold, 1996.

Scrinis, Gyorgy. "On the Ideology of Nutritionism." *Gastronomica: The Journal of Food and Culture* 8, no. 1 (February 1, 2008): 39–48.

Seggern, Harm von, and Gerhard Fouquet, eds. *Adel und Zahl: Studien zum adligen Rechnen und Haushalten in Spätmittelalter und früher Neuzeit*. Ubstadt-Weiher: Regionalkultur, 2000.

Seidel, Paul. "Der Lustgarten am Schlosse in Berlin bis zu seiner Auflösung im Jahr 1715." *Forschungen zur brandenburgischen und preußischen Geschichte* 3 (1890): 89–124.

———. *Der Silber- und Goldschatz der Hohenzollern im königlichen Schlosse zu Berlin*. Berlin: Cosmos, 1895.

———. "Die Beziehungen des Grossen Kurfürsten und König Friedrichs I zur Niederländischen Kunst." *Jahrbuch der königlich preuszischen Kunstsammlungen* 11 (1890): 119–49.

Seutter von Lötzen, Claudia Curtius. "Das Tafelzeremoniell an deutschen Höfen im 17. und 18. Jahrhundert: Quellen und Rechtsgrundlagen." Doctor of law thesis. Friedrich-Schiller-Universität, 2008.

Shapin, Steven. *Changing Tastes: How Things Tasted in the Early Modern Period and How They Taste Now*. Hans Rausling Lecture 2011. Uppsala: Uppsala University, 2011.

Shennan, Margaret. *The Rise of Brandenburg-Prussia*. London: Routledge, 1995.

Shumacher-Voelker, Uta. "German Cookery Books, 1485–1800." *Petits propos culinaires* 6 (1980): 35–45.

Simmel, Georg. "Soziologie der Mahlzeit." *Beiblatt zum Berliner Tageblatt*, no. 41, 10 October 1910, 1–2.

Siraisi, Nancy G. *Avicenna in Renaissance Italy: The Canon and Medical Teaching in Italian Universities after 1500*. Princeton, NJ: Princeton University Press, 1987.

———. *History, Medicine, and the Traditions of Renaissance Learning*. Ann Arbor: University of Michigan Press, 2007.

———. "Medicine, 1450–1620, and the History of Science." *Isis* 103, no. 3 (September 2012): 491–514.

———. *Medieval and Early Renaissance Medicine: An Introduction to Knowledge and Practice*. Chicago: Chicago University Press, 1990.

Slicher van Bath, B. H. *The Agrarian History of Western Europe, A.D. 500–1850*. Translated by Olive Ordish. London: E. Arnold, 1963.

Smith, Lisa. "The King's Dinner, Bodies in the Royal Household, and Kew Palace." Presented at the Institute of Historical Research, University College London, London, February 27, 2020. https://www.youtube.com/watch?v= MvexqtWToWE, at minute 27:00.

Smith, Pamela, and Paula Findlen. *Merchants & Marvels: Commerce, Science and Art in Early Modern Europe*. New York: Routledge, 2002.

Somerset, Anne. *The Affair of the Poisons: Murder, Infanticide and Satanism at the Court of Louis XIV*. London: Weidenfeld & Nicolson, 2003.

Southard, Robert. *Droysen and the Prussian School of History*. Lexington: University Press of Kentucky, 1994.

Spang, Rebecca L. *The Invention of the Restaurant: Paris and Modern Gastronomic Culture*. Cambridge, MA: Harvard University Press, 2000.

Spangler, Jonathan. Review of *The Affair of the Poisons: Murder, Infanticide, and Satanism at the Court of Louis XIV*, by Anne Somerset. *The Historian* 68, no. 2 (2006): 402–3.

Spannagel, Karl. *Konrad von Burgsdorff: ein brandenburgischer Kriegs- und Staatsmann aus der Zeit der Kurfürsten Georg Wilhelm und Friedrich Wilhelm*. Berlin: A. Duncker, 1903.

Spary, Emma. "Poisons and Secrets: The Court, the King, and the Problem of Drug Knowledge in Late Seventeenth-Century France." Lecture presented at the Intoxicating Spaces Lectures Series, February 17, 2021. https://www .crowdcast.io/e/poisons-and-secrets-the.

Spiekermann, Uwe, Dirk Reinhardt, and Ulrike Thoms, eds. *Neue Wege zur Ernährungsgeschichte. Kochbücher, Haushaltsrechnungen, Konsumvereinsberichts und Autobiographien in der Diskussion*. Frankfurt am Main: Peter Land, 1993.

Spies, Paul, Dominik Bartmann, and Peter Schwirkmann, eds. *Palace. City. Berlin: The Residence Shifts to the Center (1650–1800)*. Berlin: Holy Verlag, 2016.

Spiker, Samuel Heinrich. *Berlin und seine Umgebung im neunzehnten Jahrhundert.* Leipzig: Reprint-Verlag, 2004.

Spode, Hasso. "Von der Hand zur Gabel. Zur Geschichte der Eßwerkzeuge." In *Verschlemmte Welt: Essen und Trinken historisch-anthropologisch,* 20–46. Göttingen: Vandenhoeck & Ruprecht, 1994.

Stecker, Arthur. *Franz von Meinders, ein brandenburgisch-preussischer Staatsmann im siebzehnten Jahrhundert.* Leipzig: Duncker & Humblot, 1892.

Steege, Paul, Andrew Stuart Bergerson, Maureen Healy, and Pamela E. Swett. "The History of Everyday Life: A Second Chapter." *Journal of Modern History* 80, no. 2 (June 1, 2008): 358–78.

Stein, Caspar. *Das alte Königsberg: eine ausführliche Beschreibung der drei Städte Königsberg samt ihren Vorstädten und Freiheiten wie sie anno 1644 beschaffen waren.* Nachdr. der Ausg. Königsberg 1911. Hamburg: Selbstverl. des Vereins für Familienforschung in Ost- und Westpreußen, 1998.

Stein, Robert, and Judith Pollmann. *Networks, Regions and Nations Shaping Identities in the Low Countries, 1300–1650.* Leiden: Brill, 2010.

Stengel, Walter. *Alte Wohnkultur in Berlin und in der Mark im Spiegel der Quellen des 16.–19. Jahrhunderts.* Berlin: B. Hessling, 1958.

Stillfried-Alcantara, Rudolf Maria Bernhard von. *Ceremonial-Buch für den Königlich Preussischen Hof.* Vol. 1. Berlin: R. von Decker's Verlag, 1877.

Stokstad, Erik. "Bringing Back the Aurochs." *Science* 350, no. 6265 (December 4, 2015): 1144–47.

Stolberg, Michael. *Experiencing Illness and the Sick Body in Early Modern Europe.* Houndmills, UK: Palgrave Macmillan, 2011.

———. *Homo patiens: Krankheits- und Körpererfahrung in der Frühen Neuzeit.* Cologne: Böhlau, 2003.

Stollberg-Rilinger, Barbara. *Der Staat als Maschine: zur politischen Metaphorik des absoluten Fürstenstaats.* Berlin: Duncker & Humblot, 1986.

———. *The Emperor's Old Clothes: Constitutional History and the Symbolic Language of the Holy Roman Empire.* Translated by Thomas Dunlap. New York: Berghahn Books, 2015.

———. "Höfische Öffentlichkeit: zur zeremoniellen Selbstdarstellung des brandenburgischen Hofes vor dem europäischen Publikum." *Forschungen zur brandenburgischen und preußischen Geschichte, Neue Folge* 7 (1997): 145–76.

———. "Kneeling before God—Kneeling before the Emperor." In *Resonances: Historical Essays on Continuity and Change (Ritus et Artes: Traditions and Transformation),* edited by Nils Holger Petersen, 149–72. Turnhout: Brepols, 2011.

———, ed. *Was heisst Kulturgeschichte des Politischen?* Berlin: Duncker & Humblot, 2005.

———. "Zur moralischen Ökonomie des Schenkens bei Hof." In *Luxus und Integration: materielle Hofkultur Westeuropas vom 12. bis zum 18. Jahrhundert*, 187–204. Munich: Oldenbourg, 2010.

Streich, Brigitte. "Fürstliche Repräsentation und Alltag am Hofe Herzogin Elisabeth von Braunschweig-Lüneburg (Calenberg-Göttingen)." In *Herzogin Elisabeth von Braunschweig-Lüneburg (1510–1558): Herrschaft, Konfession, Kultur*, edited by Eva Schlotheuber, 138–66. Hanover: Hahn, 2011.

Strong, Roy C. *Splendour at Court: Renaissance Spectacle and the Theater of Power*. Boston: Houghton, 1973.

Stürmer, Michael. *Herbst des alten Handwerks: Quellen zur Sozialgeschichte des 18. Jahrhunderts*. Munich: Deutscher Taschenbuch-Verlag, 1979.

Stürzbecher, Manfred. "Zur Geschichte der brandenburgischen Medizinalgesetzgebung im 17. Jahrhundert." In *Beiträge zur Berliner Medizingeschichte*, 1–67. Berlin: De Gruyter, 2018.

Suden, Marina thom. *Schlösser in Berlin und Brandenburg und ihre bildliche Ausstattung im 18. Jahrhundert*. Petersberg: Imhof, 2013.

Süssenguth, Mario. *Der kulinarische König: Essen und Trinken wie August der Starke*. Berlin: Eulenspiegel, 2004.

Symons, Michael. "Simmel's Gastronomic Sociology: An Overlooked Essay." *Food and Foodways* 5, no. 4 (January 1, 1994): 333–51.

Tannahill, Reay. *Food in History*. New York: Crown, 1989.

Taylor, Valerie. "Banquet Plate and Renaissance Culture: A Day in the Life." *Renaissance Studies* 19, no. 5 (2005): 621–33.

Teuteberg, Hans Jürgen. *European Food History: A Research Review*. Leicester, UK: Leicester University Press, 1992.

———. *Historical Diet Research in Europe: Problems and Development since the Beginning of Modern Times*. Leicester, UK: Leicester University Press, 1991.

———. "Periods and Turning-Points in the History of European Diet: A Preliminary Outline of Problems and Methods." In *Food in Change. Eating Habits from the Middle Ages to the Present Day*, edited by Alexander Fenton and Eszter Kisban, 11–23. Edinburgh: J. Donald, 1985.

Theibault, John. "Germany, Early and Medieval Periods." In *The Oxford Encyclopedia of Economic History*, edited by Joel Mokur, 406. Oxford: Oxford University Press, 2003.

Thielen, Peter Gerrit. *Die Kultur am Hofe Herzog Albrechts von Preussen (1525–1568)*. Göttingen: Musterschmidt, 1953.

Thomas, Andrew L. *A House Divided: Wittelsbach Confessional Court Cultures in the Holy Roman Empire, c. 1550–1650*. Leiden: Brill, 2010.

Thorndike, Lynn. *A History of Magic and Experimental Science*. Vol. 7 of 8. New York: Columbia University Press, 1958.

Thornton, Peter. *The Italian Renaissance Interior, 1400–1600*. New York: H. N. Abrams, 1991.

Tielhof, M. van. *The 'Mother of All Trades': The Baltic Grain Trade in Amsterdam from the Late 16th to the Early 19th Century*. Leiden: Brill, 2002.

Tlusty, B. Ann. *Bacchus and Civic Order: The Culture of Drink in Early Modern Germany*. Charlottesville: University of Virginia Press, 2001.

Topolski, Jerzy, ed. *The Manorial Economy in Early-Modern East-Central Europe: Origins, Development and Consequences*. Aldershot, UK: Ashgate, 1994.

Toussaint-Samat, Maguelonne. *A History of Food*. Cambridge, MA: Blackwell Reference, 1993.

Trentmann, Frank. *Empire of Things: How We Became a World of Consumers, from the 15th Century to the 21st*. New York: Harper, 2016.

Trubek, Amy B. *Haute Cuisine: How the French Invented the Culinary Profession*. Philadelphia: University of Pennsylvania Press, 2000.

Unger, Richard W. "Dutch Herring, Technology, and International Trade in the Seventeenth Century." *Journal of Economic History* 40, no. 2 (June 1, 1980): 253–80.

Urkunden und Actenstücke zur Geschichte des Kurfürsten Friedrich Wilhelm von Brandenburg. 23 vols. in 27 bks. Berlin: G. Reimer, 1864–1930.

Valenze, Deborah M. *Milk: A Local and Global History*. New Haven, CT: Yale University Press, 2011.

Veblen, Thorstein, and Stuart Chase. *The Theory of the Leisure Class: An Economic Study of Institutions*. New York: Modern Library, 1934.

Vehse, Carl Eduard. *Die Höfe zu Bayern*. Edited by Wolfgang Schneider and Annerose Reinhardt. Leipzig: G. Kiepenheuer, 1994.

———. *Geschichte der deutschen Höfe seit der Reformation*. Hamburg: Hoffmann & Campe, 1851.

———. *Illustrierte Geschichte des preußischen Hofes des Adels und der Diplomatie vom großen kurfürsten bis zum Tode Kaiser Wilhelms I*. Vol. 1. Stuttgart: Franckh'sche Verlagshandlung, 1902.

———. *Preussische Hofgeschichten*. Munich: G. Müller, 1913.

Verk, Sabine. *Geschmacksache*. Berlin: Staatliche Museen zu Berlin, 1995.

Vermeir, René, Dries Raeymaekers, and José Eloy Hortal Muñoz. *A Constellation of Courts: the Courts and Households of Habsburg Europe, 1555–1665*. Leuven: Leuven University Press, 2014.

Vickery, Amanda. *Behind Closed Doors in Georgian England*. New Haven, CT: Yale University Press, 2009.

Vierhaus, Rudolf. *Germany in the Age of Absolutism*. Translated by Jonathan B. Knudsen. Cambridge: Cambridge University Press, 1988.

Voinier, Sarah, and Guillaume Winter, eds. *Poison et antidote dans l'Europe des XVIe et XVIIe siècles*. Lettres et civilisations étrangères. Arras: Artois Presses Université, 2020.

Wacker, Gabriele. *Arznei und Confect: medikale Kultur am Wolfenbütteler Hof im 16. und 17. Jahrhundert.* Wiesbaden: Herrassowitz, 2013.

Waddington, Albert. *Histoire de Prusse.* Paris: Plon-Nourrit, 1911.

Wade, Mara. "Festival Books as Historical Literature: The Reign of Christian IV of Denmark (1596–1648)." *The Seventeenth Century* 7, no. 1 (Spring 1992): 1–14.

Wagner, Wulf D. *Das Königsberger Schloss: eine Bau- und Kulturgeschichte.* Regensburg: Schnell & Steiner, 2008.

Walsham, Alexandra. "Eating the Forbidden Fruit: Pottery and Protestant Theology in Early Modern England." *Journal of Early Modern History* 24, no. 1 (February 20, 2020): 63–83.

Walters, Arthur Harry. *Ecology, Food & Civilisation.* London: C. Knight, 1973.

Warde, Paul. *Ecology, Economy and State Formation in Early Modern Germany.* Cambridge: Cambridge University Press, 2006.

Watanabe-O'Kelly, Helen, and Anne Simon. *Festivals and Ceremonies: A Bibliography of Works Relating to Court, Civic, and Religious Festivals in Europe, 1500–1800.* London: Mansell, 2000.

Wegführer, Johann. *Leben der Kurfürstin Luise, gebornen Prinzess von Nassau-Oranien, Gemahlin Friedrich Wilhelm des Grossen, Kurfürsten zu Brandenburg u.s.w.: treu geschichtlich dargestellt zunachst für religiöse Freundinnen vaterländischer Vorwelt.* Leipzig: C. P. Melzer, 1838.

Weindling, Paul. "Medicine and Modernization: The Social History of German Health and Medicine." *History of Science* 24, no. 3 (September 1, 1986): 277–301.

Wendland, Folkwin. *Der Große Tiergarten in Berlin: seine Geschichte und Entwicklung in fünf Jahrhunderten.* Berlin: Gebr. Mann Verlag, 1993.

Weyrauch, Erdmann. *Man nahm [. . .]: ausgewählte Kochbücher vom 15. bis zum 19. Jahrhundert.* Wolfenbüttel: Herzog August Bibliothek, 1993.

Wheaton, Barbara Ketcham. *Savoring the Past: The French Kitchen and Table from 1300 to 1789.* Philadelphia: University of Pennsylvania Press, 1983.

White, Richard. "American Environmental History: The Development of a New Historical Field." *Pacific Historical Review* 54 (1985): 297–335.

Whited, Tamara L., and ABC-Clio Information Services. *Northern Europe: An Environmental History.* Santa Barbara, CA: ABC-CLIO, 2005.

Wiedl, Birgit. *Alltag und Recht im Handwerk der Frühen Neuzeit: Schmiede, Wagner, Schlosser und andere Eisen verarbeitende Handwerke in Stadt und Land Salzburg.* Salzburg: Archiv und Statistisches Amt der Stadt Salzburg, 2006.

Wiegelmann, Günter. *Alltags- und Festspeisen in Mitteleuropa: Innovationen, Strukturen und Regionen vom späten Mittelalter bis zum 20. Jahrhundert.* 2nd ed. Münster: Waxmann, 2006.

Wiegelmann, Günter, and Ruth-Elisabeth Mohrmann, eds. *Nahrung und Tischkultur im Hanseraum.* Münster: Waxmann, 1996.

Wieringa, W. J., ed. *The Interactions of Amsterdam and Antwerp with the Baltic Region, 1400–1800: De Nederlanden en Het Ostzeegebied, 1400–1800.* Leiden: M. Nijhoff, 1983.

Wiesinger, Liselotte. *Das Berliner Schloss: von der kurfürstlichen Residenz zum Königsschloß.* Darmstadt: Wissentschaftliche Buchgesellschaft, 1989.

Wiesner, Merry E. *Early Modern Europe, 1450–1789.* Cambridge: Cambridge University Press, 2006.

Wiggin, Bethany. "The Politics of Coffee Consumption: Leipzig Coffeehouse Culture at 1700." *Wolfenbüttler Barock-Nachrichten* 31, no. 1 (2004): 25–36.

Willan, Anne, Mark Cherniavsky, and Kyri Claflin. *The Cookbook Library: Four Centuries of the Cooks, Writers, and Recipes That Made the Modern Cookbook.* Berkeley: University of California Press, 2012.

Williams, Gerhild Scholz. *Ways of Knowing in Early Modern Germany: Johannes Praetorius as a Witness to His Time.* Aldershot, UK: Ashgate, 2006.

Wilson, Bee. *Consider the Fork: A History of How We Cook and Eat.* New York: Basic Books, 2012.

Wilson, Peter. *Absolutism in Central Europe.* London: Routledge, 2000.

Winau, Rolf. "Leibärzte des Großen Kurfürsten." In *Medizingeschichte in unserer Zeit. Festgabe für Edith Heischkel-Artelt und Walter Artelt zum 65. Geburtstag,* edited by Hans Heinz Eulner, 213–22. Stuttgart: Enke, 1971.

———. *Medizin in Berlin.* Berlin: De Gruyter, 1987.

———. "Medizin und Botanik am Hof des Großen Kurfürsten." In *Schön und nützlich: aus Brandenburgs Kloster-, Schloss- und Küchengärten: Begleitbuch zur Ausstellung des Hauses der Brandenburgisch-Preußischen Geschichte; 15. Mai–15. August 2004,* 100–107. Leipzig: Henschel, 2004.

Wintzingerode, Heinrich Jobst von. *Schwierige Prinzen: die Markgrafen von Brandenburg-Schwedt.* Berlin: Berliner Wissenschafts Verlag, 2011.

Wirth, Irmgard. *Berlin 1650–1914: von der Zeit des Grossen Kurfürsten bis zum Ersten Weltkrieg: Stadtdarstellungen aus den Sammlungen des Berlin Museums.* Hamburg: Christians, 1979.

Wiswe, Hans. *Kulturgeschichte der Kochkunst: Kochbücher und Rezepte aus Zwei Jahrtausenden mit einem Anhang zur Fachsprache von Eva Hepp.* Munich: Moos, 1970.

Withington, Phil. "Intoxicants and Society in Early Modern England." *Historical Journal* 54, no. 3 (2011): 631–57.

Wittenauer, Volker. *Im Dienste der Macht: Kultur und Sprache am Hof der Hohenzollern. Vom Großen Kurfürst bis zu Wilhelm II.* Paderborn: Ferdinand Schöningh, 2007.

Wolters, Friedrich. *Geschichte der brandenburgischen Finanzen in der Zeit von 1640 bis 1697: Darstellung und Akten.* Vol. 2. Munich: Duncker & Humblot, 1915.

Wunder, Heide. "Agriculture and Social Change." In *Germany: A New Social and Economic History*. Vol. 2: *1630–1800*, edited by Sheilagh Ogilvie, 63–99. London: Arnold, 1996.

Würgler, Andreas. "Bitten und Begehren. Suppliken und Gravamina in der deutschsprachigen Frühneuzeitforschung." In *Bittschriften und Gravamina: Politik, Verwaltung und Justiz in Europa, 14.–18. Jahrhundert*, edited by Cecilia Nubola and Andreas Würgler, 17–52. Berlin: Duncker & Humblot, 2005.

Zahn, W. *Die Altmark im Dreißigjährigen Kriege*. Schriften des Vereins für Reformationsgeschichte 80. Halle: Kommissionsverlag von Max Miemeyer, 1904.

Zanden, Jan L. van. "Wages and the Standard of Living in Europe, 1500–1800." *European Review of Economic History* 3, no. 2 (August 1999): 175–97.

Zeeden, Ernst Walter. *Deutsche Kultur in der Frühen Neuzeit: Handbuch der Kulturgeschichte*, Frankfurt am Main: Akademische Verlagsgesellschaft, 1968.

Zeev, Gourarier, and Jean-Pierre Babelon, eds. *Versailles et les tables royales en Europe XVIIème–XIXème siècles*. Paris: Editions de la Réunion des musées nationaux, 1993.

Zelck, Agnes, ed. *Bei Tisch—Essen und Trinken in der Frühen Neuzeit*. Altena: Verlag Fotoforum SchwarzBunt, 2016.

Zepernick, Bernhard, and Else-Marie Karlsson. *Berlins Botanischer Garten*. Berlin: Haude und Spener, 1979.

Zieschka, Siger, et al., eds. *The Dining Nobility. From the Burgundian Dukes to the Belgian Royalty*. Brussels: Brussels University Press, 2008.

Zischka, Ulrike, Hans Ottomeyer, and Susanne Bäumler. *Der Anständige Lust von Esskultur und Tafelsitten*. Munich: Edition Spangenberg, 1993.

Zumthor, Paul. *Daily Life in Rembrandt's Holland*. Stanford, CA: Stanford University Press, 1994.

INDEX

Studies in Early Modern German History

The Fuggers of Augsburg: Pursuing Wealth and Honor in Renaissance Germany
Mark Häberlein

"Evil People": A Comparative Study of Witch Hunts in Swabian Austria and the Electorate of Trier
Johannes Dillinger, translated by Laura Stokes

Witchcraft and the Papacy: An Account Drawing on the Formerly Secret Records of the Roman Inquisition
Rainer Decker, translated by H. C. Erik Midelfort

The German Discovery of the World: Renaissance Encounters with the Strange and Marvelous
Christine R. Johnson

Cautio Criminalis, or a Book on Witch Trials
Friedrich Spee von Langenfeld, translated by Marcus Hellyer

Bacchus and Civic Order: The Culture of Drink in Early Modern Germany
B. Ann Tlusty

Shaman of Oberstdorf: Chonrad Stoeckhlin and the Phantoms of the Night
Wolfgang Behringer , translated by H. C. Erik Midelfort

Obedient Germans? A Rebuttal: A New View of German History
Peter Blickle, translated by Thomas A. Brady Jr.

Lost Worlds: How Our European Ancestors Coped with Everyday Life and Why Life Is So Hard Today
Arthur E. Imhof, translated by Thomas Robisheaux

Mad Princes of Renaissance Germany
H. C. Erik Midelfort

Printed in the USA
CPSIA information can be obtained
at www.ICGtesting.com
CBHW030849100924
14325CB00002B/92